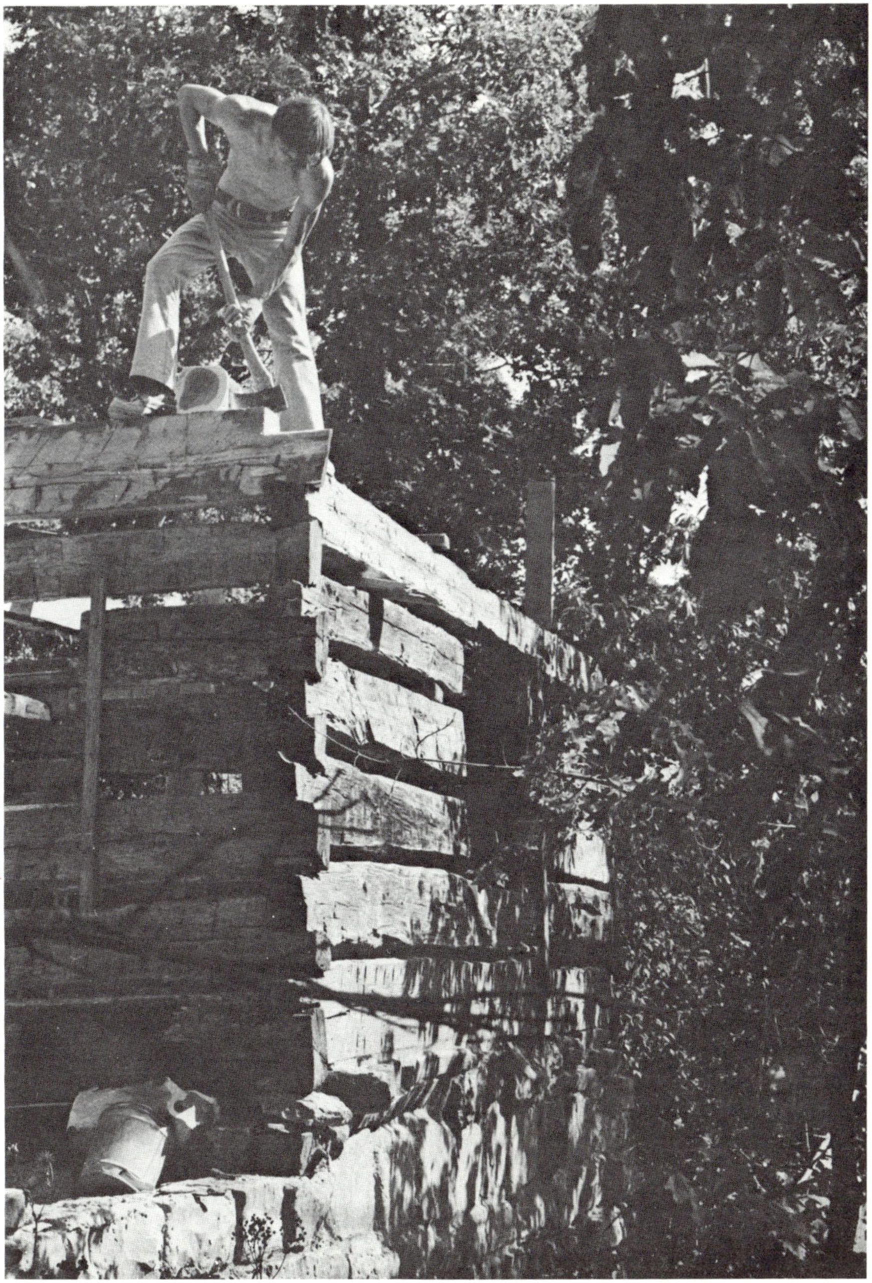

BURKHART

Building The Hewn Log House

By Charles McRaven

PAINTINGS BY
James Burkhart

PHOTOGRAPHS BY
Linda Moore McRaven and the Author

ILLUSTRATIONS BY
Chandis Ingenthron and the Author

Thomas Y. Crowell, Publishers
Established 1834   New York

Dedication

To Linda, who helped build our log house in the woods, and to Amanda, who is growing up in it.

BUILDING THE HEWN LOG HOUSE. Copyright © 1978 by Charles McRaven. All rights reserved. Printed in the United States of America. No part of this book may be used or reproduced in any manner whatsoever without written permission except in the case of brief quotations embodied in critical articles and reviews. For information address Harper & Row, Publishers, Inc., 10 East 53rd Street, New York, N.Y. 10022. Published simultaneously in Canada by Fitzhenry & Whiteside Limited, Toronto.

ISBN: 0-931158-00-1
LIBRARY OF CONGRESS CATALOG CARD NUMBER: 77-085768
79 80 81 82 83 10 9 8 7 6 5 4 3 2 1

Table of Contents

FOREWORD		6
INTRODUCTION	**Hewn Logs and Houses**	8
CHAPTER ONE	**The American House**	15
CHAPTER TWO	**Pioneer Building**	30
CHAPTER THREE	**Restoration**	44
CHAPTER FOUR	**Land and Site**	55
CHAPTER FIVE	**Design**	66
CHAPTER SIX	**Acquiring Materials**	77
CHAPTER SEVEN	**Foundation**	89
CHAPTER EIGHT	**Hewing, Notching, Log Raising**	98
CHAPTER NINE	**Roof**	119
CHAPTER TEN	**Stone Fireplace**	137
CHAPTER ELEVEN	**Floors**	148
CHAPTER TWELVE	**Windows and Doors**	156
CHAPTER THIRTEEN	**Porch, Lean-to, Loft**	165
CHAPTER FOURTEEN	**Water Supply and Waste Disposal**	179
CHAPTER FIFTEEN	**Utilities**	191
NOTES		199
REFERENCES		200
GLOSSARY		201
INDEX		206
ACKNOWLEDGEMENTS		208

Foreword

Books about traditional folk houses in general and log houses in particular have been published before. There have been "how-to-build" books, historical-geographical surveys, even studies of the personality of those people one hundred years ago who built and lived in traditional forms of housing -- based entirely on the house forms themselves. Charles McRaven, in **Building the Hewn Log House**, considers all of these approaches to the description and understanding of the hewn log house.

This is, primarily and without apology, a "how-to" book, and in the course of telling the reader how hewn log houses were built by the pioneers and how he himself builds and restores them today, McRaven also places the Ozark log house within the broader context of log house building in North America. Most interesting, I think, are the historical and personal ramifications of McRaven's work. Here is, in essence, a book written from the perspective of a log hewer and builder skilled as one a hundred years ago but who has the advantage of the improvements and refinements made in the building industry during the past century. Thus he achieves a vantage point on building with logs that is both structural and historical. Cultural geographers and folklorists can study traditional house types till all the timbers rot, but until they do the hewing and house-raising dozens of times themselves there will be something missing of lasting value -- something that Charles McRaven has to tell us all -- about our heritage, about a sense of time and history, about our great-grandfathers' blisters and calloused hands.

As I have said, the principle intent of this book is to tell you how to build your own log house. The work involved, however, suggests to a mechanical illiterate like myself that not everyone who picks up this book will rush out to build a log house. The true worth of McRaven's work does not depend on how many authentic hewn log houses begin to dot the landscape; rather, the main point of such a work is that it shows us how the cultural landscape of the Ozarks was shaped by the generations of log hackers who first came to these hills.

All of this would seem to imply that the author is an American primitive, a salty old eccentric who lives off the land and has refused to join the twentieth century. Not true. McRaven is forty-two years old, taught at the university level for several years, and stopped just short of earning his doctorate in journalism because he felt more comfortable wielding a broad axe than a Ph.D. He and his wife and baby girl do live in a log house, way down in a holler, but they commute daily to a business they own and operate in Hollister, Missouri. He also has been a regular contributor to **The Ozarks Mountaineer** for several years. McRaven knows the ways of the early Ozark settlers, from his years of building and restoring hewn log houses, and knows log houses well, having even grown up in a round log house in Saline County, Arkansas. As often as not, however, his anecdotage is of both his work and his time -- cutting and hauling logs in a sleet storm, overturning a four-wheel drive vehicle on the way home from a house-raising, driving an old truck loaded with logs down a muddy mountain. There is much here for the general reader as well as for the scholar and potential house-builder.

This book is the first volume in the Arkansas College Folklore Monograph Series, the purpose of which is to publish regional studies in Ozark folklore and folklife. Initial funding for the series has come from the Rockefeller Foundation; we gratefully acknowledge the support of the Foundation, both for the series as a continuing annual publication and for partial funding for the publication of this first number.

Richard S. Tallman
Folklore Archivist and General Editor
Arkansas College Folklore Monograph Series

INTRODUCTION

Hewn Logs and Houses

With so many available publications on building your own shelter, using everything from plywood to old car bodies, it seemed to me fitting that a detailed work on traditional log houses was in order. Of course there are "log cabin" books in every bookstore, but these invariably deal with the round-log, "modern" cabins. Somehow, we seem to have come to accept these pole cabins of sapwood logs, stacked schoolboy fashion, as the shelters America grew in.

Not so. Historians and folklorists have established reliable records of the growth of log housing in this country, beginning not long after Jamestown and Plymouth. With few exceptions, the pioneers built hewn log houses.

Although its origins may be traceable to the Scandinavian mead halls or the old English half-timbered cottages, the squared-log homesteaders' house of this country's uplands is an architectural form entirely its own.

The use of round logs was limited mostly to temporary cabins, barns, forts and hastily thrown up shelter. Our forbears built with much more skill to house their families. Hewing, adzing, notching, mortising, riving--all these skills reached a high level in the building of a settler's permanent home.

And the labor involved was staggering. If there is a single reason hewn log houses are so rarely built today, it is that just too much work is required. Everyone who attempts a log house today tries to avoid the very investment in painstaking, hard work that gave the hewn log house its heart. Builders devise crack-brained schemes to shape logs mechanically into identical, fit-together games. The purveyors of log cabin kits peddle their Lincoln-Log wares to nostalgia buffs who want their houses assembled quickly if not authentically.

The hewn log house survived the seasons and the wear of generations because it was best. Best for the needs of the people, in best harmony with the land, the best use of the materials at hand. With its easily-rotted sapwood hewn away, its corner notches locked rigid, its thick walls holding heat in or out, it stands as a beautiful part of our heritage, best because it has lasted, and served.

Of course today we can render those same massive logs into skinny two-by-fours, plywood, fiberboard, particle board and fake paneling, and build several dwellings. I can only say that a log house I build will house many generations, as have those of the pioneers. The modern thin-walled, thin-roofed, thin-floored house may shelter one, or two.

To build or restore a hewn log house today, you must first come to terms with the materials and the way they must be worked. Study the settlers themselves; by understanding their way of life you can come to understand their homes. Do not make the common mistake of assuming that you have the advantage of modern machines and technology. Or that, if done well with hand tools and limited knowledge in 1800 it will be done much better today.

The very use of machines has dulled our self-reliance, our inventiveness, our ability to think in harmony with the materials and with the earth. When you can learn to select the right wood for each purpose, knowing how it can be worked, how it responds to shaping, stress, seasoning, dampness, you have only begun. You must then learn to cut that particular tree, hew or rive your timber, shape, smooth, fit it to its use, all by hand, before you begin to achieve the viewpoint necessary for this kind of work.

Then you must learn thousands of long-forgotten building pitfalls, common knowledge to those same settlers. You must make mistakes serious enough to be remembered.

Not all of us will shape and drive a wooden peg equally well. Some of our forefathers too, were terrible at building, and most of their flimsy efforts have fallen down. Those that remain are usually the best, and you can learn from them.

If you plan to build, start with something simple. Try shelves, a doghouse, a small barn. You may in the process remove all doubt that you are indeed a bumbler, and only the cows will know.

Do not hurry. Almost all the problems modern owners of hewn log houses encounter stem directly from their own frenzy to get inside. We are too conditioned to paying our money for instant gratification. Even the kit houses must be given time to settle, although their buyers may not be told this. Allow a year. Or two. Take time to savor this experience; you may not repeat it.

When I begin a hewn log house, it does not matter that this is one of many I have raised or restored. The thrill of beginning a new affair returns, in the feel of worn tools in my hands, in the sight of new foundation stones rising from the ground. And the first long broadaxe strokes wake an old fever inside me. My hands harden again to the feel of wood and stone. And I look forward to the long months of building.

I tell first-time builders to begin in the fall, when the crisp air makes handling the broadaxe a form of joy. Hew a few logs at a time, maybe one a week, or one a day. Work through the cold months. When the ground is too frozen to dig foundations, the big axe will have you in shirtsleeves. And by spring you will have a pile of hewn logs, partly seasoned, lighter in weight, ready to be notched and raised on your new foundation stones.

Settling and shrinking will go on through the summer as you labor. Roof as soon as possible, but leave verticals like door and window facings, staircase uprights, studs for the lean-to, till a year has passed. Two years is better, but most of the settling will be over by the second fall. Chink last, when the logs are completely seasoned.

The driving of the final wooden peg, the placing of the last chimney stone, is for me never an occasion of pure joy. It is inevitably an anticlimax, an aimless gathering of tools and leftover pieces in the unaccustomed quiet, a sad time of leave-taking.

I become quite involved with my houses, to the extent that I will no longer build for a client. It's something like the relationship an antique car enthusiast has with his treasures. The 1850's pine log house I recently acquired will ultimately become half a dogtrot, in a glade on 40 acres we own in a notch of National Forest. Sometime later, when the icy air has the other squirrels home in bed, I will hew out a matching pen, and once again put my skill up alongside that of some nameless settler.

And of course, I will probably continue to write about these houses. The history and background in these chapters comes from my own research and observation, and through the kind assistance of the Folklore Department of Arkansas College at Batesville. Professors Dick Tallman and George Lankford made available to me a great deal of pertinent material I would otherwise have missed.

Most of the history and reference information is concentrated in the early chapters, which chart the evolution of the log house. Subsequent chapters, beginning specifically with chapter four, are the how-to section.

The chapters are arranged in a sequence to yield information about this very American house: its origins, types and locations. Then the business of how to build or restore one is dealt with from site selection to final details such as plumbing and utilities. It is designed to be the source book as well as the handbook of hewn log building.

I tell you about the evolution and growth of this type of house, its sizes, shapes, traditions. I tell, piece by piece, how to build one, and why it must be done this way. I have swung an axe since I was nine, and have made all the mistakes I warn of, rejecting systematically the methods that did not work.

I have built and restored several hewn log houses over the years (and a few round log ones) and there is no part of the work I do not do myself. I have forged nails and hinges, hewn logs and riven shakes, laid the stone and raised the beams by hand. I have gone into the forest with an axe, and built from the standing trees. My writing is from experience, from blisters earned, and judgment sharpened in use. I do not work from someone else's plans. My tools are old tools, partly because I like old things, and partly because, like the log houses themselves, old tools seem to work best.

But I learn many things new each time I begin the labor of long love with the first foundation stone of another log house. I rediscover truths perhaps known by my ancestors, facing the forests of the frontier.

I must confess that, from the laying of the first stone for a log house, I work in close harmony with images of my own great-grandfathers. One, David Saxon, traveled from South Carolina in the 1850's to hew out a pine log house among the low hills near Camden, Arkansas. Another, Daniel McGraw, left the cotton-sun of Mississippi in 1878 to settle a long slope of mountain above the Mulberry River near Turner's Bend, in a cabin with a deerskin for a door.

And generations before them, west from the Carolinas the ghosts of earlier ancestors move through the forests on silent feet, axes on their shoulders, into the new land. Up the lost creeks and the narrow hollows, sometimes to the very hillsides where I have hewn long after.

We may meet them, you and I, in some clear October dusk down in a beechwood glade, among the smell of clean wood and the bright chips scattered. They will look long at the work of our hands, measuring in the wisdom of their incredible years. And we will need no words.

                                        Roark Creek
                                        Taney County, Missouri
                                        August, 1977

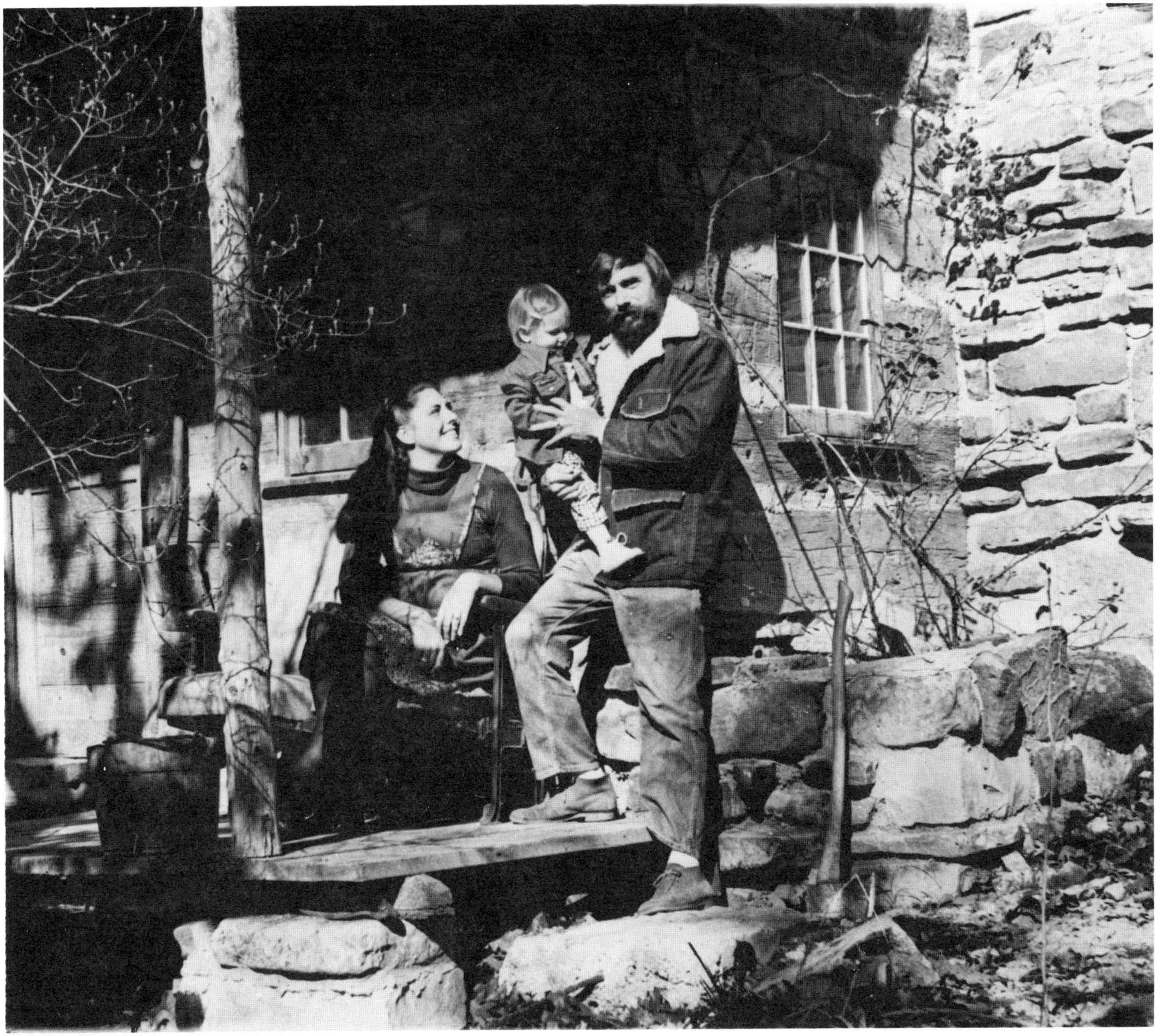

14

CHAPTER ONE

The American House

The settler who swung his long axe in the clearing to shape the logs for his pioneer home, established a tradition curiously American: The log cabin. Even the term calls up mental pictures of open fireplaces, long rifles and coonskin caps. It has launched presidential aspirations, and been the setting for a hundred years of hillbilly stories. But in this age of temporary housing, it retains its dignity.

Usually a hastily put together and sometimes crude shelter, these houses still conformed to a building method that had its solid roots in European soil. And the hewn logs stood the tests of Indian attack, of winter and of rain and of the advancing years. Listen now, to the story the old logs have to tell.

The American log house is by historic definition a structure of hewn logs, corner-notched to form one or more pens, chinked with split boards or thin stones, and mud or mortar, covered on top with split shakes. It has one or more fireplaces, stone or mud-and-stick chimneys, and is intended as a permanent home.

The log cabin, by contrast, is often of round logs, and is of less careful construction, being generally built as a temporary or occasional residence. Size has little to do with the basic difference between house and cabin, although this is the definition basis most people today would use -- our "bigger is better" society speaking.

"Cabin" is from the old French term "Caban." Eugene Wilson writes the earlier "Capanna", which may be the forerunner of these names, has Neolithic connections.[1] American cabins have been mostly one-room structures, evolving from the "bay" or "rod" dimension, 16 feet, of English rural housing.

The 16-foot measure, perhaps originally from the width required by four oxen, recurs again and again throughout the growth and spread of log housing. That's largely cultural; the isolated pioneer as often measured his house using his three-foot axe handle. But the fact remains that logs of greater length were heavy and awkward for the lone settler to handle. His need was for quick shelter, so a small structure of the materials available--logs--filled that need best.

This settler often dreamed of a substantial country house like those of the gentry that rose along the rivers of the East. This log building would be temporary, and when his fields ran wide and the roads reached out from the teeming towns, he would build again. And the log house would be put aside, for use by visiting relatives, or as servants' quarters, eventually even to be stuffed with hay.

A historic comparison of log house vs. log cabin is from D.A. Hutslar, who quotes Thaddeus Harris, writing in 1805 of the trans-Alleghany territory. Cabins, Harris wrote, were of unhewn logs, chinked with rails and moss, straw and mud. Roofs were covered with long staves with weight poles. There were no windows or chimneys. Log houses, on the other hand, were hewn, with stone and plaster in the chinks. The roofs were shingled, there were glass windows, and chimneys.[2]

It's a bit difficult to imagine a cabin with no chimney, yet the early ones often had no more than a hole in the roof for the smoke from the dirt-floored fireplace to escape through. This was common in the peasant cottages of Britain. The gable-end fireplace so common in America developed in 15th Century England. Shortly thereafter, with the upper area now free of smoke, lofts became common. In central Europe, the chimney was usually in the center of the house.

The settlers from the tall ships anchored off Jamestown and

Plymouth had been for the most part town dwellers. Although many were skilled carpenters with tools at hand, they had no knowledge of, or experience with, log construction. They set about reducing the formidable forest trees to whipsawn boards and riven clapboards to nail onto hewn timbers, just as they would have done in Europe. Housed temporarily in huts of sailcloth, branches and thatch, they endured rain, cold, and Indian depredation while laboriously fashioning houses they were familiar with.

They could have had snug, safe quarters of logs almost from the first had they so chosen. Most historians are of the opinion that these immigrants just didn't know how to build with logs until the Swedes, Finns and Germans brought their skills with them later in the 17th century.

However, since logs were used early for stockade walls, forts and even jails, it's more likely that the first settlers clung to their complicated house construction practices more as a link with a culture they feared would soon fade in the wilderness. History is full of accounts of civilized people thrust into the wilds, clutching remnants of their ordered, familiar pasts.

The very persistence of hewn logs instead of round in the log houses of the pioneers is more a cultural than practical matter, given the relative labor and skill involved in building this way. Barns, corncribs, even temporary dwellings and hunter's shacks could be of round logs, but not the house the pioneer wife was to keep and raise her children in. It must have some pretensions to gentility, if only flat walls.

Remember, she was probably the moving force behind those pioneers-turned-planters who rose from owning nothing but wild land, to the ranks of the new gentry. And until she had her painted rooms and her plastered walls, she'd have them hewn as smooth as possible, thank you.

But of course the availability of so much timber, and soon the influx of log-wise Scandinavian and middle European craftsmen, saw the log house emerge as **the** frontier structure. It could be built with only an axe if need be, and built well with an axe, auger, broadaxe, drawknife, hammer and nails. No whipsawn boards, complicated mortising or carefully finished woodwork went into the average frontier log house, although some finely crafted specimens were built.

The settlers of New Sweden, on the Delaware River, are credited with the beginning of log house construction in America. Fort Christina, at what is now Wilmington, was built in 1638. C.A. Weslager says half of the first settlers in New Sweden were Finns, whose building techniques were closer to the later styles here than those of the Swedes.[3] Log houses were built inside a log stockade wall for protection, and soon others spread out into the countryside.

It takes some imagination, today, to envision this land blessed with straight trees that fit so well into the building traditions of these new Americans. With what impatience these settlers must have ventured farther and farther from the fort's walls to raise their log houses and establish their farms. Up the Delaware, out into the waiting wilderness, the Indians, the wild game, the good land.

Some of these early dwellings were of round logs, some of hewn. Corner fireplaces were a Scandinavian feature different from either the German or Scotch-Irish log houses soon to appear.

The influx of Germans into Pennsylvania, and the advent of large numbers of Scotch-Irish into the region by 1700, combined with the spread of the Scandinavian influence to create the log house as it has become known. Fred Kniffen makes the significant statement that "building with logs was a mode of construction, not an architectural type. Log, frame, stone or brick may all be the material for a type."[4]

But it wasn't that simple. Corner-notched log pens just about mean square or rectangular houses or sections of houses, so the choice of types is limited somewhat. I do know some zealots who've built odd, multi-sided log houses in an attempt to be "different", but some other material would have been better. I think the materials -- logs -- influence type considerably. More about this later.

Warren Roberts discusses similarities in and differences between Scandinavian log houses and those in America, and concludes that there is little resemblance, overall.[5] Montell and Morse say the Pennsylvania

Germans introduced the classic American log house.[6] Henry Glassie states that "the log cabin stands as a symbol of this meshing of German and Scotch-Irish cultures."[7]

We can say safely that the cultural building patterns of the Scandinavians, Germans, Scotch-Irish, English and even the Dutch underwent some necessary modifications to fit the conditions and materials available. The New Sweden houses were not of the careful oval-log, tightly fitted, chinkless style Roberts found where these people came from.[8]

The Scotch-Irish must have been overjoyed at tall, straight trees to build with, instead of the mud and stones and thatch of Ulster. And the Germans set to work building those wonderful barns of log and stone, along with their substantial American log houses with the Old Country touches. In this land of trees, our ancestors naturally used them freely.

The spread of log housing followed the flow of settlers to new territory. Germans, traveling to the Shenandoah in 1732, passed through Maryland, and of course many settled along the way. The Scotch-Irish moved into Virginia, too, and to the Carolinas. Ohio, Kentucky, Tennessee and north Georgia were penetrated as the 1700's wore on. Even during the Revolution thousands of land-hungry pioneers moved West, into the rich lands of the Tennessee River basin, fighting their own battles with Indians, the ever-encroaching forest, and the elements.

By 1800 the tide had reached into Alabama, where Eugene Wilson divides the folk house types into first, second and third generations.[9] He identifies first generation houses with fine craftsmanship, built with skill, to endure. These were built until around 1840, when the second generation saw commercial hardware, windows and doors appear. Less attention to quality craftsmanship is evident here. In the classic dogtrot house, Wilson notes a shift from the two front doors to entry ways off the open passage during the period 1840-1890. The houses also are not as tall as those built earlier. Third generation houses, to 1940 or so, embody most of the modern rural building techniques.

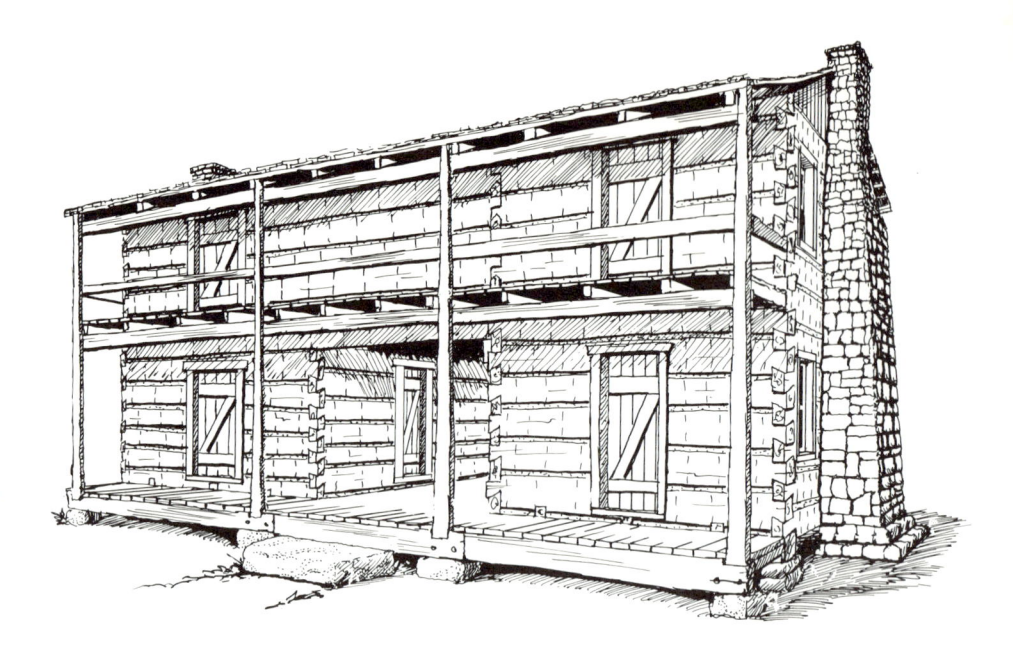

The two-story dogtrot house, with interior log partition upstairs. This is similar to the Wolf house in North Arkansas, and epitomizes the height of log house craftsmanship. Its ground floor plan is below.

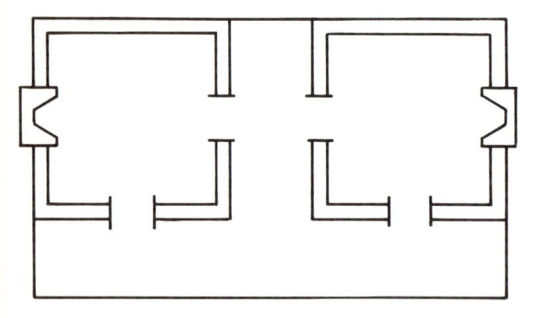

Mention of the dogtrot house brings us to the question of log house types or styles. Beginning with the basic one-room structure of one story, with gable-end chimney, and door on the side parallel to the ridge, the types evolved in several directions.

A loft was the feature most often added, requiring perhaps three more courses of logs above the ceiling joists and a combination ceiling and upstairs floor. Given a relatively steep roof pitch, the living area was essentially doubled with the loft addition. These 1½ story single-pen houses were built from the 1600's onward till perhaps the 1940's, when traditional log construction can be said to have ended.

That's a date out of the air, but it's close. Certainly during the Depression lots of hungry folks back from the city hacked out log houses for themselves on the folks' back forties. There, as before, that loft was the place the kids were stowed. Being a child of that period, I escaped sleeping in the loft of the cabin my father built probably only because it was never finished. Curiously, forty years later mine isn't, either.

A full two-story single-pen log house required only a few more logs, and these became common as permanent farm houses, principally in the East, and West into Ohio and Indiana. Like the loft house, the two-story required a peg ladder or narrow stair for reaching the upper floor.

Double pen houses were logical expansions, given the weight of the logs. By building two separate pens, the settler could enlarge his house with easily-managed short logs. He either built directly against his existing house at the gable end, or set up the second pen some distance away and connected the two with one roof.

A double pen log house joined at the gable opposite the chimney is called just that--a double pen house--although it can have other names, bestowed by historians. The double pen house usually has two front doors, and a second chimney may be added at the gable end of the new pen. An example I am quite familiar with is the Beaver Jim Villines house at Ponca, Arkansas, now being preserved by the National Park Service as part of the Buffalo National River. The original pen logs are of hewn oak; the added pen is of cedar.

When the added pen was joined at the chimney end, the house was called a saddlebag. The chimney was often rebuilt or added to, to allow a fireplace to open into each pen. It should be noted here that double pen houses of all kinds were quite often built all at once, not added later. The double fireplace is a good reason why, since it's harder to add a second one later in the center of the house.

This building all at one time was also the case with the dogtrot house as often as not, which has the two separate pens, joined by a common roof. Montell and Morse tend to believe both halves of the dogtrots they studied in Kentucky were built at one time.[10]

I know of as many dogtrot log houses with pens built at different times, as I know of those built all together. Quite often a second pen would have different notching, indicating either another date, or even transfer of the pen from another site. It should be pointed out that the more hard-nosed scholars insist that a true dogtrot have pens of identical dimensions, and that the breezeway be floored. Since it is a colorful pioneer house type, modern rebuilders have certainly taken farfetched liberties with non-dogtrot cabins to achieve the general effect.

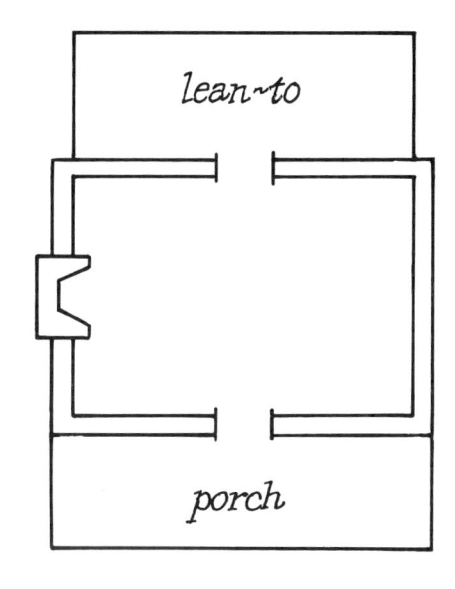

The basic one-room floor plan was enlarged in the double-pen, below, and the saddlebag, bottom. as well as the dogtrot. Additional wings and ells were also added.

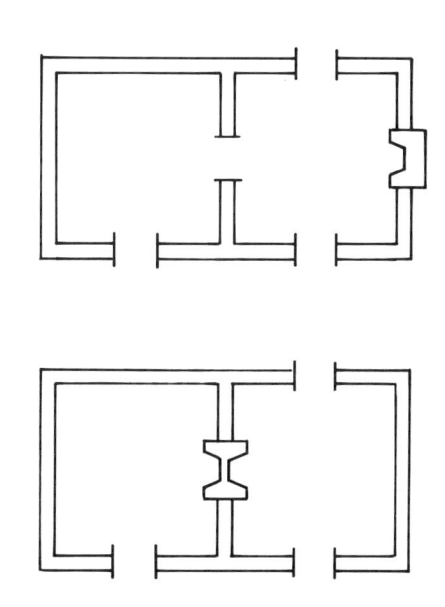

Many dogtrots have been closed in for more living space, and many boarded up entirely in complete camouflage.

The Ingenthron log house north of Forsyth, Missouri shows a way many dogtrots were enclosed for more living space.

Wilson points out that the early Norse often utilized separate buildings for separate functions, and that these were often joined with a covered passage.[11] Certainly the open passage house was known prior to its appearance in this country as a log house.

The earliest example in my region is the Jacob Wolf house in Norfork, Arkansas, built in 1809. I have read of examples in the Tennessee Basin in the late 1700's. But whatever its origins, and whether built together or separately, the double-pen dogtrot house has become the stereotype of the substantial pioneer farmer's dwelling.

J. Frazer Smith[12] sees the type as an evolutionary link between single-room log cabin and central-hall plantation house. With the passageway enclosed, and perhaps two rooms on each side of the hall thus created, you do have the basic planter's house of Tennessee. But the English Georgian houses of Sir Christopher Wren and their counterparts in Virginia had already set the pattern for the central hall "big house" of the upland South.

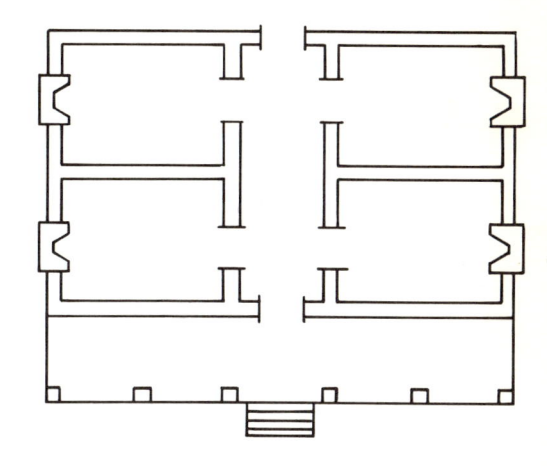

Yet another form of the double-pen house, and somewhat of a riddle in itself, is the Whitaker-Waggoner log house which stood in Morgan County, Indiana, before its removal to Indiana University. This house was of two V-notched pens across the front, with a common log partition notched by means of a combination V- and half-notch, into the joined double length logs of the front and back. Warren Roberts[13] dates the house reliably at about 1820, at which time apparently a rear wing, partially of frame and partially of log with single dovetail notching, was also built. Interlocking foundation stones place the coincidence of construction dates, and Roberts conjectures that perhaps the rear log portion of the wing was moved from another site on the place. An old barn on the farm was of similar notching.

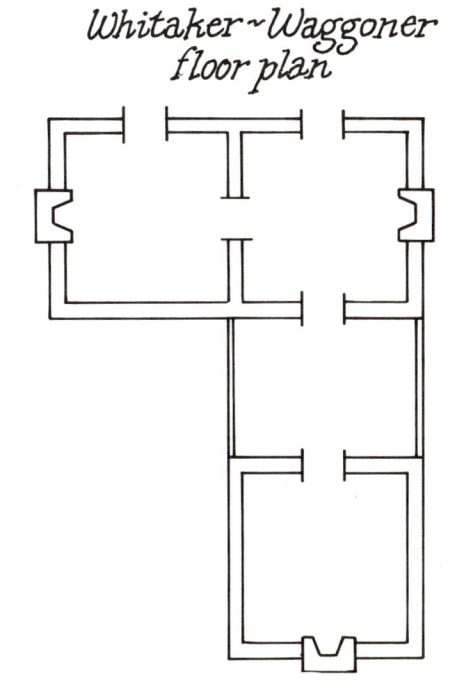

This particular house showed a high degree of craftsmanship in several features. The joined interior log partition was rare, as was the continuous foundation. Extended top gable-end logs supported the 18-inch wide plates, which extended outward to form overhanging eaves. The rafters were fitted to these plates. The plates were kept from bowing out under the roof weight by timbers mortised and pinned between them, at each end of the front section, and in the center, over the partition. Roberts gives no details regarding a doorway between the upstairs rooms, since this timber would have spanned the building at the plate height of four feet. Perhaps a separate stair or ladder, not shown in the plans, gave access to the second upstairs room.

This house also furnished convincing proof that many Indiana log houses, at least, were sided soon after construction.[14] Clapboarding here went on before the end chimneys, and when removed, showed little weathering of the logs underneath. This seems to have been a practice that did not reach into the Missouri and Arkansas Ozarks, although boards were quite often nailed over the logs in later years to keep out

Planter's House

Whitaker-Waggoner floor plan

Dogtrot with separate rear ell.

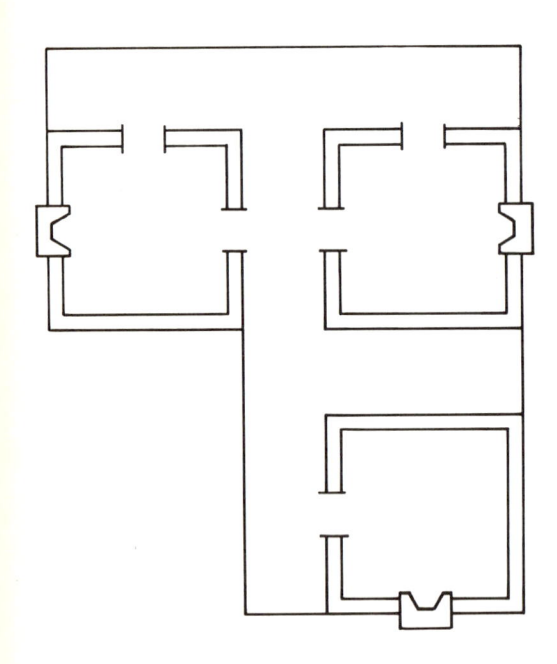

drafts and unwelcome fauna.

The interior partition log house, whether two full pens or with a common wall, is often referred to as a hall-and-parlor house. It has two rooms on the ground floor, and may or may not have a loft.

Two-story versions of the double-pen house fall into the 'I' house type. This house is one room deep and two or more long, but is always two-story. It has gable-end chimneys and in the early versions, assymetrical plans, according to Glassie.[16]

Fred Kniffen[17] calls the "I" house (not necessarily the log version) "The most widely distributed of all folk types" and sees it as the "symbol of economic attainment as a rural dwelling." The "I" plan often evolved as the earlier small farmers grew prosperous and their owners wanted more pretentious dwellings. It's significant that this basic plan is also seen very early in French Louisiana, with a liberal use of galleries and French windows for circulation of air. Here the upper level became the main floor, with utility rooms brick or tile-floored near ground level to contend with periodic flooding.

All the basic types of log houses were added to in other ways. The rear wing of the Whitaker-Waggoner log house, with its ridgeline at a right angle to that of the main house, is typical. This rear wing was usually aligned with one pen of the double-pen house, to form an ell, and was almost always one-story. Similar wings were added to single-pen houses, also. Usually the rear unit was separate from the main house, it being difficult to join logs to an existing structure. Another reason for a breezeway between the main house and rear wing was for fire protection, since this was often used as the kitchen.

A shed-roof lean-to was another addition common to all the basic log house types. It often became a kitchen, too, but was invariably attached directly to the house. The lean-to was usually of rough-sawn lumber.

The lean-to wasn't limited to log houses. This logical appendage appears on frame houses, brick houses and even barns. I just wish whoever sells that brick-patterned tarpaper so many lean-to s are plastered with, would stop it.

Just as the log house itself emerged as the logical house type for the new country, peculiar local treatments evolved. Social custom and tradition mixed necessity, skill and available tools and materials to produce local characteristics. As a general rule, as the generations passed, less care was given to log building techniques. As sawmills became common, fewer craftsmen learned the finer points of hewing and shaping wood. And the use of hardware, milled doors and windows lessened the need for close work. Probably because fewer log houses were being built as permanent dwellings by the "modern" farmers, the finished work was saved for the ultimate frame house. Logs in houses became smaller in general, too, whether for lack of good timber or ease of handling.

But there are peculiarities from region to region. Glassie tells of the uniqueness of "catted" mud-and-stick chimneys in the Ouachita Mountains of Arkansas,[18] an area of excellent building stone. So does Nancy McDonough.[19] The half dovetail notch was almost universal in the Ozarks log buildings, whereas the V-notch was prevalent farther East. An exception is the square notch, favored in the White River Valley around Batesville, Arkansas, where many house logs were also hewn evenly on all four sides.

Ozark roof pitches were predominantly 45° or a 12" drop in 12", but Hutslar reports the Ohio average as 9" drop in 12".[20] Some historians try to link roof pitch to age, but this, as with notching methods, is at best inconclusive.

In a given locale, builders might have favored the log gable (mostly evident in early buildings) while elsewhere the gables are framed. In Kentucky, Montell and Morse found windows in the fireplace gable ends of many houses,[21] but Roberts states that this was rare in Indiana.[22] It was also rare in the Ozarks, except in more recent houses.

The practice of covering newly-built log houses with siding seems clearly to have been practiced in areas where sided frame houses were common. It was seldom if ever done on the early frontier, for the obvious reason that siding was not available to the harried hunter settlers.

House Age

Perhaps a discussion of determining log house age is in order here. You will find that local inquiry unsupported by responsible records is almost worthless for houses built before the generations now living. Common responses are "It's 'way over 100 years old," or "My grandad remembered that house when he was little, and it was real old then." Any building weathered gray is taken as being old, and folks have a fondness for perpetrating myths about the age of things. Let me warn you that they may also become vehement and even violent about the veracity of their pet versions of history (as any of you who have researched local precedent already know).

In general, there are a few obvious things to look for if no reliable records exist. For instance, round wire nails came into use around 1890,[23] although cut nails can be found in houses built later. (They can still be bought today). The cut nails appeared around 1820.[24] Of course hand-wrought nails were used on the frontier after 1820, but, this being a high priority item of trade, they were rare. Cut nails are those tapered, blunt-ended ones with two rounded sides and a symmetrical oval head. Wrought nails will show the hammer marks on the irregular heads. So a log house peppered with round nails dates since 1890, unless they've all been added later, and their application will tell you that. Cut nails in strategic places such as original door facings put your house roughly in the 1820-1890 range. Pegging of rafters and window and door facings, with maybe a few forged nails, can mean you have a really historic log house. That is, if it is located in an area of early settlement.

I dated a log house near my home at 1850 at the latest, because two of its four layers of roof were nailed with cut nails, and the shingles were of heart cedar. This wood lasts easily 40 years, properly applied, so even if the second roof had been put on in 1890 I shouldn't be far off. This house was also of pine logs, in an area where only the earliest houses were built of pine, since this wood was and is rare here. Of course the house could be older, but back to the roof: the one layer of shingles fastened with round nails would have deteriorated around, say

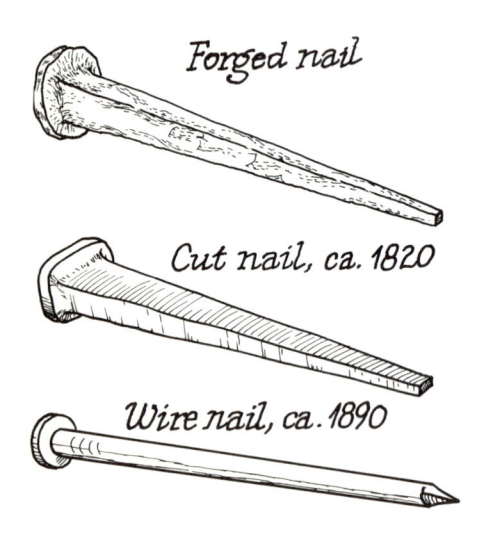

1930, and the latest roof of corrugated iron was still serviceable, with probably 45 years of age on it. The original circle-sawn (probably since 1840) lathing over the cedar-pole rafters was also from large pine trees, and showed the marks of just those roof nails mentioned.

The use of lime mortar in chimney stones and chinking means either that a house was built before modern concrete (1900-1920, roughly) or that it could be much older, since lime and sand mortar have been used for centuries. Mud chinking could mean only that the house was remote, or that its builders couldn't afford lime.

Pegging usually dates a log house before mass-produced hardware was readily available in that specific area. Again, the penury of the builder is a factor. Cast door locks became common around the 1840's, as did the pointed wood screws for attaching them and door hinges. Look for evidence of original doors, hinges, latches and fastenings. Many of these will have been replaced, but you will almost always be able to detect this in hinge strap mortises and perhaps old peg-holes.

Many log houses were moved, or recycled, since it is much easier to disassemble one and reassemble it, than to start from scratch. My own log house in Southwest Missouri has both oak and cedar logs, hewn differently and both half and full dovetail notching. I suspect the few full dovetails are evidence of reworking during an early reassembly.

Log gable ends instead of frame were used in early houses, with lengthwise roof poles, or purlins, for the shakes to be fastened to. I know of a few late (1870's) examples of this type, however, so the method is not sound for determining age.

Whipsawn boards almost always place a house as being built before 1850. True, some vertical sawmills were in use afterwards, but the circle saw, with its efficiency, had replaced most of them by then. Straight, uneven cuts indicate a man-powered pitsaw; regular patterns mean mechanical power, usually water or steam. I know of many dated houses from the 1850's in the Ozarks with rough, circle-sawn boards and beams.

Older houses had almost no eave, whereas 20th century versions

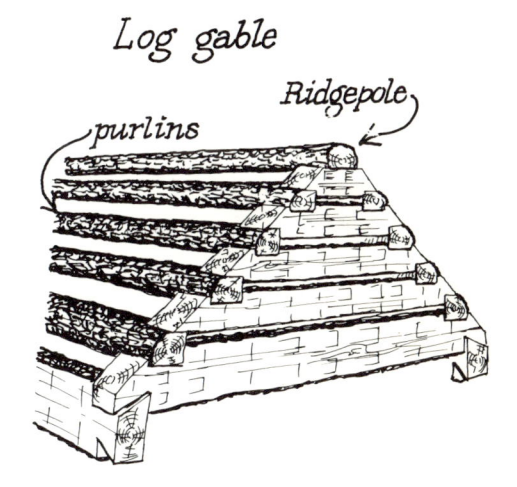

This is the basic one-room log house, with loft and porch. It remains the starting point for the hewn log house today, proven by 300 years of survival.

project all around. The exception was the early house with a catted chimney, where the builder often projected the eaves on the chimney gable end only to keep the mud dry.

    Study the history of the area to determine settlement dates. A claim of 1790's age in an area not settled till 1840 is obviously farfetched. There were isolated early houses built, but an abstract of the actual property will determine the homestead date, if nothing else.

    Hutslar mentions the science of dendrochronology,[25] or comparison of log growth rings to established regional patterns. If a log's rings extend to the bark edge at any point, the exact year of its cutting can be established. You can assume that the original construction, or at least the hewing, took place the same year, since no log-hacker in his right mind tackles seasoned timber. Check your state university for a possible growth scale.

Perhaps the most involved search for a log house's origins was that concerning Lincoln's birthplace. Weslager traces it through moves, reassemblies, rebuildings and changes of hands to its present, largely accepted status as Abe's first home.

Whatever its age, its origin or precedents, and wherever a hewn log house stands in America, you may be certain that it has become a classic of the pioneer era. A symbol of an age of timber, of hand craftsmanship, of our country's broad-shouldered youth.

The "I" house. Many farmers left their log houses for this style frame house, symbolic of their acquired affluence.

CHAPTER TWO

Pioneer Building

In the long move Westward, the custom of building the hewn-log house came into the new territory along with the settler's hunting skills and his other crafts for survival. He might camp for months on his new land in any sort of shelter, clearing and planting, building rail, stone, or pole fences for his stock. But his permanent dwelling, in the Smokies, the Tennessee Basin, in the Bluegrass, or on into the White River Ozarks to the West, was of hewn logs.

Certainly the earliest houses of this type in the new country were built with only the simplest of tools. We know of settlers having put up their houses with only the axe, and no hardware at all. To that tool was usually added at least one auger, and whenever at all possible, nails for the shakes on the roof. Indeed, many settlers possessed or had access to the tools of blacksmithing, which made available nails, and even hinges and the swinging crane for the fireplace. Plowing the new ground, replacing the axes, knives, shovels, and parts of harness, horseshoes, and wagon tires all depended on a smithy somewhere within reach.

31

We know the split shakes of early cabins were held in place with no nails, being weighted with butting poles, weight poles and knees, or they were wedged under saplings laid across them and bound at the ends with rawhide. But my experience with shake roofs in wind and rainstorms leaves me no doubt that these cabins were drafty and damp.

The building of the hewn log house was usually then, done with a limited but useful set of tools, and with handmade nails at least for the roof. With a felling axe, broadaxe, froe, augers, hand plane or drawknife, chisel, hammer, shovel, knife and perhaps a saw, adze and prybar, the pioneer could construct a house quite adequate and comfortable.

Poll axe

Log House Building Tools

One-man crosscut

The site chosen was usually on a rise of ground, above high water of creek or river. Rarely was it placed in a level spot with good soil, and indeed, it appears that the site most chosen was the one least desirable for cultivation. A rocky bank above a spring was a favored spot, or rough ground between newly-cleared fields. Outbuildings were scattered nearby: barn, smokehouse, corn crib, root cellar, henhouse. The hewn log house was only one of several structures necessary to sustain the settler.

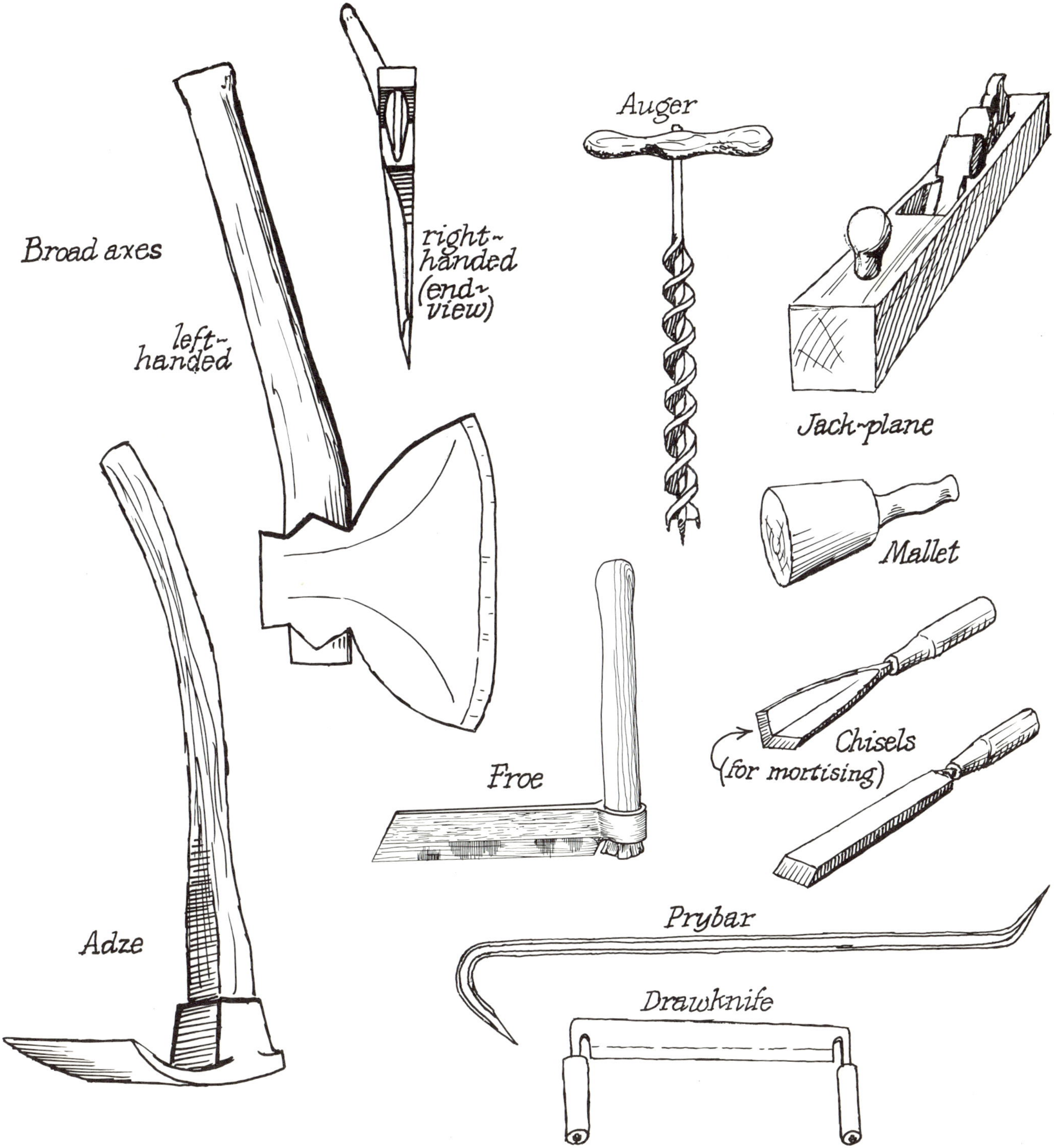
Broad axes
left-handed
right-handed (end-view)
Auger
Jack-plane
Mallet
Chisels
(for mortising)
Froe
Adze
Prybar
Drawknife

The actual construction began with cutting the trees, usually a continuing chore anyway, as fields were cleared. The man and older sons, if any, hewed the house logs on two sides while green, often adhering to the signs of the zodiac. March and May were supposedly good months, Eric Sloane tells us, to keep hewn timbers from warping. The logs were hewn to a thickness of 6 or 8 inches, with the heart in the center, to further reduce warping. Sometimes logs were split and each half hewn, but this was rare. Each family usually did its own hewing, over a period of perhaps months, and the logs were skidded to the house site where they seasoned, at least partially. Then, when enough logs were ready and time from farm work permitted, the house was raised.

The Raising

A house raising was held if other settlers were near, and this custom was as colorful a part of the pioneer's life as we know of. Neighbors began arriving at daybreak in wagons, on horseback or on foot, bringing their tools, the wives laden with food, children and dogs scampering everywhere. The air of festivity was that of a social occasion, as the women caught up on their gossip, the men competed good-naturedly in feats of strength, the girls and young men courted behind their elders' backs, and the children played and shrieked over everything.

If the logs had not been hewn ahead of time, crews were put to work with broadaxes, squaring the logs, sills, joists and beams. Then the men notched and fitted the logs, laying them on the stones of the foundation, prepared ahead of time. Notches were worked by eye, as was everything about the early log house. Everyone knew what he was doing; they all lived in houses like this one, after all, and had all done this many times before.

Sometimes the stone fireplace and chimney went up along with the logs, but this was usually added later. Sometimes the shakes were riven as the logs were laid, and clay and grass mixed for chinking and doors built. Rafters were laid out, and long slats split or poles cut, to go on them.

The noon meal was a feast combining the efforts of all the

women, and was as impressive as an outdoor church dinner. Favorite dishes combined and competed in bewildering volume, and many a stalwart lad found it hard to return to work afterwards.

Walls up to ceiling height of seven feet or so, the joists were notched in. Ceiling joists were usually broadaxe-hewn on all four sides, since they were to be visible from below. Sometimes they were dressed further with the adze, and (rarely) they were even beaded with the shaping plane. Often a mortise was cut into the front and back logs through which the joists extended to the outside. Weslager shows examples of this technique in New Sweden houses from the 17th Century. Wilson observes the custom of mortised ceiling joists in those log houses in Alabama with half-dovetail notches, and notched joist ends in V-notched houses.[26]

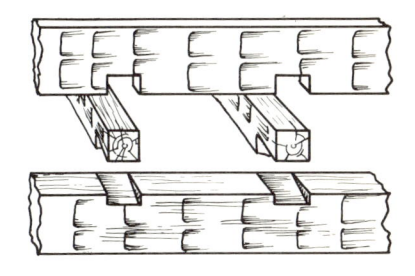

Ceiling joists half-dovetailed into wall logs. At left is a house in East Tennessee that shows clearly the joist ends in place.

Above the ceiling joists, two, three or even four courses of logs were laid to give more room in the loft. The walls terminated with heavy front and back plates hewn on all four sides, which were pinned at each end, down through at least one set of gable-end logs. These heavy wooden pins were known as "trunnels" (tree nails) and were whittled of tough locust, oak or hickory.

Trunnels were sometimes purposely square, to be driven into the round hole for a tighter fit. Sometimes notches were cut into them to help hold them tighter. A trunnel must be of dry seasoned wood or it will shrink and allow the timbers to come loose. It should be split out of heartwood, and never the slender sapwood branches.

35

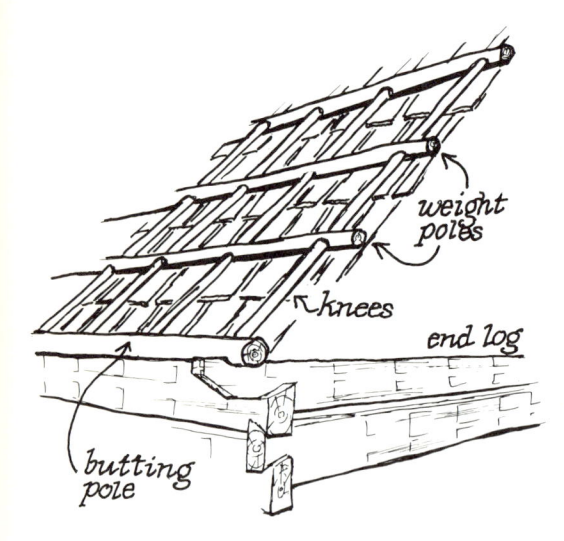

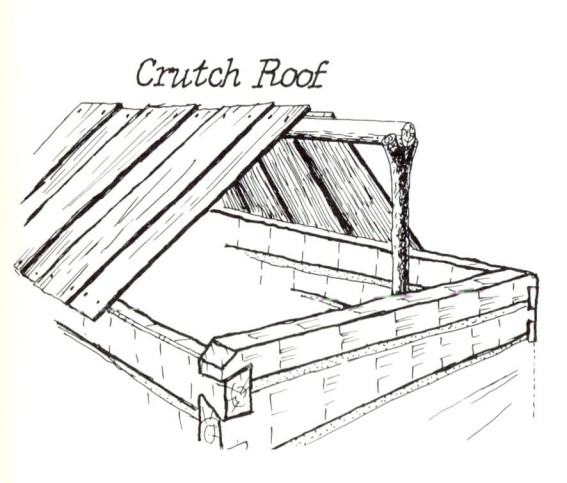

A final pair of end logs were notched into the ends of these plates. These logs were extended, in very early, nailless houses, to support the butting poles which held the knee and weight poles for the shakes. These end logs were sometimes carried on up to form the gable, becoming successively shorter to the ridge. This log gable method utilized lengthwise purlins, logs fitted to the ends of the gable logs. The top purlin became a ridgepole. Shakes were laid onto the purlins, and no rafters were used.

Still another very early method is quoted by J. Frazer Smith[27] as involving the use of a forked pole at each gable with the ridgepole laid in the fork. Then long clapboards were laid all the way from the plate to the ridge. Weslager tells of this "crutch" roof in early Jamestown.

With the availability of hardware, the framed gable became common, used with rafters, and long laths fastened across them. These rafters were usually poles, flattened on top, and the laths were split or sawn. Traditionally, when sawn lumber was used, it was not edged, but laid on full-width.

Shakes were usually riven ahead of time and allowed to season before the house raising. Shakes, like all timber, shrink when drying, so were never nailed up green. If laid with weight poles and knees, however, the shakes could be riven and laid green. Under the weight poles they could shrink without splitting. Traditionally, they were laid while the moon was on the increase, to avoid curling.

The window, fireplace, and door openings were sawed out, with either a partial saw cut having been made as the logs went up, or a series of auger holes bored to insert the saw through. Doors were put in place, and the cracks chinked.

Then, as a final christening, a dance was often held at dusk, in and outside the new house. Records show that a good deal of homemade whiskey was consumed at these raisings. Indeed, Hutslar quotes an early observer as estimating that the cost of refreshments might equal that of hired labor, had that been available.

At last the neighbors left, scattering by pine-knot flare and lantern light, to their own houses in the hollows. As social gatherings, house raisings were welcome, festive occasions.

I have participated in several modern cabin-raisings, and these differ only in mode of transportation and dress, from those of the pioneer. I hope this custom endures forever.

Too often early cabin logs were laid right on the ground, with the good earth for a floor. More substantial houses were laid on large stones at the corners, sometimes set down into the ground on firm subsoil. A column of sorts was built up to a sight level, which might be less than a foot high on flat ground, or three feet at the lower end of a hillside site. Stones were laid dry, with pebbles wedged between to stabilize them.

Sill logs were laid, usually as the first front and back logs. Unless a log house was square, it was almost always longer down the ridge line, so the floor joists, if any, were laid front-to-back, the shorter dimension, on the sills. These sills could be and were sometimes laid as end logs, but not generally. If a raised floor was to be built, joists were notched into the sills at regular intervals, from two to four feet. Sometimes small split logs or puncheons were notched and laid side by side on the sills with the flat sides up, to form the floor itself. These were worked with the adze when in place, and fitted to each other at the edges. As they seasoned and shrank, they could be slid together and another added to take up the space.

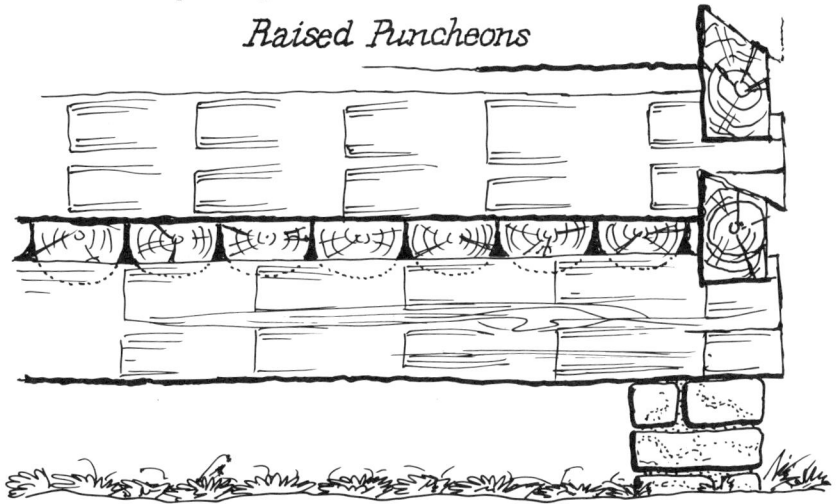

Raised Puncheons

Notch types

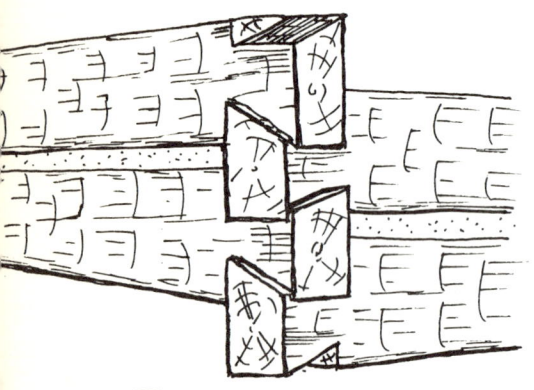

Half-dovetail

V-notch

If dirt or puncheons in the ground were to be the floor, the log walls went up all the way to the ceiling joists without interruption. The logs were notched either full-dovetail, V-notch, square-notched, or most often in later years, half-dovetailed. In rare cases in the early Midwest and East, a beautiful form of the full dovetail was used, in which each log was worked with notches of the same compound angle. Rarely, too, the diamond notch, half notch, and other experiments were used.

Logs were raised into position most often by hand. Most log houses were 20 feet or less long, or were two or more log pens of no more than that size. A man at each end of such a log, perhaps with the aid of skids, could just manage the job of raising it if no neighbors were near for a cabin-raising. Let's picture the pioneer father at one end, with perhaps his sturdy wife and a half-grown boy at the other. Or the team of oxen or horses could be used to cross-haul the logs up skids, into place, with the final fitting done by hand.

At ceiling height, usually six to seven feet, joists were notched in, again from front to back. Upon these, as upon the floor joists, would be laid the split or rare sawn boards of the ceiling and floor.

Above ceiling height and two or three more courses of logs, was laid the heavy top plate. In the finest tradition of log building that has survived, the rafters terminated at this plate, which was thicker than the wall under it, often projecting out to form a minimal eave. Sometimes the plate projected inwards, and the rafters were notched into it or over its outer corner to extend to form eaves.

The real function of the heavy plate, which was usually of oak, even in pine, poplar, or other soft wood houses, was to help take the outward thrust of the rafters under the roof weight. Where there were no log courses above the ceiling joists, these joists held against this thrust, but some log wall above the ceiling was common.

If the house were of the log gable type, the top plate need not be heavier. No rafters were used here, so there was no outward thrust.

With rafters, split slats or poles were fastened lengthwise to them for the shakes to be laid upon. These pieces were sometimes bound with rawhide or pegged, as were the rafters. Pegs were often square, to be

Full Dovetail

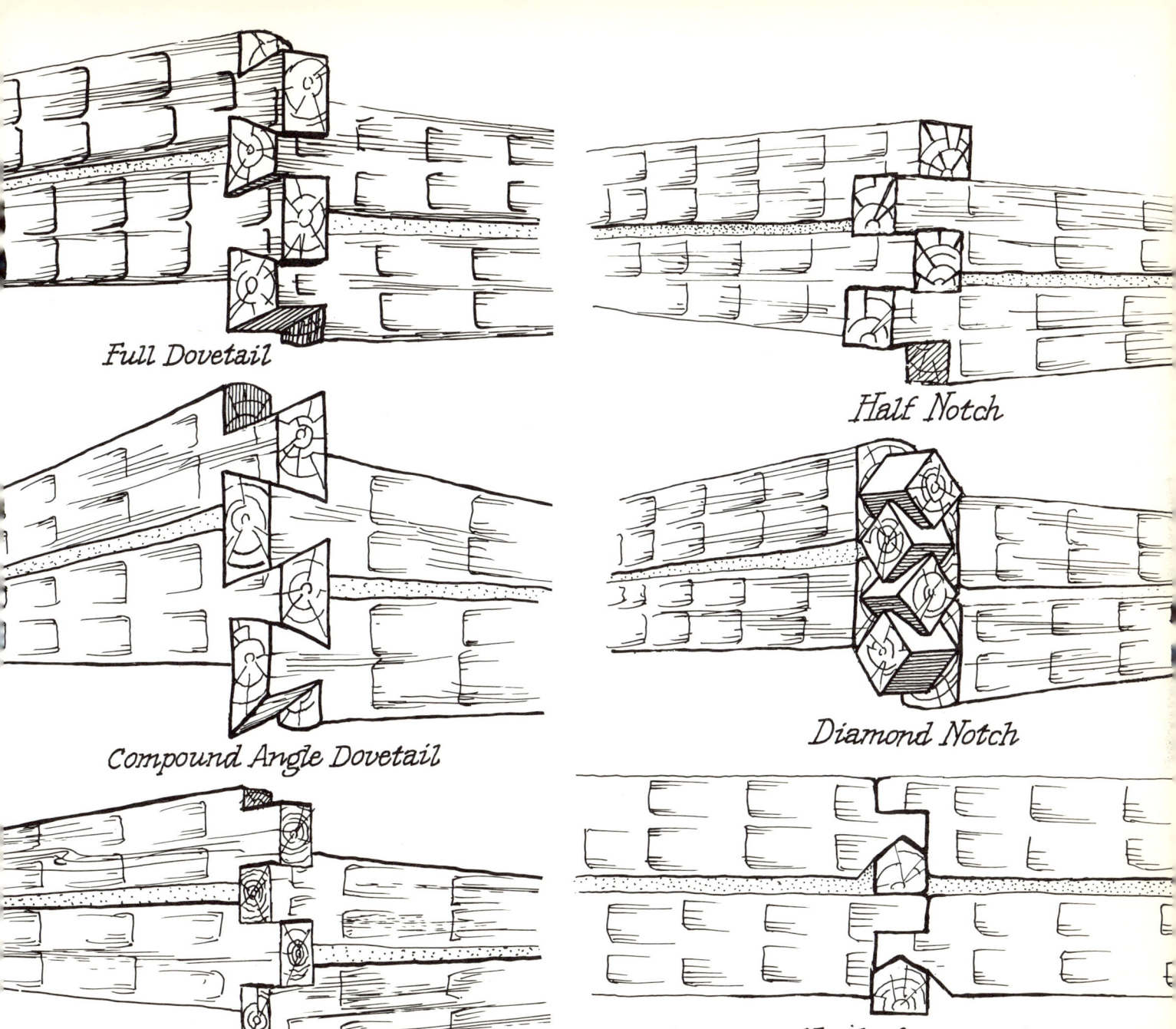

Half Notch

Compound Angle Dovetail

Diamond Notch

Square Notch

Partition Notch for extending walls

Pole rafters

Blacksmithing Tools

driven tightly into the round auger holes.

The rafters themselves were poles, sometimes worked flat on top with the drawknife or adze. They were fitted together in pairs at the peak with no ridgepole. Most often a 45° roof pitch was used, making figuring angles much simpler. Some steeper roofs were built, and many less steep. Often the pitch was a matter of guess, or of the builder's eye, as were the very dimensions of the house itself.

Shakes for the roof were split with the froe, an L-shaped tool driven with a heavy mallet. Early shakes were quite long, often three feet or more, of the prime timber the pioneers found. If laid without nails, the shakes could be riven and used, green. Nailed shakes had to be seasoned to prevent splitting at the nails as they shrank. Some early craftsmen split shakes of green wood, others of seasoned. Oak, cypress, and cedar were most used.

If the settler had the knowledge and materials, he could forge his own roof nails from bits of worn metal. Even half a horseshoe, worn completely through at the front, could be drawn out easily to produce a handful of nails. Early blacksmiths used charcoal where coal was not available, in a simple sand-filled forge charged with a wood-and-leather bellows. A nail heading bar, hammer, and anvil with cutoff hardy were the only other tools necessary for this and most other simple iron working.

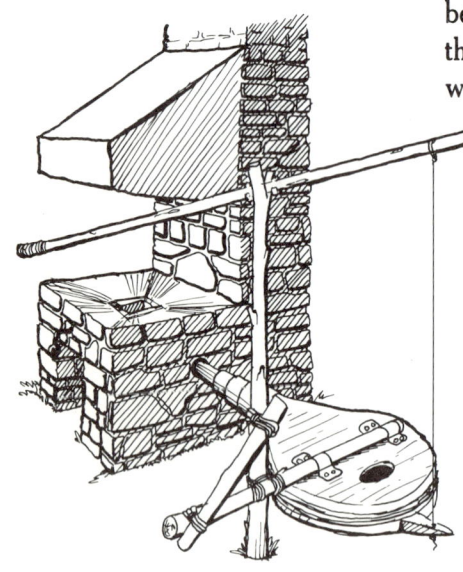

Forge and bellows

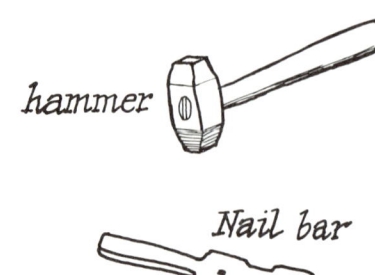

hammer

Nail bar

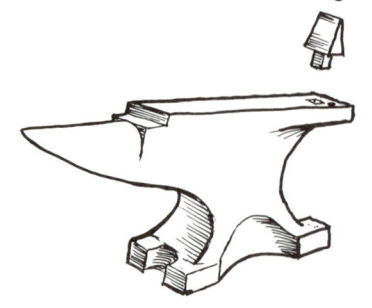

anvil and hardy

Occasionally these large split shakes were pegged in place with small wooden pegs,[28] but this was rare. Pegging was most effective as friction fastening, on the principle of a headless nail, and was not suited for the flexing of shakes in wind.

Where a log gable was not used, a gable framework of poles was pegged in, and shakes or riven clapboards used as covering. This allowed the house to be put under roof sooner than the log gable, and the whole was lighter. As sawn lumber became available, the log gable was even less common, boards being easier than shakes or split clapboards to work and to apply.

Doors and windows, if any, were sawed with the crosscut saw, starting in either partial cuts left for the purpose as the logs were laid up, or in a row of auger holes forming an opening. Into the cut log ends, facings of riven boards were pegged or nailed which were necessary to hold the logs in line. Then shutters and doors were hung with leather, wood, or iron hinges. Shutters were of split boards, or sometimes tightly stretched animal skins were used. Rarely, the first settlers had glass for windows. When they did, it was usually fastened in place instead of being hung to swing open, to avoid breaking it. The wooden shutters let in light only with the outside air, and were often kept shut all winter. In hot weather they let in gnats, flies and mosquitoes.

Doors were low affairs, made of split boards nailed or pegged together, seldom angle-braced. To keep them from sagging, the settler often used many of his precious nails in a heavy pattern, clinching them on the other side. The door was hung, and secured usually with the simple lift latch with its latch string hanging outside.

Board floors downstairs and up were often riven, though sometimes a primitive sawmill or whipsaw, powered by two men or a water wheel, produced sawn stock. As early as the settlement of Jamestown these saws were used and they were quite often added to water-powered gristmills in the new settlements. A board floor was a source of pride for the pioneer wife. It was pegged or nailed, with cracks lessened during installation by prying with a bar set in bored holes in the joists. Smoothing the rough lumber was accomplished sometimes by

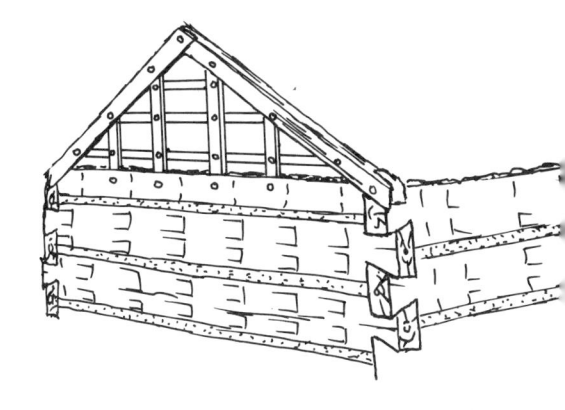

A mortised and pegged frame gable. These largely replaced the log gable and preceded the nailed framing. Below is a wooden shutter on a house on Bryant Creek in South Missouri.

rubbing with sand and stones.

The pioneer fireplace was of stone with clay or mud mortar. The chimney was often of sticks laid like the logs of the house, lined with "cats" of mud or clay. These chimneys were firetraps and unless used and maintained constantly, they fell apart in the rains. But they were easy to build, went up fast, and could be built with no special skills. As the mountain settlements became less remote, itinerant masons began building stone chimneys of really fine craftsmanship. Many older cabins had new chimneys of stone added after years of life with catted or loose stone work.

Chinking the early cabin was a continuing process. Short split boards were often laid at an angle in the cracks and a mud-and-grass mixture plastered into them. Sometimes thin poles were wedged in and covered with the mud or clay. Timber being plentiful, the earlier cabins tended to be built with wide logs, leaving little space for chinking, and only later were the wide cracks of 3 to 6 inches much in evidence.

Chinking, along with the hard work of hewn log building, has probably been the major reason for the near-disappearance of log

A catted chimney, often the original chimney which was later replaced with stone, this type persisted in such areas as the Quachita mountains in Arkansas. At right is traditional chinking in an 1850's pine log house being dismantled in South Missouri.

houses. Always the logs shrink away from the filling, as they season, or anytime dry weather or heat contract them. The drafts that result are likely to be the most memorable aspect of cabin living recalled by an old-timer. Shakes, slats, boards, and later tarpaper, were nailed over the chinked cracks. Mud, clay and lime mortar were patched and replaced season after season. According to Roberts,[29] hewn log houses in southern Indiana had clapboards nailed over them as soon as they were finished.

Wall paper, newspapers, canvas, old sacks were applied to inner walls. Often both the inner and outer walls of log houses were covered to stop the wind, and sometimes still, a sturdy older house will surprise the remodeler or wrecker with log walls underneath.

Once complete, the early log house often continued to grow with the family. A lean-to was often added at the back, of logs or rough lumber. A second complete cabin was sometimes added, either on the chimney end, flush, to form the saddlebag house, or separated by a few feet, on the end away from the chimney, with roofs joined over the resulting breezeway or dogtrot. A separate chimney at the opposite end completed the dogtrot house. Sometimes the saddlebag or dogtrot had a wing extending to the rear, with a roofline at right angles to the original.

Taken altogether, the hewn log house built by the pioneers grew as a logical, practical product of the materials at hand, the environment, tools and skills of the people. These were influenced heavily by custom and tradition. The very fact that the logs were hewn flat on at least two sides was largely social, adding to the families' community status. A round-log building was faster and easier to build, and was often used in barns and outbuildings. True, the sapwood of the round logs rotted away, and true too, round logs of the size of the hewn ones commonly used, would have been unmanageably heavy.

The resulting house has survived the generations simply because it was best, the poorer efforts have disappeared because of their inadequacy. The hewn log houses we see today are evidence of the finest of the pioneer builder's craft, weathering even the centuries. Proud, strong, an almost permanent feature of the hill country, beautiful even in decay.

CHAPTER THREE

Restoration

    This book is devoted largely to the process of building the hewn-log house today. We discuss just about evey step in the process, from site selection to door-latches. But among the problems you'll encounter is that of obtaining logs, which we also talk about in Chapter Six.

    Given the difficulty in obtaining materials, and a justified concern for dwindling forests, you might consider seriously a log house restoration. Certainly you will save a lot of time and labor, using seasoned, fitted logs instead of laboriously shaping them yourself. Whether the house is to be restored at its site, or moved to another, you're often three months or more ahead in acquiring materials.

    But that isn't the reason I like to restore old log houses. Perhaps I can best tell it this way: a good friend and I were dismantling a long-abandoned house I'd found for him, which he planned to move and rebuild. In the attic, still dry under its replacement tin roof, was the castoff accumulation of over a century of living. Faded scraps of letters, gnawed by mice, told bits of history. We were able to trace the growing of a lad named John, born just after the turn of the century. Some school records, letters reporting his staying with relatives out of state--fragments. We thought it quite fitting that my friend's son, then six, would also grow within these old walls.

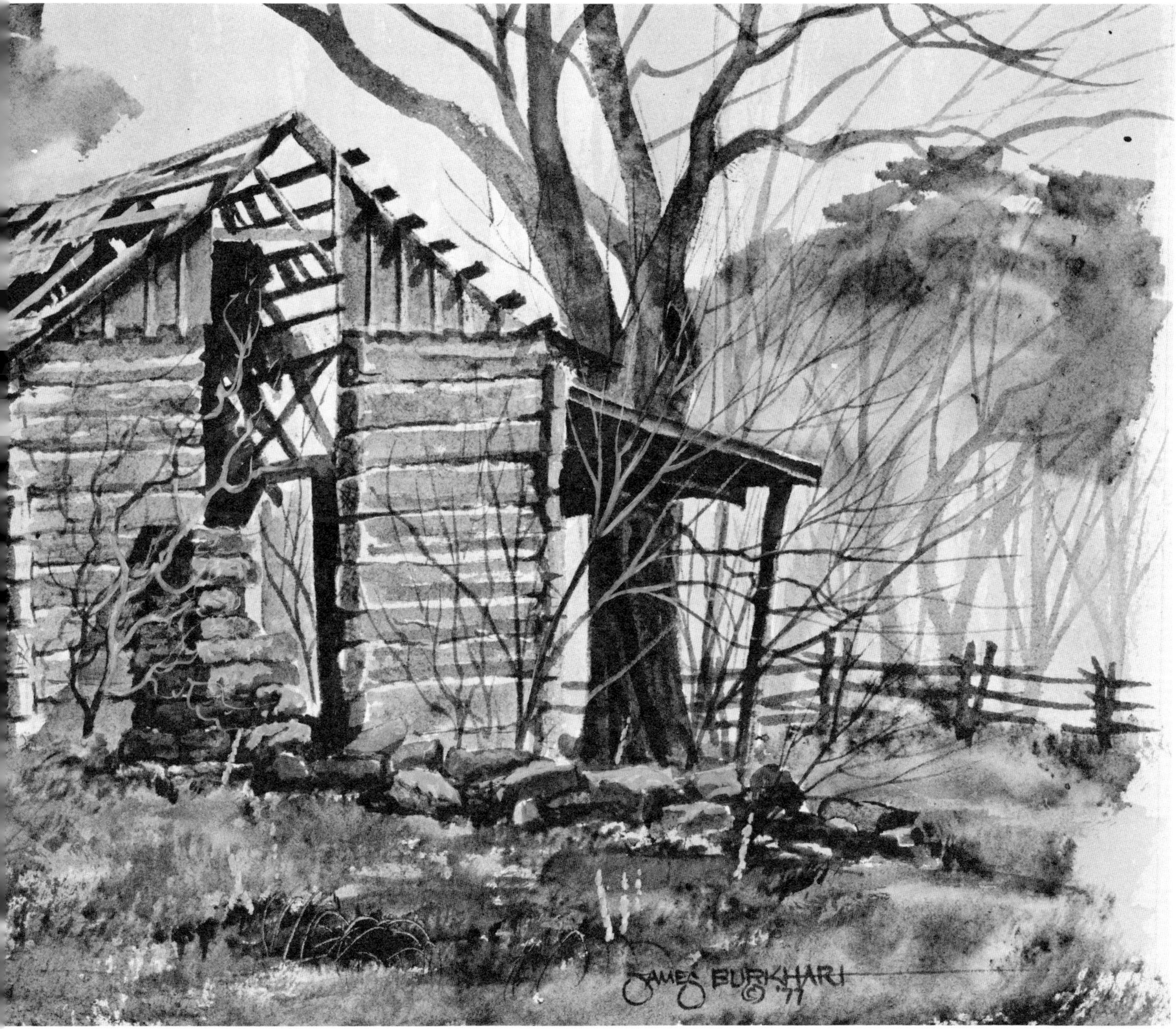
JAMES BURKHART
© '77

People come from everywhere to watch a log house being built, rebuilt, or torn down. The young ones are usually just curious, but the older ones almost always have a store of log house memories of their own to relate. The old man who shuffled up as we removed the last of the roof was one of these.

"This house used to belong to my folks," he said, "I grew up here."

"Your name isn't John, is it?"

"It sure is. How'd you know?" He was genuinely glad we were going to rebuild the house again, and promised to visit later. For my part, I considered it something of a privilege to have been a part of the restoration.

I have sketched bits of family history from old cemetery stones, and tried to match the bornings and dyings with additions and changes in the nearby houses that still stand. A lean-to may have been added, for instance, about the time of the birth of twins now in their 80's. Or the building of the second half of a dogtrot may coincide with a settler's marrying a widow with children.

Different broadaxe strokes also bear the tale of patient craftsmanship or of hurried shelter construction, as do marks of other tools, details of foundations, care in stonework. Sometimes there will even be penciled notes on walls. I recall a house in the Buffalo River country of Arkansas that has a regular diary written on the outside wall, dry under the porch.

Of course the best reason for restoring a log house is to preserve a bit more of our vanishing heritage, reflecting so well the American pioneer culture that has allowed us to grow, for better or worse, into what we are today. If you believe in vibrations, they are certainly abundant in the silvering logs and old hearthstones laid so long ago.

Finding a restorable log house is first. Then buying it or, less likely today, getting it for the act of removal and cleaning up the site. Then there's dismantling, pulling lots of nails and removing the inevitable additions of years, then transportation. Then you're about ready to begin at square one.

This log house hidden under clapboard was a rare piece of early craftsmanship near Kirbyville, Mo. Below is a restored log house with additions, at Dawt Mill in Ozark County, Mo.

You will hear endless tales about log cabins, most of it blurred by fading memories and wishful thinking. Many times I've tracked down reported rare specimens to find corncribs, barns, pole shacks or modern attempts instead of the real thing.

Locate your house by asking, driving around, or tracking down newspaper photographs. On a slow day the editor of a weekly will often run a feature on somebody's grandfather's house, and maybe it can be had. I will say that cabin hunting cannot be a used-car-lot pursuit. It takes time, and you should never roar up to a backwoodsman in your shiny vehicle and grill him impatiently. About log houses or anything else.

My friend Bill Cameron, now almost 80, for whom my brother and I helped restore Turnback Mill, near Halltown, Missouri, is the finest hand at discovering antiques I know. Be it old millstones, log houses, lost cemeteries or sorghum mills, I have seldom known him to fail. It goes like this: we approach a farmhouse or country store in the prerequisite battered pickup truck, and he visits with whoever is there. In maybe five minutes he's found that some old friend or relative is a mutual acquaintance (sometimes I wonder if he invents these people), and reminiscences follow. We are soon invited to join in anything from dinner to a hunt for just what we came after, or we are referred to someone else who can supply it.

I suppose the best introduction to country folks who know about log houses is, finally, being obviously country folks yourself (not hobbyists) with callouses to prove it--which you never have to.

The first enemy of your restoration is the very work of time that may appeal to you most. Unless your find has been boarded over and roofed with tin, the materials can be pretty crumbly. A log house can look sturdy as it stands, but come to pieces when dismantled. Most alarming is the way bark and rotted sapwood flake off, leaving you with 6-inch chinking cracks where the originals were 2-inch.

Check your prospect for soundness. If a log looks rotten or termite-infested, it probably is. Held in place by the comfortable stresses of years, logs and beams can look solid when they're not. Poke, pry, hammer on and stick your knife into everything you can reach until you're satisfied. I recall how solid the old Howard cabin near Kirbyville, Missouri, was when we took it apart. Then someone dropped a heart cedar rafter, and it snapped like a match stick.

A house that has no roof left is a risk. The old, dry logs go to pieces very quickly when exposed to weather. As little as 3 or 4 years uncovered can reduce log walls to rubble. And if some of the walls have caved in, forget it. Once apart, the logs will be worthless.

Look for houses with wide logs. That means more heart wood and less chance for rot. The chinking may be gone or intact, but chances are you'll lose some sapwood either way. Pole cabins of less than eight inch logs aren't usually worth the effort.

Now, acquiring a log house you've found can be harrowing. Often the least desirable hulk becomes suddenly treasured beyond price (almost) when you evidence interest. Having established a good down-home relationship with the folks helps. So does the fact, if made visibly obvious, that your resources are modest (which is why you want that old cabin, anyway--to save the cost of a new house).

I have acquired log houses free, just ahead of a developer's bulldozer. I have paid more than they were worth for desirable specimens and I have just plain talked my way into possession.

Perhaps the most involved experience I can relate was in Searcy County, Arkansas. The cabin I wanted was just about roofless, but had a wealth of history, some recorded on century-old tombstones in a nearby cemetery. Inquiry through a friend who was related to just about everybody in the county revealed that two brothers owned it, along with other abandoned farmhouses. But these were only two of eight heirs to the holdings, scattered from there to California. Neither brother would sell without everyone's permission.

I found that a Fourth of July reunion was scheduled for that summer, and got the brothers to agree to ask the others. Meanwhile the cabin was mouldering. No help for it, though. I was off to college that summer to try and finish an elusive degree, and heard no more till late August.

Seems when the kinfolks realized which cabin I wanted they had all said yes, and so I tried to strike a price with first one brother, then the other. Neither wanted to say, and each referred me to the other. Finally my friend and I set out to dismantle the cabin, taking along most of a jug of relatively good homemade whiskey some local candidate for office had given us. They still did things like that in the early 60's, after you got to be known as good old boys.

You see, one of the brothers liked a nip now and then, so this was the one we went to see. Well, he helped with the jug some, and finally allowed that I could just have the cabin, since he'd probably only use the logs for fence posts, if that, even.

True story. I wrote an article about that cabin for the September, 1969, **Ozarks Mountaineer**, under a pen name.

If you buy a log house from an absentee owner, get a letter authorizing you to remove it. Muskrat Murphy bought his cabin from a doctor in Michigan, and her letter kept us out of trouble with zealous neighbor folks who weren't right sure we should be taking it apart.

Don't even fondly imagine you can slip in and whisk away an abandoned log house undetected. First of all it takes lots longer than you think and everyone in the country will know about it. Some students of mine and I once 4-wheeled down a non-road miles beyond the reach of most folks, to dismantle a one-room cabin in two hours flat. But we encountered an entire horseback riding club, a hunter, some canoeists and a farmer on foot, in the time we were there.

A final word on buying your cabin. It will be quite expensive to dismantle and transport to your site. So unless you buy the land and restore it on the spot, don't pay much for the house. I was offered a borderline condition dogtrot log house for $1600.00 in 1976, 200 miles from home. All told, I'd have had probably $25,000.00 in a total restoration before I was through, so I said no, thank you. If it had been free I might have taken it, more to preserve it than as a bargain.

Dismantled, you're talking about nearly 100 logs up to 20 feet long, in this example, plus perhaps good rafters and possibly rare, whipsawn roof slats and handworked beams. That's several truckloads, for a long truck.

If you pay anything at all for labor, you'll have more than you'd like to admit tied up in just getting the logs to your site.

Buy cheap. How cheap is up to you, but always multiply a

reasonable sum by three, whenever building, to arrive at what you'll probably spend.

Once bought, you have two options in moving your house. A house mover will move it intact, but it costs lots of money. The Grigsby dogtrot log house on the Arkansas College campus in Batesville was moved 12 miles intact, except for the chimneys. Cost was around $10,000.00. That's not unreasonable for a 50-foot building.

This house had original chinking with diagonal splits largely intact, which was one reason for this type of move. Being square-notched, the non-locking corners did not hold together well enroute or as the house was being set down.

The usual method is to location-code each log as you dismantle the house, using a carpenter's crayon so rain won't wash off your code. The third log up on the east side could have a 3EN on one end and 3ES on the other. You can do this with chimney stones, too, and joists and rafters.

Dismantling is slow and dangerous. Heavy logs, sometimes with nails protruding, are prone to fall on the unwary, and more than once I have encountered snakes reposing in hollows where chinking had fallen out. Rats and birds have left their spoor everywhere, and dust is usually thick. I even removed a roof once to let the rain wash down the rest of the cabin, but it didn't help much. Respirators do help.

A restored log house with dogtrot enclosed, in the city park of Forsyth, Missouri. Thanks to government agencies and civic groups, a few log houses are being restored and preserved.

51

Perhaps more involved than most dismantlings was the Murphys'. It was a community affair; sort of a house-razing, if you will. We converged on the impossibly high mountain in Newton County, Arkansas, with an assortment of 4-wheel drives, one heavy pickup truck, and several trailers. It was a weekend in May, just after a lot of rain, so several folks got stuck in mud holes in the old logging road that wound up the hill. It was here we were challenged by a neighbor who informed us the road was closed to the public, and who never really believed the letter we had from the former owner.

I spent most of an hour trying to convince him we were all good old boys, not being helped at all by the sunglasses and colorful garb of the others, while they got their vehicles unstuck. Finally he and I recalled a mutual bulldozer operator acquaintance, who was then in jail, and talked about some other folks I thought I dimly remembered. He finally even offered to help us out of the mud, except that his back was sort of out, from having "drove fence posts yesterday" but by then we were ready to go, anyway.

Well, it rained all weekend. I was more or less gainfully employed at the time, and was expected to be on hand for a special event at work, so Linda and I visited the site each afternoon. We witnessed the soggy camp as it grew soggier, the demolition of the cabin and of the foodstuffs, the dampening spirits.

By Sunday we decided to evacuate the pickup and its tandem-wheeled trailer before the alternate road became impassable, too. This road ran straight down the mountain over boulders higher than the red clay was deep, so of course we high-centered often. Then we winched back up to bring down most of the short logs on a trailer behind my Land Rover. On the way back up I slid into a ditch and overturned, which delighted the owner of a Japanese 4-wheel drive, until he tried unsuccessfully to pull me upright.

That's Chapter One. A couple of weekends later Muskrat got together another set of friends and rented a huge truck to complete the move. But no one would drive it up that gullied road, so I volunteered. Never have I been so banged about as I was inside that metal cab. The

Dismantling Murphy's cabin during a rare lull in the rain. Ropes help keep from breaking weak logs or splitting off the notches.

steering wheel cracked me around like a whip, but we got to the top of the hill.

Then, after we'd loaded many thousands of pounds of logs on the beast, everyone sort of looked at me again. Well, so much for a misspent youth driving log trucks. In I climbed and down the mountain we lurched. That truck was never the same, after that.

The story would not be complete without the house-raising that followed, some months later. A third set of friends (notice how all but a couple of them seem to have learned from experience?) gathered on one of those rare sunny November days to raise the cabin.

There was lots of good food, hard work, camaraderie, and even suspense (Murphy had coded more than one log with a given code number). We almost flattened two of our number under a plunging 400-lb. log from high on one wall. The kids and dogs loved it all. Later there was some fine mountain music around the campfire.

Murphy's house-raising, clockwise from top: carrying the logs to the site; Murphy officiating; raising a hewn oak plate; figuring new rafter length; John marking a joist notch.

54

You may not be able to find a suitable house for restoration, and probably won't, within reason. Most of the ensuing chapters are devoted to building your own, step by step. If you restore, you can pick up construction details at any point you choose, which will apply as well to restoration as to new building. If you need floor information, refer to Chaper Eleven. Roofs always need replacing, so thumb the pages of Chapter Nine. I've arranged the book this way partially for this purpose.

There are compensations for the rigors of log-house restorations. Lots of them. Since either building your own house from scratch or restoring one will be lots of work and take lots of time or money, or both, you have a choice. Of the sense of history, good vibrations and the knowledge that you have, by restoring, saved an important part of our past, and saved some standing timber, too. Or, you have had the tremendous satisfaction of hewing your home from the forest. Every bit of it, and laying the clean, bright wood together to start its new life as your shelter.

The crew goes to work on ceiling joists, at left, notching, fitting and lifting into place. Above, Quinn Murphy, then two, stokes the campfire as the day's raising ends.

Trees are a renewable resource. Intelligently thinned, they can provide lots of material or fuel. Unfortunately too many of us are radicals about trees, either ravaging the forest or treating them like sacred cows.

55

56

CHAPTER FOUR

Land and Site

White canvas-topped wagons wound into the Ozarks a hundred and fifty years ago, up the rivers and the little lost creeks, past laurel thickets and into the beechwood glades.

The settlers stopped their tired teams beside clear pools and springs; they camped and looked around them. At the black soil, at the mountains rolling to the sky. And sometimes, when the mists had blown out of the hollows next morning, they stayed. And built.

A clearing for a garden, with the inevitable stand of corn, was first in order. Shelter was often an overhanging bluff for many months. Sometimes it was a tarpaulin stretched from the wagon bows to the ground. For days and weeks the sound of axes echoed up the spring creeks, and threads of woodsmoke rose from the new campfires.

Logs were burned on the spot, or rolled aside to be hewn for the house. Then, sometimes a year or more later, the settler and his wife and older children raised the cabin, or if neighbors were near, a community raising was held. Logs had been squared over the months, in bits of spare time, by the man and perhaps older sons, using the broadaxe. Hewn on two sides, the logs were carried or dragged to the chosen site.

Water was the first consideration for that site, and early cabins were located near springs or streams. A favored location was against a rise of hill, overlooking the sloping floor of a hollow which was to become fields, down to a creek or river. If a side branch or spring ran by even better. Curiously, these were also the sites favored by the Indians for their hunting camps and villages, and many a pioneer homestead was littered with broken shards of pottery and bits of stone bowls. I have found deeply hollowed stone mortars in old stone fences throughout the mountains.

The evening damp brought chills, and settlers tried to build on higher ground, even if it meant carrying water. But the blufftops, far from bottomland fields, and exposed to winter blasts, were also avoided. Only after successive generations pushed their claims up the ridges, were the rocky tops cleared and homesteaded. As the first settlers' children and then their children grew and spread back up the mountains, sites became more remote, less ideal.

Many of these ridgetop cabins still survive: tumbled ruins left stranded when the automobile came, with its inability to follow the wagon roads up the hollows.

Today the same requisites for a cabin site apply as they did a hundred and fifty years ago. There just isn't much of that prime spring creek land available. The springs have all been found, been polluted or have gone dry as the water table has lowered. The fields are modern farms, and about all you'll find for your dollars is rough woodland: dry, hard to reach, and generally thought unsuitable for anything but logging. Or glades, with only a thin skin of topsoil over stone ledges, and maybe scatterings of small cedars.

Small acreage is generally hard to find. The expense involved in dividing a large holding, surveying, providing abstracts for every piece (the record of all transactions in the past) makes most owners want to sell in a large unit. Tracts of 160 acres or more are easier to find, and usually much cheaper per acre.

If you look long enough, you will find a good tract, for a price. There may be an old foundation there, or perhaps jonquils in the spring,

Keep looking for the site that is so right you can grow to belong to it. The right spot is worth a lot of inconveniences.

gone wild from some settler's path no longer visible. For enough money you can still find a prime location.

And that leads us to the inevitable question: How much?

Land is worth whatever you think it is. Owning an acre of ground, to do with it what you wish, is worth thousands to some. And small parcels often cost more than $1,000 per acre. As part of a large, remote holding, the relative cost of a few acres diminishes. For insulation against the rest of us, you should have five acres or so, on which there may be one or several acceptable house sites. Unfortunately, everyone wants five-acre plots, and that puts the price up.

Consider a large tract, and find friends to buy the rest of it, keeping your choice plot. Or consider ruining your bank account for larger acreage, with the idea of selling off some later. Or buy it anyway, and sell your second car, then give up all your other expensive habits. Land and a log house will take all your energies, anyway.

Land purchase is a one-time outlay, unless you later mortgage it to pay for the kids' college. You can find out current prices from those deceptively attractive real estate catalogs, from local realtors, and from just asking around. But in the end, this one big expenditure is your choice, and is worth it or not to you alone.

The right land must be so right you just can't let it get away. Then price becomes less awesome. You get this feeling of belonging to this one hill, of wanting to dig your hands into its soil and become a part of it, and you know this is the place. If you don't, you probably shouldn't even entertain the prospect of log building.

So the land doesn't have a spring. It could be full of phosphate, anyway. Maybe that wet-weather branch runs only four months out of the year. Invite friends only on wet weekends. But that white oak tree is 200 years old: Daniel Boone's contemporaries scouted around it.

You can always drill a well, and maybe push in a road without ruining the whole mountain. You can get the local cooperative to extend the electric line, or use kerosene lamps (avoid most schemes for generating your own). And you've searched for a year, and argued with your spouse, and you're tired.

A hazard of the lime rock country is that polluted water runs for miles in underground channels with almost no filtration. It is unfortunately common to find soap suds in one's remote shallow well or spring from the rest of civilization's effluent.

Above all, your house should look as if it belongs where it is. Visualize the approach to it; you will make that approach many times.

So buy it. If you can live with it, whom do you have to justify it to? Well, the banker, mother-in-law, the guys at work . . . Nonsense. This place has the right vibrations. It's your personal statement. Here is where you build your log house.

A couple of things to watch for: Whether or not you buy through a realtor, insist that anything questionable on the abstract be cleared up. Read all fine print. That option to drill for oil, or other evidence of mineral rights foregone by previous owners, could still be active. If there's any doubt about property lines, have the land surveyed by a licensed surveyor. It costs, but your site should not be too close to the line. Who knows what may become of the adjoining land. A hog farm? Chemical plant?

Watch for liens; make sure you have good, legal access; don't take any rights for granted. The romance of opening three pasture gates to get to your haven, pales in nocturnal sleetstorms. And a new owner next door may have other ideas about the route he will provide you access on. If you buy with others, get it all down in writing: when George and Sally split up, she may end up with it all, and sell it to a paper mill. On this note, it's better to own your part free and clear, and keep a friendly relationship with the others. Ideals wear thin when it's mortgage payment time.

I might mention that my wife Linda and I found 200 acres bordering the National Forest which we decided we must find a way to own. At least part of it. After much balancing of eggs, cajolery, drawing and redrawing of imaginary division lines, we were able to get a brother and three close friends to buy parts of it, leaving us with our choice of some 40 acres of clear creek, waterfalls and bluffs. We go over that a lot and swim in the creek and listen to the silence, now. Someday I'll build a dogtrot log house there, very near the site of a 100-plus-year-old settler's cabin.

That's one way the land purchase can be done in a group, and there are certainly others.

All right, the land is yours. You have several sites in mind. Most books say to pick level land because it's cheaper to build there. Right, but you'll spend a lot of time here. Find the spot you want, the view you want, the approach to your house you want, and unless it's physically impossible, build there. (If it's level, you'll never pass for hill folks-- one leg shorter than the other from walking around hillsides.)

Points: Can a well driller get to it? Or close enough for you to pipe water? Those rigs are enormous, and their drivers seldom respect a graceful limb that's in their way, or want to risk their equipment on a pitching road. Will you have to carry materials in? Logs are heavy, and don't bend well around tight turnings of your path. Is there room to maneuver a small trailer?

Is there good, porous soil for sewage drainage and filtration? The limerock ledges of the Ozarks are terrible for effluent filtration. So you'd have to make plans and budget for a more efficient sewage system. Does the land slope too much? I've built five-foot stone walls on the downhill side to perch a 16' square cabin on, but wouldn't want to go any higher. You wouldn't either.

How about shade in summer and exposure to the wind in winter? A ridge top will give you power for a windmill on your well, and maybe a nice view, abut it will frost you out, too, in winter. Too close to a creek or wash can leave you soaked, or with your foundation washed away. Watch for loose rock up steep mountainsides, too.

And access. We finally gave up trying to drive the last few yards to our log house, and built a stone retaining wall up the slope. We filled in a turn-around area above, with steps down. It isn't far to walk, and those last vertical feet were hard on clutches and tires. Besides, we'd rather have the mossy rocks and plants than a vehicle at the door, with muddy ruts all around.

Whatever you do, don't turn a bulldozer operator loose to build you a road and level your site. Be there every minute, and yell loud. I've operated dozers, and can't explain the power thing, but it's there, and it's hell on trees and earth. It's your land. These are your plans, With care, a dozer can be made to work for you. If you must level, do so sparingly, remembering that torn soil washes away badly.

Follow contours for your road; ditch, and use culverts at low

Land-clearing for a log house is the first concrete step in construction.

places. A good road should be functional, and still have that series of unusual surprises, as natural as possible. A fourwheel-drive vehicle is handy if you don't or can't level much, but they're expensive.

A pickup truck with snow tires and some weight in the back will usually get you in and out, and they're so handy. I own a very narrow, very old Jeep pickup with a minuscule engine, that winds in and out of our trees with some agility and all sorts of cargo, as long as we don't hurry. And not hurrying is something you must learn in this business of modern homesteading.

The best way to handle a steep site is to build a high downhill foundation, instead of cutting down into the uphill side. You get mud, clay and erosion by digging and leveling. We did both, since we have a flagstone floor and had to level. It was a cut-and-fill operation, done by hand, but it's taken years to heal the scars.

It also seemed to take forever before we saw any progress. Much easier & faster to raise a natural stone foundation on one side and build a wooden floor, with steps up. Of course our floor is indestructible, and we have heating cable underneath, which is delightful for bare feet in winter, so it was worth it.

Site problems, from a money standpoint, blow up your budget. Consider stone ledges, marshy land, steep slopes, all hazards. Every obstacle, however scenic, increases your cost in money or time, taking away from what you have to spend on the whole project. I do not agree with the modern builders who level everything first, or build in a flat field, but they do save money that way.

Site selection is not usually so complicated, but it gets more limiting if you must be near fields for farming, or available electricity or water, or a road. But in general, it must be a place you want to be, to look out over and to come home to. A place you can disfigure as little as possible, leaving it as nearly as it was before you came, and still love it.

Now, plan to spend a lot of time at your chosen site or sites. Camp there. Wake up early enough to watch the mists lift from the hollows. See where the sun will rise and set. Can you stand that wind in winter? Will August bake you, here? Get to know the moods of the place.

And finally, when you can feel that this spot is home, start visualizing your house. And keep in mind that it can be only what the site will allow. It must fit as if it grew here, of the materials that are naturally here. An artist friend of ours said that our log house looked like a mushroom. That's close, since a mushroom is never out of place in the woods. Nor is a stone, or a tree. Work toward that, and see how close you can get.

CHAPTER FIVE

Design

Hewn log houses, weathered gray in rain and seasons of sun, cracked and aged in old axe marks and lichened stones, blend into the mountains as a fact of history. They follow a few basic designs that have endured as the most useful.

Of course, your own house should be a personal statement, not necessarily an established building style. But architecture should fit, growing as naturally from the ground as possible, using natural materials in a harmonious, serendipitous complement to surroundings. If you choose variations on the basic designs--and you will, as surely as did the early settlers--let them be subtle, in keeping with a use of surrounding materials and hand craftsmanship. You will approach your finished house many times, and you must always be happy with what you see.

67

The classic log house was of hewn logs, "V" or half-dovetailed notches, shake roof, stone foundation and chimney, raised wood or puncheon floor, pole rafters, small windows, maybe a loft and lean-to, and certainly a roofed porch. Most of the wood was worked by hand, although rough-sawn lumber, available generally for nearly a century, was often used.

This house had a transverse ridge, with the chimney always at one gabled end, and the door near the center of the sloped-roof front, which was sometimes longer than the gable dimension. (Public buildings--schools, churches--often had the front door or doors under the gable, possibly because they rarely had fireplaces. The peak also made a nice place for the belfry, up front and on display.) This was the basic mountain cabin, with lots of variations which we'll talk about later.

Farther south, and north, and west you'll find round-log work,

The logs in our house have been recycled at least three times since the 1840's. Here it's under temporary roof, awaiting porch, fireplace and gable covering.

different notching, different woods, reflecting different backgrounds and customs and availability of materials.

And everywhere you'll see modern adaptations and slipshod imitations, with their inevitable picture windows and green plastic skylights. I shudder.

Don't jar the landscape. Look for natural lines, such as the slope of a distant hill or framing by trees. Pitch a roof a little more, or less, to blend with the terrain as well as to give you the upstairs room you need. Consider switching the chimney to the other end where the road winds, to catch it in your first view. Watch how the sun hits your site, and put more or fewer windows accordingly. Raise your foundation another eight inches to give yourself a view into the next valley. Your house should look as if you expected to find it there, looking just as it does.

The basic log house is traditionally 16 to 20 feet square. Maybe it's a bit of a rectangle, longer across the front and back to balance out an added lean-to or porch. But it's pretty small, as we view houses today. Full length logs are necessary, to bind it all together above and below windows and doors. And you'll find it difficult to locate, transport, and handle anything longer than 20'. So did the pioneers. Most settlers' cabins were about 16' square. A larger house also takes a lot longer to build, and costs more.

A loft is very little more trouble, and if high enough, doubles your floor and storage space. Lean-tos, often kitchens and now bathrooms, can be built along with the basic cabin or added later, just as the settlers did. The size and shape of a lean-to, like a porch, is a matter for your eye, in relation to the rest of the house.

Often the pioneer built the one-room cabin with fireplace, then when the family expanded, built another, separate one with its own chimney at the opposite end, and joined the roofs, for the breezeway or dogtrot house Sometimes both were built together. One section was for cooking and sleeping; the other was for general living and sleeping. The upstairs, under the not-very-tight shake roof was for sleeping, too. Our forefathers had lots of kids, and sometimes maiden aunts and widowed grandmas.

Jacob Wolf's house served as Indian agency, store, courthouse and home. It is perhaps the oldest log house in the region.

These dogtrots were sometimes two-story, with an upstairs porch running the length of the house, over the open area, and were large, substantial farm houses. Perhaps the finest and certainly one of the oldest examples of this style is the Jacob Wolf house, at Norfork, Arkansas, built in 1809.

Curiously, the two front doors of the dogtrot have survived this style house in the mountains. Logically, each separate cabin needed a front door, and the dogtrot retained both, even with additional doors to the breezeway. But where the builders of the central-hall house, which may have evolved from it, favored an impressive single entry, the mountain house clung to the separate front doors. A notable variation is the 1870 Grigsby house, now being restored on the campus of Arkansas College, in Batesville. Its entry doors open on the breezeway.

Later builders abandoned log construction, closed in the breezeway, and even did away with it as a hall or room, but kept the two front doors. I have a file of pictures of Ozarks houses, some built as late as the 1960's, with dual front doors. Scholars hasten to inform me that this practice was continued in churches and schools to separate the sexes with a few feet of wood. J. Frazer Smith suggests that, when company stayed over, this was also the case with dwelling houses.[30]

In all, this double-pen log house was and is a picturesque style. If you need the space, consider the one- or two-story dogtrot, and count on a lot of labor and material.

The saddlebag house requires less roofing but it's difficult to join the two log pens snugly. The partition as used in the Whitaker-Wagoner log house referred to in Chapter One is a nice solution, although this is not a saddlebag house.

For really irresponsible numbers of offspring, the settler often added a wing to his dogtrot or saddlebag, or even his "I" house, sometimes behind one half, with a side porch. I've just finished designing one of these for a family who wanted all the rooms of their dogtrot on one floor. Quite organic and fitting, and historically accurate.

That turns out to be a great deal more important to me than to the people I have built for. And while I urge regional and historic integrity in log house architecture, it need not dismay you. You need live primitively in your house only if you choose. Such niceties as bathrooms have become necessities in our modern culture, and properly constructed, are unobtrusive, efficient, and nonpolluting. So are kitchens.

Many log dogtrots have been boarded up to cover cracks, and the style persisted for many years in frame versions.

I prefer to locate these more or less modern rooms in lean-tos, to make it evident that they are part of the added-on construction, not jarring instrusions into the historic-appearance of the house.

And insulation is a useful, invisible, and comfort-producing material that you'll find very helpful and economical. A number of other modern conveniences, such as electricity, can be built in tastefully without offending most purists. If, in fact, your log house is to be your permanent home, it's better to build in wiring, plumbing and insulation, than to add it when you come to the realization that roughing it becomes a chore, year in and year out.

I do not pretend that these conveniences are entirely in keeping with the spartan pioneer cabin, of which we have built several. People managed without plumbing for thousands of years, and if you so choose

I applaud your decision. I just don't envy you on wintry nights.

The basic cabin, electrified and plumbed or not, remains the starting point, whichever way you choose to add on. As a somewhat askew example, I had planned to rebuild the transplanted log house we live in as one-half a dogtrot, adding the other half as the material and time became available. My wife, who at the time had never seen a dogtrot house, decided that going up, across and down, or out through the weather, in order to reach point B from point A, was a masochistic trip. So we located the cabin in another spot which has allowed a lean-to but would have been impossible to build a dogtrot on. Now, after two extensions of the lean-to, both of us are sorry. Moral: build where you can add, in one way or another, without removing select trees or parts of a mountain.

We've talked more about variations on our basic cabin in Chapter One. Essentially we're still working from a one-room building, just as history has left it to us. You may add and expand in lots of traditional ways.

To decide on a basic style, look at pictures. Get in your car, on your bicycle or horse, and go hunt up some specimens. Ask around--the natives are used to cabin-hunters by now. Take pictures, visit ruins. Harass the history or folklore professors at the nearby college. Find out what you're doing before you invest part of your life in this madness.

Avoid pre-planned cabins (and pre-planned houses of any kind) as consumer ripoffs. Borrow features and ideas, none of which are new, but let your site tell you what and how to build. That goes for stone houses, too. And glass. And cathedrals and motels. You're going to live with those trees and that hill a long time, so don't Better Homes them to death.

But, of course, you will have basic needs. Your family size will dictate a need for so many square feet, divided into rooms of whatever description you require. The business of good design always means integrating the requirements of the occupants with the allowances of the site. Intelligently and artistically.

If you have a washer and dryer, for instance, you'll need a place

Don't make the common mistake of settling on a house plan clipped out of a magazine and then running around looking for a place to put it. This almost always results in the house being an insult to the site, or vice-versa.

to put them. A separate laundry shed would preserve the authenticity of your log house, but you'd clock a lot of miles over a period of time, going there and back. So put them in the lean-to.

And do something clever with the space under the low roof-slope at the outside walls upstairs, like slip in a mini-room of his own for your youngest. Give him a dormer window to let the world in through. A dogtrot house has lots of upstairs space, so maybe a sewing room for the wife, away from traffic, is in order.

In a small log house, the loft can be one open space. It's usually better to brace the joists with king posts or queen posts down from the rigid roof.

There is a myth among modern Americans that bigger is better. And while it is true that you'll use every bit of space you build, I prefer an efficient utilization of smaller areas. Up high on the cabin wall in the lean-to is a world of room for shelves, cupboards, cabinets (even a half-story sleeping space for someone small). Put your deepfreeze under the porch at one end, screened by shrubs (It's more efficient there).

A great deal of the botchery visited on old log houses has been in the form of additions tacked on at random. By all means plan your house in such a way as to allow sensible additions that will not destroy rooflines or overall appearances. Give yourself enough space, and use it wisely.

Above all, let your log house-building be an exercise in reverence. For the priceless land, for the traditions of craftsmanship and for your pioneer heritage, no matter how many generations gone. Not everyone is privileged to feel the weight of an axe helve in his hand, and his feet upon his own ground. Go quietly into the woods, and work in harmony with the trees, resisting the impulse to change and brand the earth.

The saddlebag house was built around a central fireplace, usually open to both pens. When built all together, the joining log partition was often used. When a second pen was added, double walls usually butted together at the center.

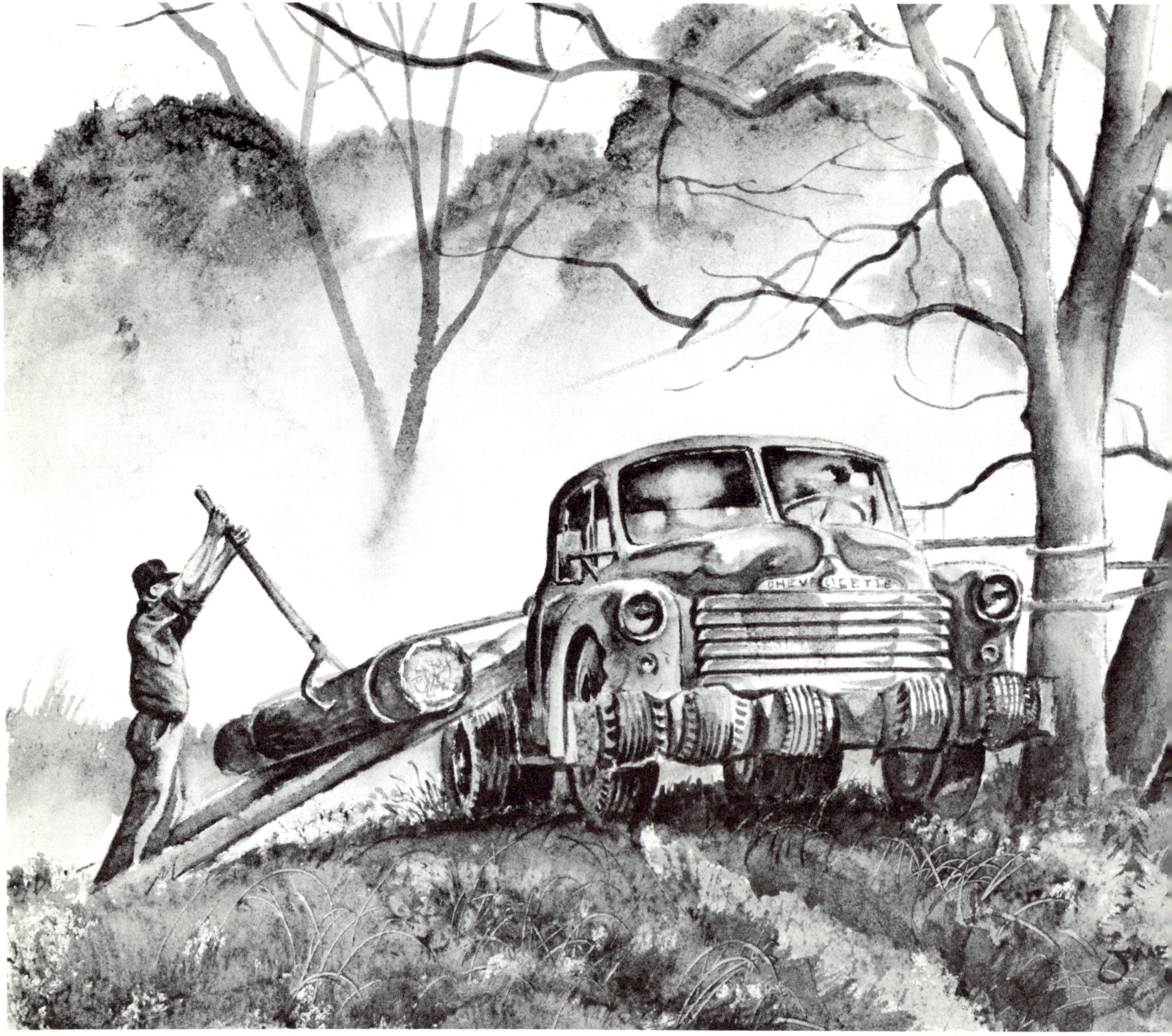

CHAPTER SIX

Acquiring Materials

The question I am asked most about log houses by serious seekers is, where do I get the logs? That's a valid concern, given the quantity of material the log house requires. Logs, beams, joists, rafters--just the names sound like massive sections of wood, and they are.

If you're lucky enough to find a site with lots of trees, give some thought to cutting your own, selectively. Wood-butchery though this may seem, careful thinning opens your site and will allow the trees remaining to spread their limbs seeking more sunshine. Logging your land does alter it, but in a few short years your woods will stop looking like a disaster area.

Felling a tree

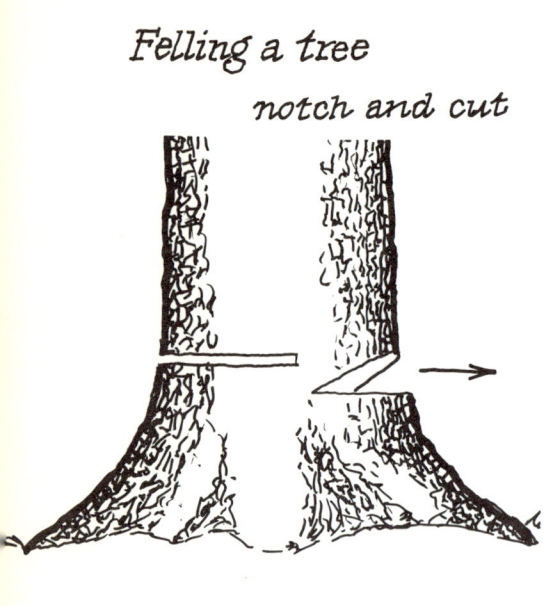

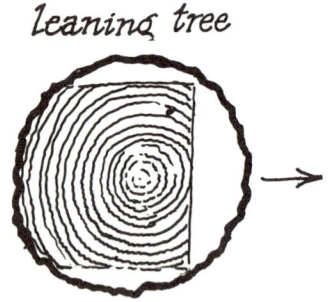

notch and cut

leaning tree

to change direction

Remember though, that you'll need probably 45 logs, anyway, including a heavy beam under the floor joists, plus overhead beams. Then there are rafters for the main house and porch and probably a lean-to. And the floor joists themselves. And that's just for the basic one-room house. You may also want to have your lumber cut from logs at the nearest friendly sawmill, a practice I encourage. So, unless your trees are very tall and very straight, you'll get maybe one hewn log and some boards, from each tree. Take a quick count and see if you really want to cut those trees and clear that much ground.

If you've never cut timber, there are a few basics to observe. The tree should be notched on the side it is to fall toward. Use an axe, saw, or both, to cut about four inches deep. Now begin the actual cut on the opposite side a couple of inches above the notch. Keep cutting till there's only an inch or so of wood left, or until the tree starts to fall. Then get your saw out and run like hell.

These hazards are common: the tree falls backward on you or your saw; the butt end kicks out as the tree falls (particularly if you've cut too much); limbs broken off the falling trunk are whipped back at you by the spring action of the surrounding trees. Any of these can kill you. Also, if the tree leans much in the direction you plan to cut it, chances are it will split before you've cut far enough through, so the butt kicks back as the split ruins your first log.

Cuts into each side three or four inches deep before you make the major cut will lessen this splitting. So will a last burst of frenzied cutting as the tree starts over, if you have the nerve.

Felling a nearly vertical tree where you want it instead of where the wind or gravity alone wants it, is mostly a matter of aiming the notch--and practice. Also, as you cut, leave more wood on the side you want the tree to fall toward. I have seen my father bring a tree a quarter-circle as it fell. My brother John delights in placing falling trunks between closely-spaced neighboring trees.

A last word about felling trees: If your saw (crosscut or chain) gets caught as the tree falls, spend a minimum of time trying to remove it. There will usually be a split-second when it's free just before the trunk jumps at you, but don't bank your life on it. Saws can be replaced.

If you cut your own nearby, skid them with a tractor, 4-wheel drive, winch, or patient mule. If you cut your own some distance away, have them hauled. More about this later.

If you have no timber, your least laborious course is to visit that sawmill operator and offer to buy logs and lumber. He'll sell the lumber and usually the logs to you for a board foot price, or refer you to one of his log suppliers. These folks who sell to mills invariably own aging trucks, live out on faint roads and haul a few logs to supplement whatever it is they live on. (I know, I grew up pursuing this very trade.) You may be eyed suspiciously at first, and you may have to wait a spell for your logs, but give this a try before you give up entirely.

Get your logs hauled to the site. Period. Do **not** go out and purchase a rusting truck, justifying it as an eventual hay-hauler, wood hauler, rock hauler or cattle hauler. The damn thing will fall to pieces at all the tense moments, either mangling your body and/or delaying your building for many weeks. The same predictions apply to good old neighbors and friends who own trucks. Avoid them.

You see, I first learned to drive--a log truck--in my tender years, and I have this battered observation: Logging takes the life out of a truck faster than any business. My own tutorial machine was soon brakeless, starter-less and cab-less. Even a pampered highway truck throws up its gears after a few bouts in the woods. An ex-garbage truck, that anonymously dependable remover of things foul, also turns mean under a shifting load of logs. The most docile flatbed rolling will seem to leap at stumps, mudholes, and precipices as soon as you declare your intention of burdening it with logs.

Have your logs hauled. You can get yourself killed suddenly, and of course permanently, fooling around with tons of loaded logs. Don't even help unload. When that strange type over the mountain you bought logs from delivers them, arrange to be gone, or find a pressing chore out of sight.

Still not convinced? Still eager to pit your mite of might against

If the tree rocks back and closes the cut on your saw, you may have to wedge it over. If there's no room for a wedge and the saw blade, try springing a sapling at an angle between the tree and the ground, or use it as a push pole to free the saw.

the timber (cutting, skidding, loading, hauling, unloading)? You got a real ego problem.

All right. I'll relate a simple logging trip from a recent log house job. You'll notice right off I never take my own advice, but you just keep your eye on the point, not the inconsistencies.

A Logging Tale

Three of us set out for a stand of near-perfect trees some 85 miles from the site (too far) and over a hundred from our homes (entirely too far). We're minimizing the cost by taking a second vehicle, a pickup truck, that one of us will fill with free building stone at odd moments. Also, when our 19-year old White log truck grinds to a stall, we can abandon it easier.

I drive the White, which after all those years of logging, still looks like a garbage truck. My nephew Danny, and a friend Brad, who's working this summer to learn how to build a log house, go ahead in the pickup.

It is July. Morning, before the heat rolls off the green flanks of the mountains. I coast down the twisting blacktop slopes, mentally anticipating the careening return trip, laden with logs inevitably too heavy and too long. The roar and vibration and fumes successfully numb my appreciation of the scene: hollows absorbing sunlight, the last mists blowing from the deep creek bottoms.

I have hiked this country, and skimmed its rivers in canoe and kayak in less strenous times. Now I am bent on traversing it, against what are usually long odds, with some of its beauty chained to my truck bed. So much for poetry, generally drowned in the howl of gears over three hours of steep inclines.

We arrive. I regain my land legs a step at a time. Danny is overhauling the magneto on the skidding tractor. Brad is measuring and marking trees we felled last time. They dry out and lose lots of weight in a few days. Clever of us.

The tractor refuses to start, but we pull it into life with the truck. I assault the fallen trunks with the borrowed chainsaw (last time we felled these by hand with a crosscut). Brad starts to collect stone, mossy and aged, from the woods.

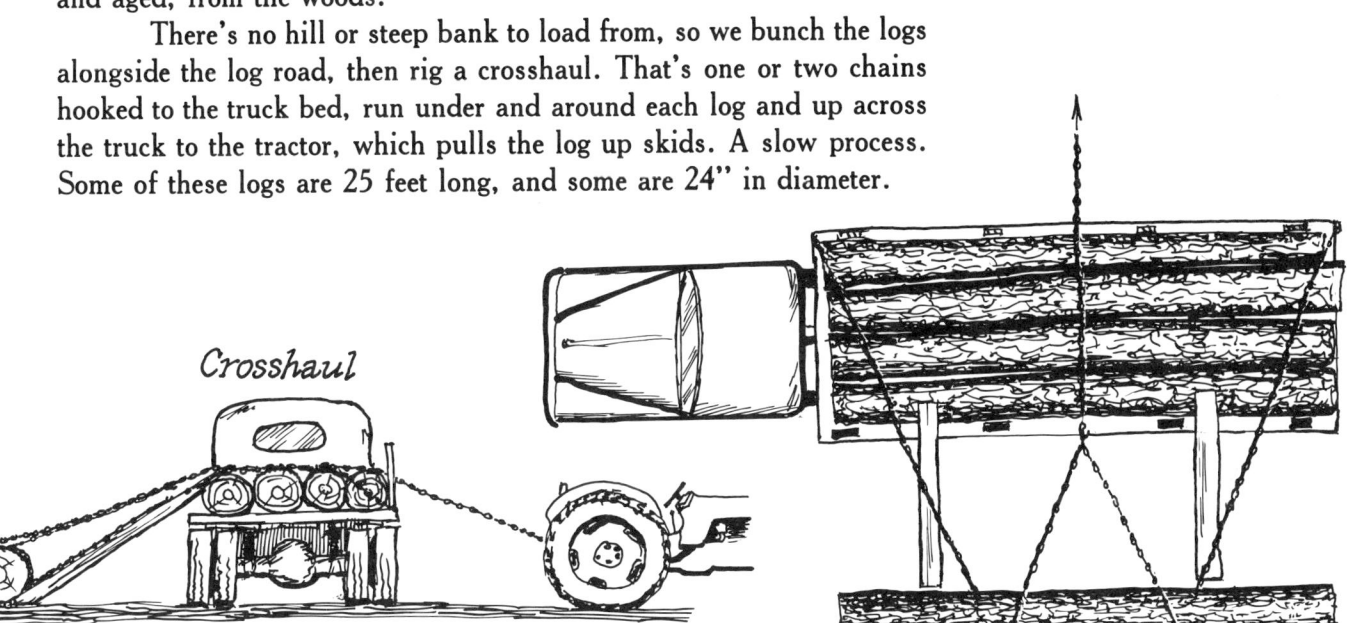

There's no hill or steep bank to load from, so we bunch the logs alongside the log road, then rig a crosshaul. That's one or two chains hooked to the truck bed, run under and around each log and up across the truck to the tractor, which pulls the log up skids. A slow process. Some of these logs are 25 feet long, and some are 24" in diameter.

Crosshaul

We are barely started loading when the tractor overheats, so we shut down for lunch. Linda has sent barbecued ribs (not a typical logger's lunch) which we devour. It is already afternoon, and heavy clouds are piling in the southwest. The tractor radiator is filled from a pond, and we crosshaul some more. It takes all three of us, two to shift each log on the way up as the big end gets ahead. Danny stops the tractor at a roared signal and holds while Brad and I strain with cant hooks to straighten the log.

Drops of rain start to spatter. We get the first eight logs on, less than half a load, as the shower stops. Now the skid trail is slick and the tractor spins its one bald tire. Danny brakes that wheel with jabbing motions, and the tractor does a series of uncontrolled lurches forward and sideways. It's uphill, and the nose lifts. That scares the hell out of me, because it can flip over on your body before you get your foot on the clutch. We clear a longer skid trail that's not as steep.

I go to drop more trees, tight business in this dense growth, when my brother John materializes. He'd thought the trip would be rained out, but reasoned that we might be fool enough to go ahead anyway. John's an artist with timber, so I give him the saw and go spell Danny on the tractor.

Now the woods come alive. I use second gear and full throttle on the skid trails, with Danny clearing and hitching at the trees and Brad unhitching and bunching with the cant hook at the truck. John moves along the fallen trunks, and limbs drop away; log sections roll apart. Everything is steamy, and wet with sweat.

The next crosshaul takes us nearly to dark. We need more long logs to span over windows and doors of the house. John has them cut, and I head the tractor into the gloom as the other two finish the load of stone. Of course no one thought to bring a flashlight.

The last logs are skidded in total darkness, John walking ahead, a dim shape guiding me around trees, stumps. The tractor has never run so well. The others wanted to stop an hour ago, but I suppose this is my macho trip. The long logs bend and bind and snap around behind my machine, but by God they come out of the woods. Branches slap me; a long greenbrier gets around my leg and rasps its welts. John hurries ahead; I ride down a brushpile by mistake; the tractor sings.

We load by the pickup's headlights. A heavy load, dangerously long off the back, but we chain it down tight. Now we scrounge every drop of gasoline from reserve cans and even drain the tractor which we will leave in the woods; no stations at all open. It's a long, deserted stretch; we'll have five hours of grinding ahead. Check and add oil. Eat the last of lunch and some granola John brought.

We'll drive the truck in shifts. I'm first, then Danny. John follows me in his VW and the boys go ahead to wait and perhaps catch a nap, at the Buffalo River bridge, less than a third of the way.

The truck is all dead weight on the two miles to the pavement, a half hour of slow churning. From there on, the long tail hangs out on curves too much and the front wheels want to paw the air. I stop and we tighten chain bindings. Gradually I get to know the load, and the truck, ancient and massive, settles into its harness and pulls its rusted heart out.

We're on Hwy. 21 now, dropping down to the Buffalo. This hill is 45 minutes of first gear, with the engine at a high singing moan, and a little braking on the steep places. It's like letting a weight down a cliff, this climbing out of the sky. I know the deep canyon below me; in daylight you catch your breath at its bluffs and distant waterfalls. Now it's all black emptiness, with maybe one isolated farmyard light, way off.

At the last switchback I shift from first gear directly to top, rushing to full speed as I straighten out. I'm carrying nearly 20,000 lbs. on a 16-foot bob truck. I must be crazy.

At the river we discover it's midnight, so we make some decisions. John heads for home and the cows he'll milk in a few hours. Danny, the shortest of us, crawls into the padded space up behind the seat of the White. Brad unrolls one of my sleeping bags on the broad hood of the pickup. And I stretch my aching bones on another, on the ground, with a poncho to help keep the mosquitoes off.

My trucks make ticking sounds, settling into sleep. I picture them both fleetingly, not as worn and rusted hulks, but as finely hammered steel, eager for work, sure under my hands and the hands of these good old boys working with me in this madness. Mosquitoes buzz, confused by the sticky repellent. Stars peep, and the nearby river murmurs.

Sudden heavy rain drops pound the thin poncho into me, and lightning silhouettes the trucks. Brad abandons the sleeping bag, doubling his length onto the pickup seat. I do not move, and soon am struck by a closeness to the elements, driven by rain that does not touch me, spread upon and flowing into the ground in fatigue. Come on, rain. It's just you and me. And these big trucks, and all these logs, and rocks. And pretty soon some more sleep, in spite of everything.

Morning sees us splashing river water in our faces and then me, grinding away up another mountain just as high. We stop at Kingston for breakfast, in a cafe in one of several old buildings put together no doubt, with money from timber when this land was first logged. The high ceiling is embossed sheet metal, and everything smells wonderfully old.

Danny takes over, and the rest is July sun and curving hills till we reach the site. It's noon as we roll in, and it takes a while for the landscape to stop moving.

We unhook the chains cautiously, because this simple operation can kill you, as those tons of logs storm loose. We pry and roll the last of them off, and the truck straightens its back. I pat it on the nose, as the boys roll two specimens onto cross beams in a sea of chips.

Then we reach for our broadaxes.

John and I with the beleaguered truck on a quieter day.

Well, that's an account of an actual logging trip. I could also tell you about the time we had a timber deadline to meet in January, and worked all night in a sleetstorm, skidding and loading, to haul next day on ice, but you get the point. Logging is **always** a lot harder and takes longer than you expect. And expensive: You see, the timber had to be bought first, at about 10c a board foot, and we paid ourselves (too modest) a wage. Add to that, eight more trips for logs, both for the house walls and for lumber. And at least two big truck tires at nearly $100 apiece. And a tractor overhaul, and a clutch job for the pickup truck. And all those trips that took two days instead of one. Or three, even.

So buy your logs and have them hauled, unless masochism really is your thing.

The logs are only your main cabin walls, so unless you have your lumber sawed from them, too, you still need many feet of boards. I favor rough-sawn boards and studding of yellow pine or oak, for just about everything in the house that isn't log or stone. If you'd rather, go to a lumber company and pay their prices for that imitation wood. You know, the forced-growth, soft white pine, spruce, western cedar or whatever, that America is built of nowadays. Just don't expect it to hold together in a windstorm.

You can, of course, use poles or hewn beams for rafters, but it's a bit hard to do a studwall for a lean-to or upstairs room without sawn dimension stuff.

I use either sawn shingles or split shakes on the roof. It takes so many, you may want to buy these, too. I just don't find enough good wood (red oak, cypress, red cedar) to split them realistically. A happy solution is the rare shingle mill that can saw cypress or cedar, knotty or not, at about what the lumber companies charge for theirs. We'll talk more about shingles in the chapter on roofs.

Stone may be free from a farmer who wants it out of his pasture, or $75 a ton from that farmer, or through a stone mason. It can cost that much even if it's free to begin with. That's with equipment rented, borrowed, fueled, and with breakdowns, other mishaps and time, figured in. Of course try to use any stone you find on your land.

Limestone and granite are heavy and not easy to shape when necessary. Porous, crumbly sandstone is weak. The best dense sandstone is somewhat heavy, but good to work with. More so if you have ledges that break off in even, stratified pieces. I like that off the top of the ground, with lichen and a patina of age on it.

Whatever you buy, be it stone, logs or lumber, ask around for competitive prices, remembering that hauling from a distance eats up savings. Inspect logs, lumber and all materials. Folks have a way of loading you up with castoff stuff when they hear you're just going to use it in an old log house.

Windows, nails, cement, all that stuff is about the same for a log house as for any other, and we talk about most of it in succeeding chapters. It's easier to find a large building supply house that can furnish you everything from sand for mortar to felt for window stripping, so you don't race around all over, searching for such goodies.

No matter how meticulously you plan, you'll never remember or budget for everything. And in the year or so you've given yourself, many of your first ideas will alter as you come to realize the size of the project. You can count on extras everywhere; if you save a bit here, something you hadn't counted on will take it, and more, there.

Here's a very partial list of materials and tools you'll need. Of course the quantities will vary so much, I'm not even estimating them here:

Materials	Tools
Logs	Hammers
Stone	Axes
Cement	Broadaxe
Lime	Adze
Sand	Hand plane
Gravel	Drawknife
Water	Saws, hand and/or power
Nails, spikes, staples	Augers or brace and bits
Screws, hinges, latches	Shovels, picks
Flashing	Hoe for mixing mortar
Tarpaper, sheet plastic	Wheel barrow
Felt weatherstripping	Cement mixer
Windows, doors (unless you build them)	Trowels
Lumber for walls, floors, decking, cabinets	Wire brushes
Beams for joists, rafters, studding, framing	Stone hammer, chisels
Steel reinforcing rods	Wood chisels, mallet
Septic tank or materials for building it	Screwdrivers, wrenches
Pipe for water and septic systems	Hoist, chains, rope
Plumbing fixtures	Prybars
Wiring and Electrical fixtures	Sledgehammer
Water heater, exhaust fan, other appliances	Level
Shingles	Chalkline
Reinforcing wire mesh	Square

And of course prices will vary so much with location and time, that any estimate I make will be immediately obsolete. You should plan and budget carefully to better realize what you're in for. If you're no planner, just jump into it, and cry a lot, later.

88

CHAPTER SEVEN

Foundation

Laying wood and stone upon the ground to start a log house was one of the things our pioneer forebears just weren't very good at. Invariably, sill logs were put too close to the soil, or right on it, which explains why so few pine cabins have survived even with restoration. Termites love pine. And pine, oak, or even the longlasting native woods such as cedar, poplar and walnut eventually rot, and it happens soonest close to the damp earth.

Many of the settlers' cabins I've found were on hillsides, so only the uphill sills were on or near the earth, and maybe the ends of the first side logs. Those high off the ground lasted the longest, so take a lesson from that. It means a high floor, usually, but is worth it after a few soggy seasons.

Some pioneers did build high to begin with, but the weight of the house, concentrated on a small area of foundation stones at each corner, eventually drove them into the ground, lowering the whole house. Certainly much of the sag and tilt of old log houses is due to settling rather than to poor workmanship.

Foundation specs

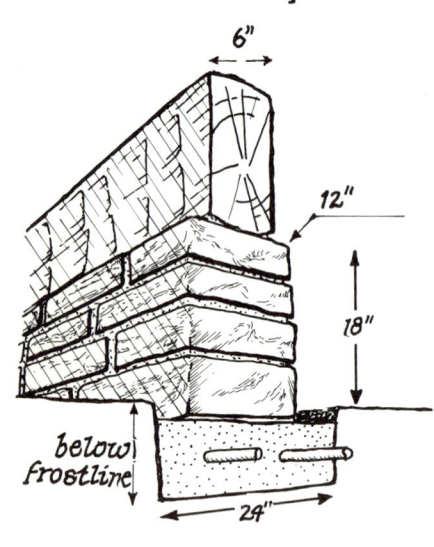

6"
12"
18"
below frostline
24"

Every so often I encounter some self-styled building sage who swears concrete doesn't need reinforcing if properly cured. Treat such suggestions as you would any other imbecilic ramblings. Onlookers are always "discovering" shortcuts the dumb builders of history could never have thought of. But they did, and tossed them out, evolving sound practices.

Too few early builders put up a wide, heavy foundation. Most stacked flat stones singly, achieving a teetery column with maybe rock chips wedged into the cracks. The Beaver Jim Villines cabin at Ponca, Arkansas, has pieces of metal from broken plow points wedged between the stones to give the piers stability.

Even stones laid on top of the ground, in a row beneath the logs with no footing beneath, will give good support if there are enough of them, because, of course, each is carrying less weight and the total load is spread over more area.

And even slender columns of stone at the house corners would be enough to resist settling, if laid on wide concrete footings. For a continuous foundation, the old builders' rule says the footing should be twice the width of the wall thickness, so if you plan only a column at each corner, you need more footing to be safe.

Fortunately, unless they built on creek bottom land, most of the mountain settlers found only inches down, very rocky, firm subsoil which really resisted settling of any kind. This soil allows a minimal footing, and will let you get past the slow, non-visible stage of building sooner, and on to the good stuff with the logs.

A continuous foundation for a log house just isn't necessary. The logs act as massive beams, to distribute the weight of the house evenly, so support can be at wide intervals.

Muskrat Murphy's cabin foundation (it's near Hilda, Missouri) is continuous, laid on a steel reinforced, foot-wide concrete footing below the frost line, with ventilation on all four sides. That can't hurt, but it cost a lot in time, cement and labor. David Darby, nearby, dug three feet each way from all four corners over a foot deep, and filled the trenches with concrete (more than needed). This supports about six running feet of stone foundation at each corner, which is plenty. Again, the footing is twice wall thickness on hard subsoil and below frost.

We built the Zent cabin near Halltown, Missouri, simply on three-foot corner angles of 16-inch wide stones, laid flat on just enough concrete to give even support. There's an additional pier supporting a sleeper under the floor joists, halfway down the sides. This also gives support to the walls midway, which is a good idea.

In yet another variation, the Kruger house near Viola, Missouri, was built on stone corner piers set on reinforced footings. Bill Kruger wanted to fill in a continuous foundation later, so we dug and poured a reinforced footing all the way for his later use. Again we built supporting piers halfway under each wall. The joist sleeper support was a pier on one end, two stone columns along its length, and another, built into the fireplace footing at the other end.

Log walls can be set on piers with as little as three feet of footing from each corner. Supporting piers at midpoint should be built. The one at left supports the joist sleeper, which is supported at the other end by the hearth foundation.

The log house my family and I live in has a continuous foundation, but only because we have a flagstone floor set on fill, and the logs begin 18" up from floor level. There is reinforced footing only at the corners, which carried all the weight during construction. Filling

Footing and foundation dimensions for an 18' x 20' log house. Horizontals on a slope should be measured with a plumb bob, center. At bottom, equal dotted line distances will give square corners.

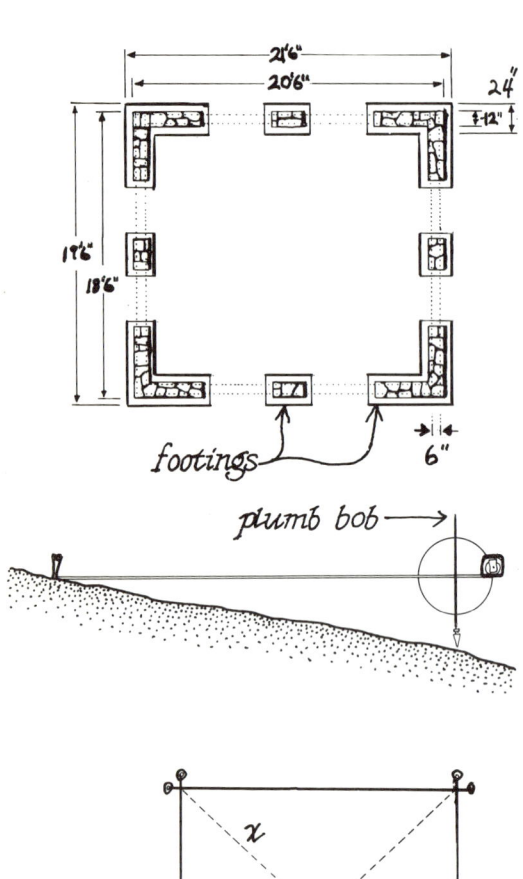

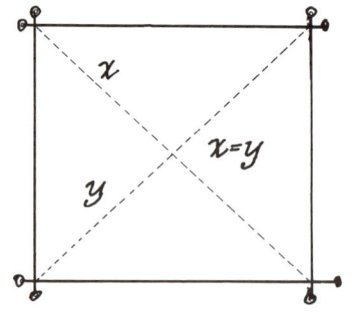

in between corners was a simple matter of laying stone up from a below-frost trench till it reached the bottom of the sill logs. The fill-in carries no weight at all. I did it a little at a time as I collected stone, and it happened that the house itself was almost complete before the foundation was.

For your own purposes, you should build a longer, wider foundation for softer ground, preferably laid on a reinforced footing. Of course you should use stone, and without the footing, settling will crack your masonry. With the logs above to distribute and bear the weight evenly, and reinforced concrete below, all the stones will have to go down together if they sink at all, and they won't go far over the years.

Settling by degrees is a fact of building, unless on solid rock. That's all right, too, if all of your foundation is on the same rock layer. Just one corner on soil will tilt the house, in time.

Lay out your foundation ditches with stakes and string, allowing for the extra width of the footing. If your house is 18' x 20' outside dimensions, you'll set those 6" wide logs on a 12" foundation, set in turn on a 24" footing. So you'll have a total of 19'6" x 21'6", with the ditches extending inwards two feet.

In measuring this out on a hillside, use a plumb bob or simply a weight on a string, to get the distances measured accurately horizontally, not at a slope. Once you've laid out the square or rectangle so that the sides are the right dimensions, you'll need to check for square corners. You can sight with a carpenter's square. Or measure a given distance from each corner to get a right triangle, square each leg, add, and extract the square root to see if the hypotenuse is correct. If not, shift two opposite walls.

I lay out the sides, simply measure from one corner to the opposite one, then measure between the two remaining corners. If the distance is the same, the corners are square. If not, I shift walls until the diagonal distances are the same.

No matter how careful you are, you will find that, by the time you've brought your foundation up three or four feet to level, you've let at least one corner get out of line. The one-foot width of the stone foundation wall gives you 3" each way for error in centering the log wall, and you'll need it. Check your first course of logs for square, too, and slide them around on the stone till they're right.

Concrete and Mortar

Your footing concrete is best mixed by hand or with a small mixer, since you'll use so little of it. If you pour a continuous footing, plus a pad for the fireplace, you might buy ready-mix from a contractor. Their trucks are big and heavy, however, and you'll need a pretty good road in, to accommodate them. I'm partial to narrow, winding, even steep approaches to sites (whatever the contour dictates) and few concrete trucks can get to such places.

Economically, you won't save much by mixing your own. For the footing and pad, it's easily possible to spend more for mixer rental, cement, hauling sand, gravel and water, than ready-mix costs. Most contractors have a minimum load, though, so make sure you'll use it all.

If you mix your own, use a 1-2-3 proportion of Portland cement, sand and gravel. Try to get gravel 1" or less in size. At no time should the thickness of the biggest stone in the mix be over half the thickness of the wall or slab to be poured.

Don't mix too thin. The water will evaporate, leaving air bubbles that weaken concrete. Mix wet enough to get all those dry pockets of sand or cement that build up in the mixer. And try to mix and pour a complete job at a time. Cold joints are weaker, so pour a complete footing or slab.

A footing on a hillside should be poured with steps in it, to give as near a horizontal surface as possible to lay stone on. Pieces of board wedged on edge into the trench at intervals do nicely. A lot of low steps works better than a few big ones, so use pieces of four-inch board. Or bricks or rocks.

I prefer ½" reinforcing bars, and use two of them in a footing six to 12 inches deep and a foot wide. Pour half your depth, then lay the bars, side by side, 4" apart and 4" from the edges, overlapping the ends. Take time to bend the bars where you need it, to keep them near the vertical center of the footing. Then put the step pieces in, if any, and

A stepped footing on a hillside, greatly exaggerated to show how boards are wedged across the ditch to form level steps of concrete. Reinforcing rods are laid below the steps.

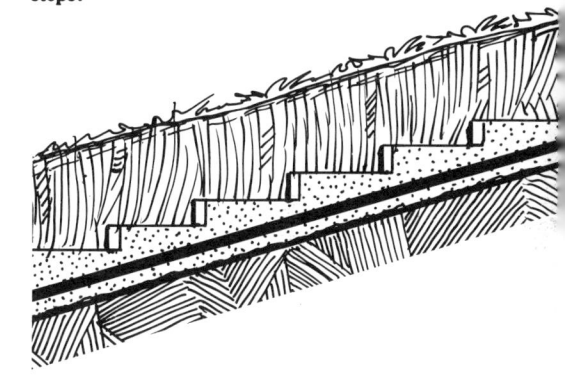

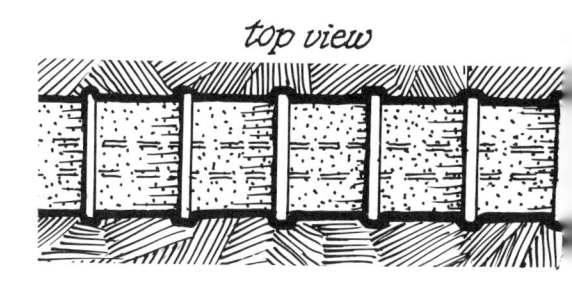

top view

pour the other half on top.

For masonry mortar, which is different from the footing mixture, I use a mix of one part masonry cement to three parts sand, and I use one part lime to two parts Portland to make the masonry cement. There are lots of other formulas, but this has worked nicely for me over several years. And it's cheaper than buying masonry cement or pre-mix. Mortar should be thoroughly mixed in a box or wheelbarrow with a hoe, using enough water for a slightly stiff mix. Most masons use it as dry as possible to avoid smearing and running, but it bonds to the stone better if it's wet; just dry enough not to run.

I don't mix masonry mortar in a cement mixer unless I have plenty of help and plan to use many batches. You'll find, if you work alone or with one helper, that it takes quite a while to use up a couple of cubic feet of mortar, and you may not mix but one batch a day. Also, a lot of it gets caught in the tines of the mixer and wasted when you wash it out.

Both concrete and mortar must be kept moist for several days for the chemical reaction that produces strength, to be complete. Just letting it dry out doesn't work. Wet burlap sacks are good to cover fresh work, or sheet plastic. Don't spray with water until the second day, or you'll wash it away.

Stones

Now, about the stones in the foundation. First of all, haul in more than you could possibly need. You'll still run short. Get stone that's flat top and bottom, if you can.

There's a myth among masons (usually beginners) that it's best to lay the first course in the wet footing concrete, but don't worry about it. Obviously you can't lay every course that way, so just one won't help much. Use a little mortar on the footing, wetting it first, just as you do for each course or layer of stone as you go up.

Lay the stone any way you choose, but cover the joints between stones with the next layer, brick fashion. You invite a cracked foundation if mortar joints align vertically. I like to lay stone flat, or ledge, with the edges showing. I vary this with a square, rounded, or

Random ledge pattern

angled stone occasionally. A wall laid with the stones standing on edge is weaker, unless very thick.

A good rule is to make sure each stone will stay where you want it before you mortar it. That way it will be there from now on, even if the mortar erodes away, as did the mud, clay, and lime mortar from earlier foundations and chimneys. Rock each stone in its bed of mortar to insure bonding, then trim the excess mortar.

Bring your foundation up a foot or more off the ground before you lay the first log. Eighteen inches is better, because termites don't like to travel far. After the logs are in place, fill in any gaps to give more support, using mortar and stone where needed.

I am occasionally asked if I set heavy bolts into the foundation masonry to anchor the sill logs. This is commonly done in conventional studwall, and in post-and-beam construction. It would be of no value in a log house, however, unless some way were devised to fasten all the logs together, from the foundation on up. The weight of the logs themselves holds the house together, and I have never seen a dovetail-notch cabin that had been blown apart by wind. In a really heavy gale the roof might depart, but we talk about preventing that, when we get to the chapter on roofs.

A dry-stone foundation is more nearly authentic pioneer, but is a haven for snakes. One advantage is that it's less work, since no mortar is used, and no footing is necessary. Since water can get between the stones and freeze anyway, there's no point in a footing below frostline. This type masonry requires good, flat-surfaced stones, however, and that means a lot of searching for the right rock, wedging between, or a lot of stone cutting and dressing. A foundation obviously shouldn't totter, or folks in your house will tend to become uneasy. So wedge dry stone work with bits of rock or metal. In the process of the ground's freezing, swelling, settling and washing, you'll notice some changes in your dry-stone foundation; but if your stones are good and wide, and the columns cover a lot of ground area, you can live with it nicely. I don't advise, however, letting your toddler stick his fingers into those inviting, dark recesses after large, curiously patterned "wiggle worms".

Dry-stone pier

In all, foundation work is singularly unrewarding. You spend days bent over, digging, prying out rocks, pouring concrete, laying stone. And not much of this is visible progress. It seems to be a fact that the builder, as well as those who inspect and criticize his work, likes to see more happening. So you might want a minimal foundation, either dry-stone or footing-and-masonry just at the corners. You can always fill in later, you know.

But whatever you do, make it solid. Cover a lot of area with the foundation, to resist settling. Get it high enough to discourage termites

Laying the continuous stone foundation for the McRaven house. Fill dirt was necessary to level for a flagstone floor.

An elaborate dry-wall foundation from underneath, in granite country. Ten foot slabs are hand-quarried.

and rot, and even grass fires. And make it look right. The neighborhood know-it-all will suggest solid concrete, but don't listen. Even faced with stone to look better, it'll cost you a mint. And don't even consider concrete blocks, or some nameless purist may visit your house and smash your offending foundation with his steel-toed boot. It wouldn't take much more than that.

Drudgery though it often is, there's still a bit of a thrill in turning the first shovelful of foundation earth. You're actually on your way now; your log house is out of your head and on its way up. Enjoy.

CHAPTER EIGHT

Hewing, Notching, Log Raising

Here is where your log house really becomes what it is. Style, foundation, roof, additions, can be similar to those in other houses, but those massive tiers of logs put your house in its own natural light.

Most mountain cabin logs were hewn, and there are lots of good reasons for this still. No matter how straight logs are, natural taper will make fitting corners, window and door facings, a pain. Hewing to a common thickness makes notching and facing easier, cuts down the work of stripping bark, and gives a flat surface inside and out. It also cuts weight, quite a factor if just one or two of you are handling those logs.

Traditionally, a hewn-log house was also a status symbol, since transient hunters and the poorest of settlers threw together huts of sapwood round-logs and mud. Barns were built this way, and what self-respecting frontier woman wanted to live in a barn? Besides, hewn logs were the style back East, and up North, and as heavy timbers in the New England clapboard houses and the English half-timbered structures. These places were where our mountaineers came from, and they brought their traditions.

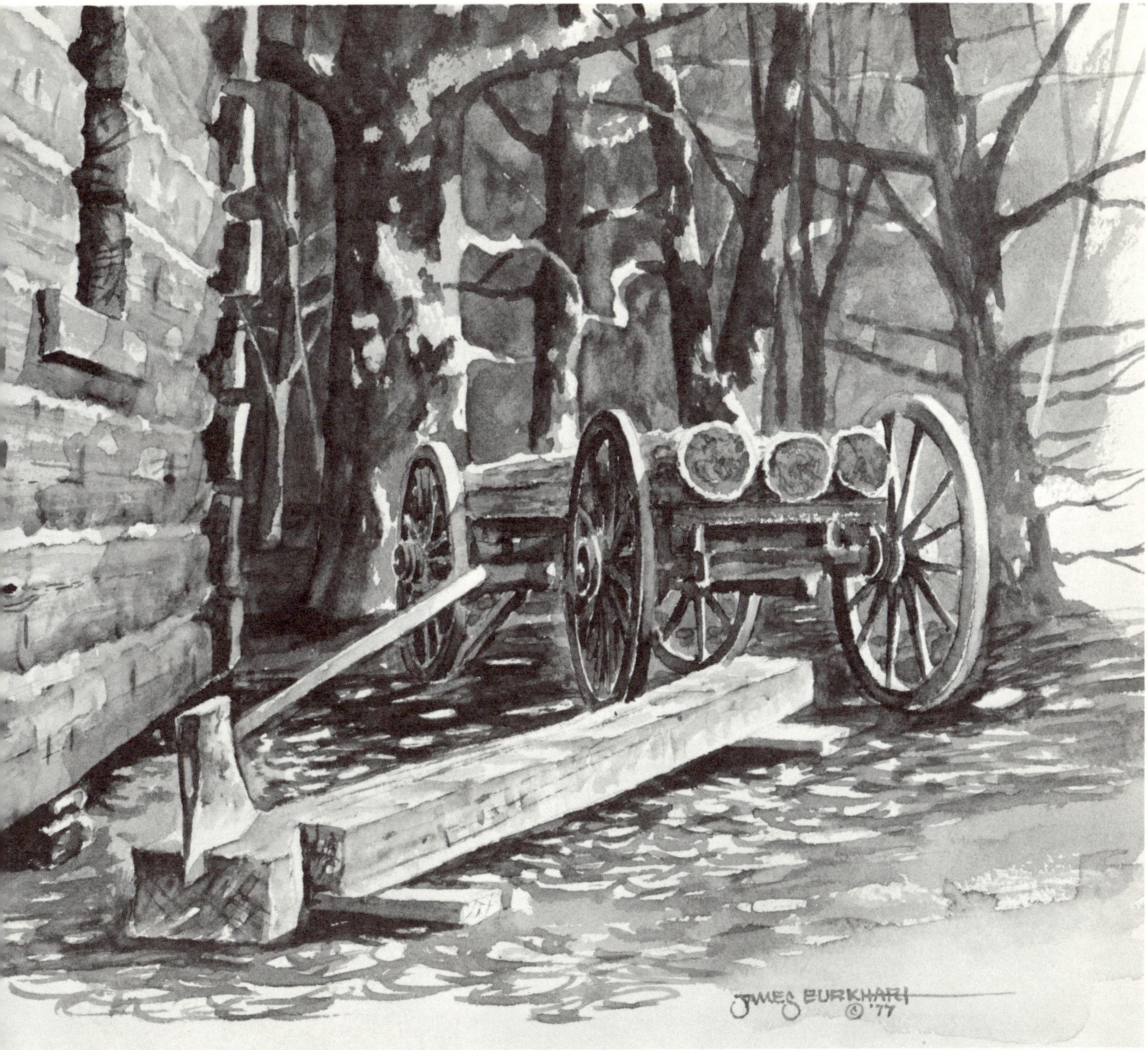
JAMES BURKHART
© '77

Exceptions were the sills and plates, which were of oak in the best examples, no matter what the other logs were. Oak resists rot, termites, and is stronger than most woods.

Oak has been the favorite for hewn logs in the Ozarks, with some pine used early, and rare examples in walnut and cedar. I delight in working in cedar, but it's hard to acquire. Our house is about half oak, with cedar having been added at some pre-1890 rebuild date, and more cedar when we restored and added to it. Poplar was favored farther to the East. Whatever wood was used, the original builder almost always stayed with the same kind throughout.

Avoid woods that rot easily, and those that are hard to work, Sycamore, elm, gum and hickory, are heavy and rot quickly, although they're generally available. Oak is not easy to work compared with cedar or pine, but is long-lasting, tough and generally available. White oak has always been the favorite, but it, too, is rare today. Red oak (water oak, pin oak, whatever your local variety is called) works well with a broadaxe or adze, being inclined to split off in chunks easily. It doesn't last as long in the weather as white or post oak, but is generally easier to acquire. Post oak is tough and hard to work. Avoid it.

Hewing

Hew your logs green. They're more inclined to crack open that way, but hacking a seasoned oak log is punishment. Folklore tells us that settlers hewed logs in the "M" months, March and May. Don't worry about the cracks; they're too narrow and shallow to matter much. Hew two sides, leaving the other two for extended height when laid up. Most houses were built this way, although square-notched houses were often of logs hewn on all four sides. The Grigsby House, on the Arkansas College campus, is square-notched, and has all the logs hewn on four sides, to a common dimension.

I prefer the broadaxe over the adze, which is more of a finishing tool. As far as I know, nobody manufactures these axes now, except for some rare and expensive hand-forged collector's items. They can still be had for a price at junk-shops and antique sales. The axe head can be handled for right or left use, and these handles **are** different.

To hew, you stand alongside the log with the flat side of the axe to the wood, and it's on the same side with you, very close to your toes. Your knuckles, too, take a beating unless the axe handle is bent away

More or less correct stance for a left-handed hewer, using a left-handed axe.

from the log. So, with the bend away from the flat side, that means a different handle if you're left or right-handed.

Novices usually devise their own variations of the basic straight-down swing, but anyone who does much axework soon returns to it. Years ago I thought I'd discovered something by using a right-handed axe (borrowed) at a 45° angle, hewing on the other side of the log with my left-handed swing. I soon abandoned that strenuous game, and I suggest you forget such variations. The heavy axe is more efficient used straight down.

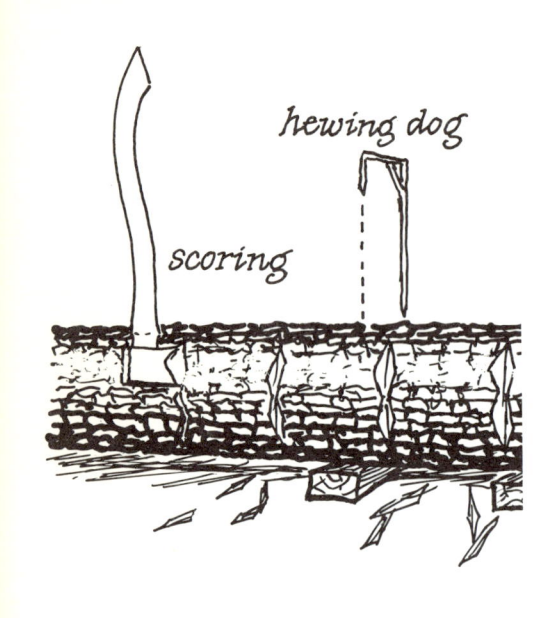

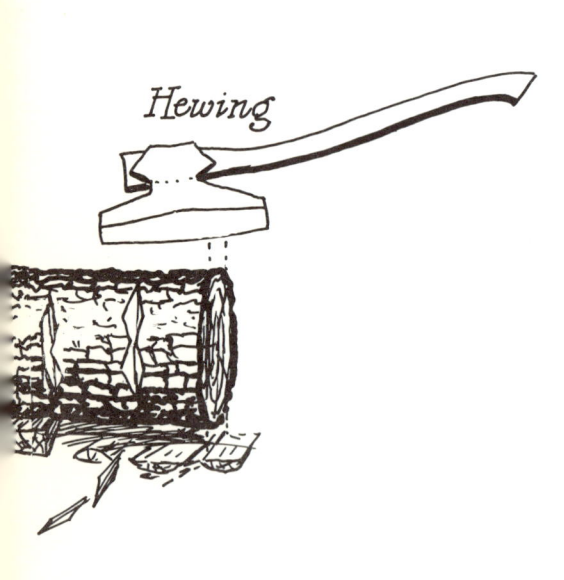

A good man often hewed a dozen logs a day using the old method, and lived. I hew two or three, then find something else to do for awhile. A good day's work for tie-hackers was also about a dozen a day, hewed on four sides, but only eight feet long. I hear tales of hackers turning out 20 ties a day, but would have to see it myself.

First score-hack the log down one side, every six inches or so with an ordinary axe. You may want to stand on the log for this, or chop from alongside, avoiding your kneecap. Then there are a couple of ways to go. One calls for splitting out the chunks, or 'juggles' with the plain axe (poll axe, felling axe, 'choppin' axe') then making a pass with the broadaxe. I score deeply, making a notch if necessary, then slice off the juggles with the broadaxe. Either way, you eventually assume the broadaxe stance, swing straight down to hit the log at about 45° and cut off everything that doesn't look like a hewn log. Lay a tough board under, to keep your axe out of the rocks. After a couple of logs, there'll be plenty of juggles to pad the ground underneath.

A log rolls around a lot while it's being hewed, and you should stabilize it. I sometimes hew the log where it falls, leaving the treetop connected and maybe even part of the stump to steady it until I'm through. If you can't do this, flatten two places on the under side of the log and lay it on crossways timbers. Or get a pair of hewing dogs, largely unheard of in this region, which were iron stays driven into the log and the timbers to hold things steady.

Some hewers snap a chalkline along the log as a guide and hew to the line after they've scored to it first. Most logs aren't straight enough to make this easy, so other hewers sort of chop a line in the bark. I just eyeball it, and make a second pass to take out any hump. You'll need at least two passes at the thick butt end, anyway.

You may have read about hewing from the top of the log down, which is fine in theory, but knots tend to head uphill, and are easier to slice through from the butt end. The swell at the base is easier to hew from the top. Switching means rolling the log over. Being able to chop either right or left-handed, I keep two axes handy and use both. That way I torture new muscles from time to time.

This is a hewn ceiling joist for the Zent cabin. Often logs with a slight bow are used, which is arched to offset sagging.

There is a mystique about converting tree trunks into hewn timbers that is quite compelling. Herculean labor, it will nevertheless remain one of the most satisfying experiences of your log house-building. In retrospect, that is. With that heavy, heavy axe, you are shaping a second life for the tree you've felled, feeling the steel bite into living wood, to ringing echoes of the hill country past.

Let me here digress to try to clear up what I regard as misinformation about hewn log walls. I have read and heard of the practice of constructing round-log cabins, then hewing down the walls **in situ.** Nancy McDonough quotes an old-timer from the Ouachitas as being familiar with this.[31] D.A. Hutslar mentions "scutched" logs as those superficially hacked after the house was up.[32]

I have used the broadaxe for many years, and have probably hewn as many logs as did the average pioneer in his entire life, yet I would not attempt to hew logs in a standing wall. I have a brother who is an artist with a broadaxe, and can shave a 1/8 inch layer end to end, and he wouldn't try it either. I know dozens of veteran hackers who would not and could not do it, and never heard of its being done.

I have visited hundreds of hewn-log cabins and have found no evidence, from a hewer's experience, that any of them were so shaped. It's the sort of thing that may have been speculated upon, since we know that logs were rolled up skids at log-raisings and maybe we assume they were still round at this point. I have used skids to get logs in place, and sometimes rolled them, but usually slid them up, always hewn sensibly, on the ground.

Of course it would have been possible, with complicated scaffolding to stand on, and a wanton disregard for digital extremities, but it would also have been somewhat self-defeating, given the added weight and difficulty of notching, etc. No, except for rare freaks, round log cabins stayed round, and hewn ones were shaped on or near the earth's surface.

When figuring log length in the woods start with your outside dimensions, and allow about 4" more at each end to extend past the notch. Most early hewn-log houses had the log-ends trimmed flush, and you may want to do this later, but allow the extra length for an error margin. So an 18' inside dimension requires at least a 19'8" log, allowing for a 6" wall thickness. Figure ahead the number and placement of windows, doors and fireplace so you can use short lengths. It seems faster and simpler to cut all the logs full length, then chainsaw out the openings, but it's not. I've done houses that way, and the pioneers always did, (sans chainsaw) but there are good reasons not to, today.

First of all, you'll need very few full-length logs--just enough to bind it all together, and it's easier to handle short ones. Long straight logs will be at a premium no matter where you are, and meandering tree trunks will afford lots of three and four-foot lengths, perfectly usable. Also, full-length logs must be notched exactly on both ends so the log won't teeter, and this takes several tries. A segment, from a corner to a window, can be a fraction off without threatening the structure, and no one will be able to tell.

So save timber, cut to length, and hew just what you need. A 19' 8" log, with a 3' door and 2' window out, becomes three short lengths, maybe 6', 4' and 4' 4". And the notching can be faster and a bit less demanding than on the necessary full-length logs. The full-length ones can also weigh as much as 600 pounds after hewing, green, so handle as few as possible.

To keep the loose ends of short logs in line, you can block the spaces between logs with 2x4 end pieces or scraps to maintain a level. Spike a board up on the outside or inside surface of the log temporarily near where door and window facings will go. These vertical boards come off later, so they can also be scrap.

Replacing a log that was notched too deep. It will be used elsewhere.

Scott Lamb uses a one-man crosscut saw to notch a corner.

Notching

Now, about that notching. You'll read about V-notching, saddle notching (round logs), full dovetail, tenon (square), also called dovetail, and probably some others. The traditional Ozarker used the chamfer-and-notch, or half dovetail, which is simply a vertical cut on the underside of the log to a depth that leaves the desired space for chinking, plus an angle cut toward the end. This is the notch. The chamfer is the sloping cut on top of the log that lets the next cross-log notch fit over it.

Our own cabin had been scrambled at least once before, in rebuilding, and several of the logs and their notching are upside down. And there are some full dovetails among the halves. We decided to leave them that way, instead of reshaping the brittle old wood. The cedar logs I added are all half-dovetail, right side up.

This half-dovetail notch pulls the corners tighter together both ways with the weight from above, which some other notches do not. The V-notch and compound-angle dovetail are the other two best choices. These also allow rain water to drain out, which helps prevent rotting. Wide eaves help here too, a non-pioneer practice that keeps making more sense as time goes on.

Notching should follow a pattern based on a set angle, and a set amount of wood left, not wood taken out. So notch a swelled butt-end deeper than the thinner top end, but keep the same angle. Cut yourself a pattern to use on the hewn logs. Make sure the pattern is laid pointing straight to the other end of the log, or curves, kinks and flaring ends will throw you. The same angle isn't essential. A friend who helped me with one cabin always worked the chamfer about where he thought it should be, then used an adjustable protractor to take the same angle to the next notch. I do it all by eye.

I use a crosscut saw to make the vertical cut, but my brother John, who has a steadier hand, likes the chainsaw. Remember to allow for the wide cut the chain makes. Then we both use an axe or adze on the angle cuts. You may not want to risk these long-handled tools while perched up in the sky, which is where we usually work the chamfers. A

Even if notching is done on the ground, final fitting usually has to be done up in the sky. Jim Maupin works a chamfer on the Kruger house.

large chisel will do nicely, but if you axe things, I suggest steel-toed boots.

You will almost certainly cut too much wood out eventually, so go light till you get the hang of it. Too wide a chinking gap means cut the notch or chamfer deeper. Unless you need a wide gap to keep the log level. More about that later.

If you do take out too much, and the log lies against the one under it without closing the notch, you can hew part of the bottom edge or the top of the one under it. Or save this log for later use. Or, you can slip a piece of board into the notch as a spacer. Not done in the best craftsmen's families, I realize, but sometimes necessary when restoring a house that has parts of the notches split off. Like ours.

In notching, keep an eye on the other corner, beyond that doorway or window, so that your logs will be the same height, as you work your way up. You'll span the opening at its top, and this spanner log should be reasonably level.

Which takes us back to the foundation. Only theorists assume that logs are straight, and of constant diameter. Lay the courses of logs alternately, with a big end one way and the next one over it, big-end the other way. And alternate opposite wall logs. The best plan is to lay each course with the big ends joining little ends all the way around. Next course should join little ends with big ends, corner for corner. This will

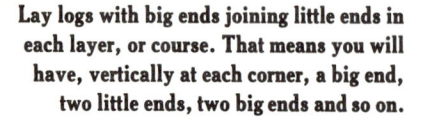

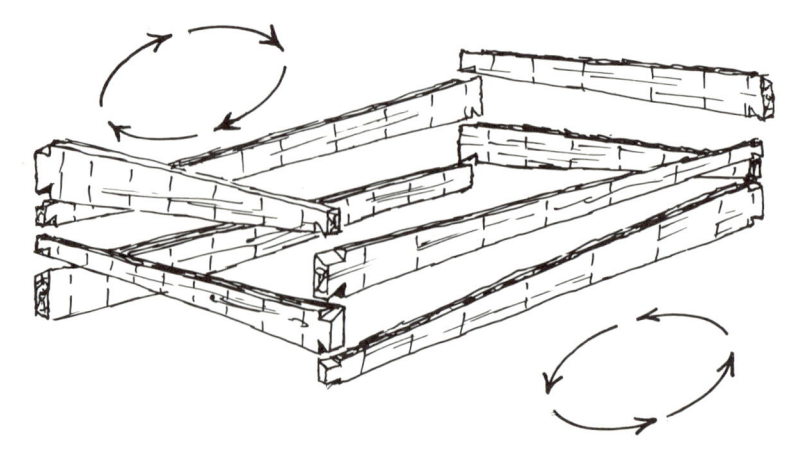

Lay logs with big ends joining little ends in each layer, or course. That means you will have, vertically at each corner, a big end, two little ends, two big ends and so on.

108

make notching much easier, and make it easier to keep all the logs more nearly level.

In a log house, your concern with levels is limited mostly to the floor, ceiling if any, and top plates. Window and door sills can be cut to a level; so can notches for floor and ceiling joists and rafters. But it's easier and less disturbing visually if the logs involved are approximately horizontal. If you notice one corner is high, notch the next log deeper, even if your have to shave off some of the butt end to let it sit down on the chamfer. Leave about 2" for chinking; more means too much mortar and looks sloppy, and much less makes it hard to get the stuff in.

Joists

I like to lay my floor joists mortised into the first two logs, or sills, at a height well below that of the second two logs, so the third pair won't have to be notched for the tops of the joists to fit into the second pair.

Shall we do that one again? It's easy to get in trouble here, trying to figure final floor height, so here's a good rule: Lay your sills as front-and-back logs, and mortise them for the joists so that only 2" of the joist is above the sills. This way your next pair of front-and-back logs will just touch the sill tops without more mortising or trimming, and still fit into the end log dovetail chamfers.

Joists can be sawn timbers, logs, or beams. I like 2' centers, and support in the middle. A stone wall, or a heavy sleeper or summer beam as this support is sometimes called, will brace the middle. Wider centers will hold the weight, but will let the floor shake and creak. For hewn or round log joists I like the same chamfer and notch into the sills as at the corners of the house. But for thinner timbers, a neat mortise is best, tight enough to keep the joist steady. If you use two-inch stock, for instance, these mortises will make criss-cross bracing between joists unnecessary.

Take a lot of care notching or mortising in your joists; you'll have to live with that sloping floor for a long time. To avoid taking out too much wood from your sills, you can cut an 8" joist down to 4" at the ends without noticeable weakening; it's only in the spans that they tend to sag.

Joists should be laid at a height to allow doorsills to be on top of, or notched into, sills. Joists can be tapered at the ends and mortised to allow a lower floor.

pegged facing

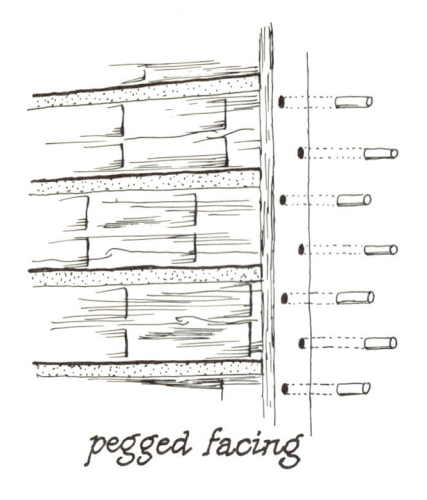

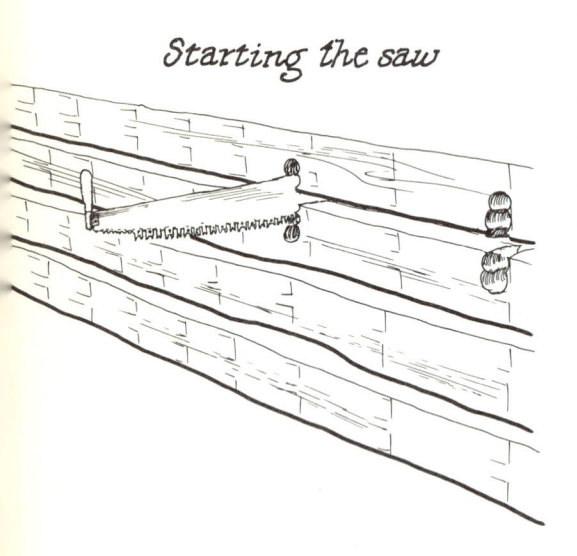

Starting the saw

I don't like to lay the floor till I have a roof on, since rain and sun will warp it, shrink it, and generally play hell with it. I usually lay some 2" boards across the joists to stand on while building. Once I covered a completed floor with black plastic for protection, which condensed moisture in gallons, swelling and buckling the floor anyway.

Spike door, window and fireplace facings directly into the ends of the logs. Make a clean cut here. I like using the crosscut saw because I can control it better, but a chainsaw is faster. Also noisier and smellier. Only the greatest need for haste drives me to use one.

One-inch oak or two-inch pine is heavy enough for the facings themselves, and a 16-penny common nail is large enough, say four per log. Don't use box nails, those slender fasteners designed for soft pine, spruce or fir, in oak. Even with common nails you may have to drill an occasional hole, especially if your logs are seasoned. I prefer the modern counterpart of the old cut nail, square, now hardened for masonry, which will go through anything. It's expensive, and you must know to drive its wedge shape with the grain, not across it, to avoid splitting. Our forefathers bored and pegged these facings with trunnels.

The facings hold the ends of the wall logs in line, and should be mortised into and fastened to, the top spanner and window or door sill log. After they're in place, you can pry off the temporary strips you nailed up as the logs went into place. It seems it would be easier to start with the facings themselves, but it's easier to trim the log ends evenly when they're all up. The pioneers had an abundance of timber, and built solid log walls. Then they bored a line of auger holes through the logs to get the crosscut saw started for the window and door cuts. Or they started a cut through as they went up, and finished it later.

Getting the logs up onto the walls is of course a major undertaking. Two to four men can wrestle 16 to 20-foot hewn logs into place if the logs are under, say 12" in diameter. But these are hard to lift to any height. Long skids were usually the answer for the early settlers, with the logs skidded up by hand or cross-hauled by oxen or horses. A block-and-tackle, although slow, will do the job, with skids or in a vertical lift from a tripod or boom.

Scott Lamb uses a come-along from gin-poles on a Jeep pickup to raise a log into place. The same setup with a winch is faster.

If you handle your logs this way, don't lift them until in position. A swinging log can overturn your rig, or punch out grille, lights, windshield or part of a wall.

The device I've developed is a full 2x4 A-frame (gin-poles) pivoted from the front bumper of my Land Rover and braced with a guy cable over the rig down to the trailer hitch. I run the winch cable up over a sheave at the peak and down to the log. Lacking a winch, a ratchet hoist or "come-along" will do it by hand. Either way, the log should be lifted at two points for balance. Once the rig is in place, it's a good idea to suppport each end of the bumper with a block, to take the weight off the springs.

At a house-raising, four men with ropes can haul each log up from the top while others push from below.

Check your log wall for vertical alignment as you go. Particularly around windows and doors, you'll have to watch a tendency to slope inwards. That's of no great consequence until you find your door won't open without swinging into the floor. Use a level, and make sure all your full-length logs are the same length from notch to notch. Some delicate adjusting for alignment may have to be done from time to time. I use a sledgehammer.

Now, at last, you're up to ceiling height. You should have at least one log spanner above windows and doors, with the facings attached. If you cut deeply into this log to get your door or window height, go up another course before laying the ceiling joists. You'll notch these joists into the log, and you must be sure there's enough wood left to support the weight.

You may not even want a ceiling or a loft, but the joists are still a good idea, run front to back, at right angles to the ridge line. They are the truss chords that tie the rafters together, keeping your ridge from sagging and the rafters from pushing the top logs apart. There is another way around this, which we'll talk about when we get to the roof.

Let's assume that you do want a ceiling, and a floor for the loft. These can be two layers, on top and bottom of the joists, with insulation between. But since you'll be using the loft, let's not insulate it from the downstairs heat. And lets keep the ceiling beams visible. Massive, hewn joists support better and look better, giving a reassuring feel of strength and shelter. I hew them with the broadaxe, then adze for additional smoothness. Fancy houses in the old days sported beaded joists, worked with a hand shaping plane.

A 6" x 8" joist is esthetically pleasing, and strong. Lay the joists a minimum of 4' apart, or three of them in a 16' house interior, four in a 20'. They should be half-dovetailed into the top front-and back logs so that they are even with the side logs. Sometimes they were simply mortised, but this gives no bracing against outward thrust. Dress the top surfaces of these logs and joists carefully, as you did your floor joists, since you'll be nailing flooring on top of them.

Probably the best flooring-ceiling combination is 2" thick tongue-and-groove lumber, which is quite expensive. A one-inch subfloor with a second layer over, is also acceptable. Tongue-and-groove helps each board support its neighbor in the spans. If

John at work notching in a ceiling joist. This half-dovetail helps tie the front and back walls together which a mortise would not, unless pinned.

The use of too many joists, if visible overhead, makes the ceiling look busy. Too few, of course, lets the ceiling sag or shake underfoot.

113

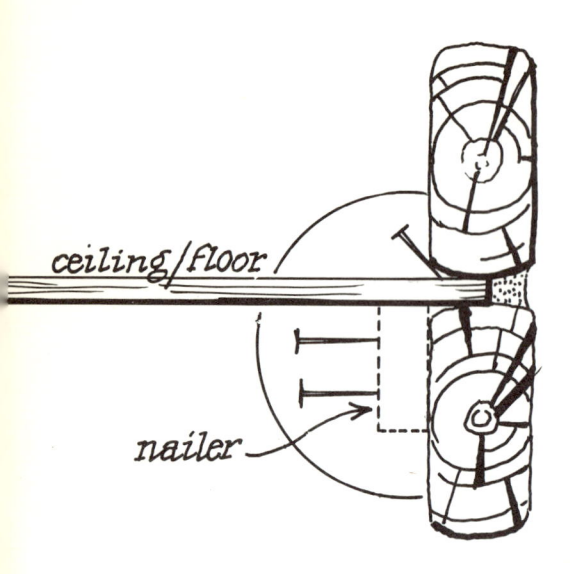

Ceiling board ends can be angle-nailed into the end logs if these are level. If not, a level mortise can sometimes be cut into the log, or a nailer spiked to it.

non-grooved lumber is used, you'll need closer joist spacing, ideally 2'.

For our house we were able to obtain, albeit at great expense, full 16' lengths of 2" tongue-and-groove lumber, which spanned the entire inside, leaving a neat inch extending into the chinking space at each end. A word of caution, however: try to lay this ceiling-floor in very dry weather. Even kiln-dried lumber can shrink enough to pull apart and leave cracks when winter heat is applied.

Again, don't lay this ceiling until you have the roof on, unless you're one of those optimists who can safely plan to have it on before the next rain. It would indeed be easier to nail the ends of the boards to the side logs if nothing were above them, but you can slant the nails fairly well.

Now, assuming you want to make full use of your loft space, you'll need to lay at least three more courses of logs above the ceiling level. Notch out the next front-and-back logs to fit over the joist ends and go ahead. Obviously, additional logs above these joists just wreck their function as chords in the rafter-truss game, but do it anyway. As I said, we'll take care of that problem later.

I once wanted a ceiling at a height that meant running the joists parallel to the ridge. And since more logs were to be laid above, there seemed no real reason not to do so. My brother John and I were building this cabin some distance from home, and left the job for the weekend. We were both convinced that the joists should be at right angles to the ridge, but neither of us could reason why, since they would give no support to the rafters. We puzzled over it all weekend.

The alternative was another pair of logs and more ceiling height, which we really didn't want. We'd already perched the cabin on four-foot foundation piers, and, only 16' square outside dimensions, it was almost too tall. Besides, I knew I'd seen houses built with the joists parallel to the ridge pole.

So we laid the ceiling joists parallel to the ridge. And it wasn't until we put in the stairs that we saw why this is a no-no. Stairs usually run along a wall, and you bump the roof if you go up parallel to the ridge. You could move to another wall and cut a couple of the joists, supporting them from below, but that's messy. In this case, we'd planned a disappearing ladder stair anyway, so we put it in the middle of the room between two joists and left everything as it was.

Stairs do take up a lot of your precious room, and many old houses used narrow, steep stairs or ladders nailed to the wall. Or disappearing stairs. With the joists laid at right angles, disappearing stairs can be along the side wall opposite the fireplace, neatly, like regular stairs. More about getting upstairs in the chapter on lofts.

Above the joists, lay as many courses as you like to help get headroom, but remember that at least the top course must not be cut into for windows. These logs need their full strength as you'll see when we talk about roofs. Finish up with a pair of end logs. These will be the chords for the end rafter trusses, and will carry a lot of strain.

Try to get all the logs level at the top; you won't be able to get a tight fit to the roof front and back anyway without chinking or boards fitted in, but it makes things easier if they're level.

If you hew a heavy plate on four sides in the old tradition, you may terminate the rafters here, or notch deeply for a tighter fit when you deck the roof.

Chinking

With the walls up, you'll have to wait several months to chink between, unless your logs are already seasoned. A year or more is better, but of course you're impatient. Let green logs stand in the completed wall at the very least through a full summer season, when they do most of their shrinking. Otherwise you will note cracks developing between your chinking and the logs, for the great outdoors to come in: drafts, spiders, centipedes, even small snakes. And vertical boards like window and door facings will buckle under the weight of settling logs.

So let the log walls stand while you labor elsewhere. There's still plenty to do. If you plan electric wiring, staple it along the open spaces to be covered with the chinking later.

A good way to keep out larger varmints as the seasons change is to prepare for chinking as soon as the logs are up. Nail strips of metal lath into the cracks on one side, set in half an inch or so. Then pack

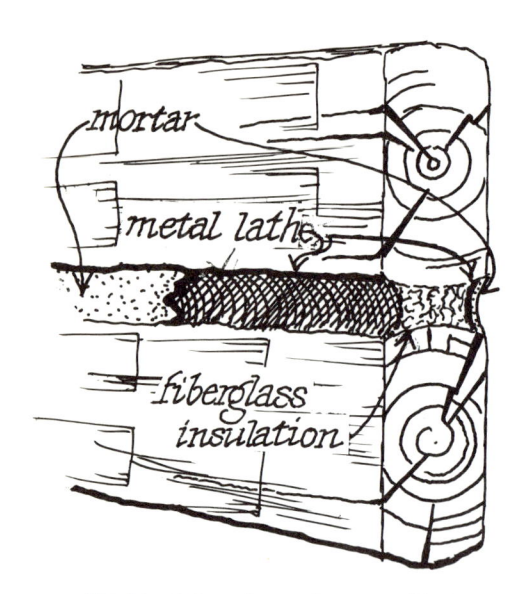

Chinking is best plastered onto metal lath or wire screen nailed into the cracks. A core of tightly packed fiberglass insulation will expand as logs shrink, and keep out drafts.

fiberglass insulation against the lath, and nail lath into the other side. Later, mortar chinking goes on nicely, and the lath keeps mice and birds from borrowing the insulation for nests before you can do the chinking.

The chinking material itself is 1:3 masonry mortar, and it needs metal for reinforcing. The lath material is more or less flexible, being a light expanded metal, and can be shaped to fit between knots and crooked places. Hardware cloth or fine chicken wire can be used, but aren't as effective. I have used rows of old nails, with a wire stretched horizontally among them, but this is slow and not as strong.

On the subject of insulating between logs, it's really a necessity. Humidity changes will swell and shrink the logs, and even the best chinking with reinforcing, pulls away slightly. It happens even with the well-seasoned, 1840's logs in our house, and only the spongy fiberglass expanding as the logs shrink, keeps out the wind.

The pioneers often used short splits of wood laid diagonally in the cracks to help hold in the mud packing, which was sometimes mixed with grass stems. With scant eaves, the mud eventually washed out, but mostly the expansion and contraction of the logs just broke it up.

A friend in Arkansas had a large house built, using old hewn logs, under the direction of one of the country's leading architects. After suffering drafts through the north wall the first few winters, he solved the problem partially with shakes nailed over the logs on the outside. This was commonly done by the settlers, too; I hardly recognized our own log house when I first saw it, covered as it was with an assortment of clapboards and shakes.

I was able to acquire an 1850's pine log cabin just for removing it recently, which was disguised by clapboarding covering the hewn log walls on the outside and many layers of wallpaper which camouflaged the inside.

So. Your walls are up, so stand back to survey the heavy labor completed. Logs up, the part of your building that gives it its character is done. Now lay aside your broadaxe with some rueful joy as you survey also the blisters, aching back and sliced boots. Looking back, you wouldn't have it any other way.

John shaping a notch on the Zent cabin near Halltown, Missouri. We were fortunate here in having the use of Bob Zent's forklift to handle these logs.

118

CHAPTER NINE

Roof

Roofing your house gives it the final shape it will wear, and of course lets you start keeping things dry inside. Any number of styles and procedures are acceptable, but I'll outline the one most used by most settlers after sawn lumber became available, which is also (you might have guessed) the simplest and most practical.

A 45° pitch was common, because it was easy to figure, was steep enough to shed rain and snow, but not too steep to work on, and gave headroom in the loft. The kids were stowed away up here, where wind whistled between the shakes in winter and only a little warmth found its way up from below.

Gable ends were sometimes just more logs, tapered and shortened to the slope with log purlins lengthwise and no rafters. This was done throughout the country, mostly before sawn lumber became available for the gables. The Henderson cabin, now in ruins near Hemmed-In-Hollow in north Arkansas, was built this way. This method requires more logs, and results in a very heavy roof.

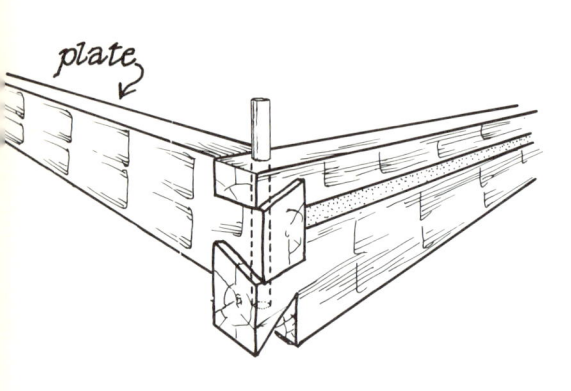

Pinning the top logs together holds against outward thrust from the roof weight. Below, rafter length can be determined for a 45° roof by the formula.

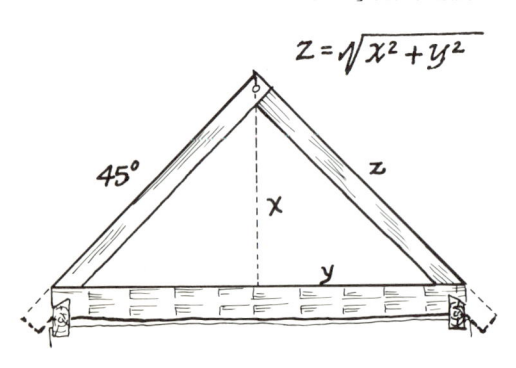

$$z = \sqrt{x^2 + y^2}$$

Let's look at the raftered, framed gable roof, gables closed with either shakes, clapboards or board-and-batten.

A ridgepole was rarely used, since the splits or slats the shakes were nailed to, served the bracing purpose. The rafters were cut to fit together at the peak, and were braced temporarily until these slats could be nailed down.

Before you begin with the rafters, bore an auger hole down through the top end logs, right in the notches, well into or through the top front-and-back plates. I use a 2" auger or expandable wood bit. Now, drive in a tight-fitting oak, locust or hickory peg, well seasoned, and cut it off flush. This is to hold the top course of logs against any outward thrusts. The settlers often used a very heavy, wide top log plate front and back to hold the outward push of the rafters, and pegged the ends this way. But even a big beam will bow out as the roof weight settles, with no chords to hold the rafters together at the eaves. Of course this is a problem only when you have a loft, and log walls built up above the ceiling joists. Otherwise as we said in the last chapter, the joists act as chords in the rafter trusses.

Cut your rafters the length of the hypotenuse of the right triangle formed by the height of the peak and half the length of your end logs, plus your eave dimension. If you didn't follow that, let's suppose your cabin is 16' deep on the outside. A 45° roof would peak 8' up, the same as the distance from the midpoint of the wall just under the peak, to the end. The high school formula tells us to square both 8' dimensions and add them to get 128. The square root of this is about 11' 5", and you'll need an extra inch or two to be safe.

Add eaves, which were almost nonexistent on the old cabins--a significant reason so few have survived. I like 2' for eaves; more makes the cabin flop-eared, and less lets the walls get wet. You don't need the extra 2' where a porch or lean-to will attach, since the rafters for these will tie in to the main ones. If you haven't decided on these additions yet, keep the 2'. It's easier to cut than to add.

Rafters were often as small as 2" x 4", (which I think was too small,) or may be as large as you want. I like a 4" x 6" dimension, either rough-sawn or hewn. I have also used round cedar, pine or oak poles. If worked by hand, hew or adze the top surface of the poles smooth for slats or decking.

Mortise the end pairs of rafters into the top end logs to give an even surface to nail gable covering to. I mortise both the rafter and the log at a 45° angle, bore and peg the joint. If you're not at ease with just this fastening, sink a few spikes or lag screws in, too. You need a strong truss at each end, pinned or spiked down at each corner.

It really takes at least two people to put up rafters. I raised the end trusses on our house, by myself, by pegging the rafters to the top log before I pegged it down. By rolling the log back out of its notch a quarter turn, I could do the whole rafter-truss operation horizontally. Then I raised the triangle with the aid of a push pole spiked to the peak, which became temporary bracing.

Space the intervening rafters 4' or less, which is about all you'll want to span, no matter what your roof is decked with. Notch the rafters where they pass over the top plates, with a shallow right angle cut at 45° You'll find, unless you've been living right, that these plates are nowhere near level or straight, so cut mortises to the lowest level. If a plate log is rounded at the outside corner, mortise deeper to get to a square shoulder.

If you've hewn the plate on all four sides and terminate the rafters against it, make sure it's level. Of course this gives you little or no eaves, but was standard practice in log house construction. A minimal eave was provided when the plate was thicker than the logs below it, and extended outward.

Assuming you're notching the rafters into the plate and extending them, use a level and chalkline, or tack a level strip along the inner face of the plate and mortise to it. Getting the rafters notched to give a uniform height is essential, to avoid a roof that humps and swells like the surf. It's easier, obviously, with rafters sawn or hewn to exact dimensions. With round poles, just notch a bit, try for fit, and notch some more.

I peg rafters, right through the notch into the plate. A 1" peg is

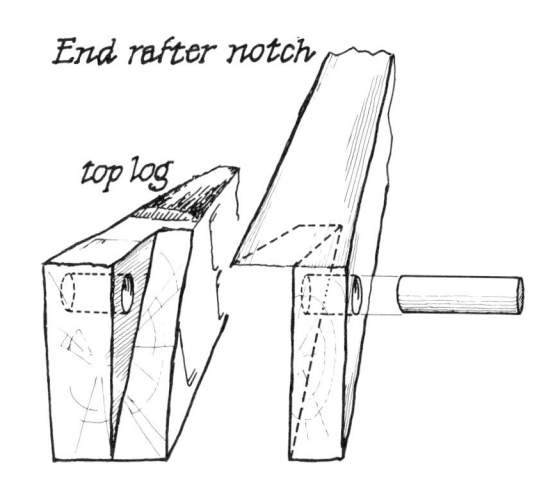

End rafter notch

top log

Traditional flush rafter

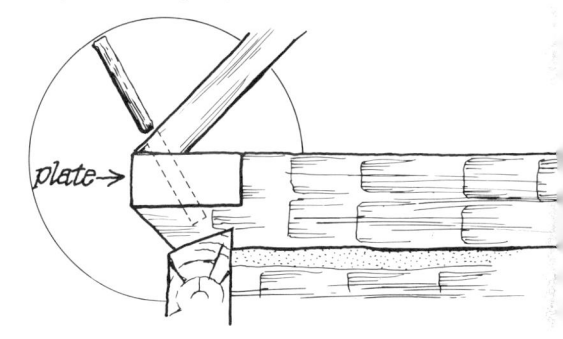

plate →

Notch to a level

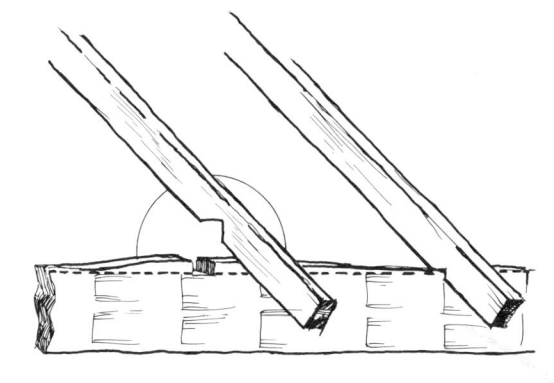

enough, but you may also toenail it with a couple of 30-penny spikes. In a windstorm, a sudden low pressure cell can cause your roof to lift off intact, if not secure at these points.

Here the ideal peg is one with a bit of a head to it, and a hole tapered out in a countersink, to hold it. A lag screw is probably better all around, but I've also used bolts driven into slightly smaller lead holes.

When measuring rafters for this plate notch, be sure to mark the apex of the notch. Almost every builder sooner or later starts the edge of the notch at the proper point, making the apex off a bit, then has assorted rafters that are an inch or two too long. It's the sort of mistake that's okay if you do it consistently, but otherwise can cause your ridge to weave. Cut the notch about an inch deep, just enough to help hold it in place till you peg it, and to help with the weight.

Now, you'll need to cut the top rafter ends to a 45° angle to fit at the peak. No matter how careful you are, there'll still be variations, so I use this method: Measure the total house depth, or the distance between each outside plate corner, at the point each pair of rafters goes. Lay the pair out with plate notches exactly that distance apart. Now cross the other ends at the measured peak point, and saw down through both at once. They have to fit, that way. A log sitter is helpful here to hold things in line--essential if you use round poles.

Now spike or pin these cut angles together, and reinforce with one or two 1"x 6" board plates, cut at a 45° angle, near the peak. That keeps the roof halves from splitting apart in a gale. It's also a good idea to nail a temporary brace across the rafters at plate notch height. Makes it easier to set in place.

Traditionally each rafter was half-notched to fit with its matching one, then both were bored and pegged. This is a simple operation for a 45° roof, but more complicated when the pitch varies. The important thing is to hold the matched rafters together at the peak, against outward thrusts from low-pressure cells in wind storms.

You'll set each rafter pair, or truss, onto the log plate at the right spot, or into the mortise you cut for it. Then level the whole thing vertically, nail a couple of angle braces up temporarily, and peg to the

Be sure to measure rafter plate notches to the center of the notch, not the edge.

plates. The first truss up is always cause for celebration, since now the vague outline of your total cabin begins to appear. I usually do the two end trusses first, but you can start, and finish, wherever you please. The last one is always hard to jockey up, whether between others or at one end.

If rafters are matched at the peak and not notched and pinned, this is a good way to be sure the angle cuts fit. With the plate notches the right distance apart, saw through both angles at once. The nailed joint, below, should be braced with a triangular plate.

Two men can raise light rafter pairs. Heavier ones need a rope to pull the peak from below, and perhaps a push pole, also from below, as well. After each pair is pegged, it should be temporarily angle-braced.

If you have help, start at one end, with stout pushes from a pole and restraining pulls on a rope. Either way someone has to climb to the peak as soon as each truss is braced, to untie the rope and/or pry loose the push pole. It's also handy to have a couple of stalwarts at each plate to keep the bases from slipping. I tied the rafters loosely here on our own house, and with the push pole nailed so that it could pivot as the truss went up, was able to do it alone, with only Herculean effort.

Now for the permanent bracing, which serves a dual purpose if your house has a loft with logs above the ceiling height. Angle four braces, say 2' x 4", from each corner up to, or near the center of the ridge. If you don't have a rafter truss at the center, go to the truss at each side.

Got that? I thought not. I've had trouble explaining this brace even to architects, unless I have a pencil and paper handy. It's an angle brace on the same plane as the roof slope, from each corner to the center of the peak. It can be spiked to each rafter on the way, or it can be in segments, between the rafters and flush with them. I like this better; it gives more headroom upstairs, allows for possible finishing inside the roof, and looks really neat.

Now, these braces eliminate end shifting, which is fairly obvious. You could also do this with braces from the ceiling joist centers up to each peak end, but not as well, and you'd cut your loft in two, for practical purposes.

The real benefit from these braces is that they carry the weight of the center of the roof out to the ends, where to the top log chords can brace it. So, no swaybacked roof, no bulging top plates, however thick, from roof weight pushing down and out.

When building the Kruger house, two carpenter friends working with me doubted this strongly. More so when I announced that we were going to drop kingposts from the peak, becoming studs for a dividing upstairs wall, to support the 20' span of the ceiling joists.

My skeptical friends chained the log plates together in the middle to keep them from bulging, then went ahead with the bracing, roof decking, kingposts, upstairs subflooring (which was also the downstairs

The roof angle brace carries weight to the end where the top log braces it against outward thrust. The brace can be pieced between rafters or continuous, extending to the peak near the center of the ridge.

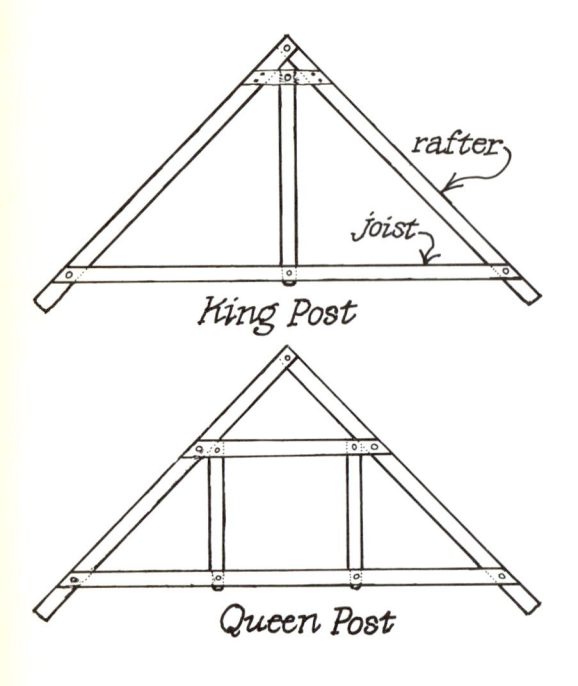

ceiling), reminding me often of the weight we were adding, and of my folly in general. Finally we loosened the chain, to the accompaniment of only minute creakings. Everything stayed true.

I will point out that these braces must be spiked into place very securely, and that each board of roof decking or slatting be nailed to them as well as to the rafters. In a large house, they can carry several tons, all to the corners, where the logs themselves would have to stretch, for the roof to sag. In the Kruger house, I used steel pins at the corners to better take the stress.

True, the pioneers didn't do any of this. But your roof won't sag or lean, or domino over in your average typhoon.

Either kingposts or queenposts are important, to keep the ceiling joists from sagging. No matter how massive, these joists will tremble under foot unless braced in the center, and the alternative is posts downstairs, right in the middle of things, or a summer beam.

This beam performs exactly the same function as the sleeper under your floor joists, but to be effective, it too should be braced at least at one point. These beams were common in New England clapboard houses, framed as they were in heavy, hewn oak. There's a good feel about a summer beam overhead, holding up the joists, but it reduces headroom, too. They were rarely used in mountain cabins.

Let's get things under roof. If you're a purist, you'll slat your rafters with split boards, poles, or rough-sawn boards with the bark edges left on. For evenness the settlers used sawn lumber here very early, since you get a much better fit with shingles on a flat surface. I know of several old houses in the mountains slatted with edge lumber sawed with a pit or whipsaw, before circle sawmills came. These old saws were powered by muscle, water or steam, and utilized a long blade that went up and down through a horizontal log.

I nail slats, which are 1" x 4" or more, about 4" apart. This lets air circulate around the shingles to help keep them dry, and holds off rot.

Of course, purism notwithstanding, a slatted roof with wood shingles **will** let in cold air, hot air, wasps, lizards, spiders and if you're not the best shingler, some water. The alternative is solid decking, with a strip of tarpaper laid under each course of shingles. Solid decking gives you a mite of insulation, too, but not enough to count on much. It does keep the great outdoors out there where it belongs.

If you plan to spend more than fair-weather holidays in your house (and you will, no matter what you plan now) deck solidly, insulate, and tarpaper under the shingles. If you want to see the undersides of those shingles between the slats, slat just your porch roof, where it doesn't matter as much.

Rafter pairs in place, ready for angle bracing and decking. Note the triangular bracing at the peak joint.

About decking. Forget plywood, because, unless it's very thick and too heavy to handle, the horizontal joints between rafters, will tend to buckle and hump and sag. Of course there are metal fasteners used by the building trade to take care of this, but remember, I'm prejudiced.

I like 1"x12" boards, which go up fast. You can find large lumber yards that stock a utility grade in long lengths that's cheap and usable, if you pick and choose a bit. I've been able to throw out half of it sometimes and still be ahead of the price game. Or get your local sawmiller to cut you some decking. If put up green it'll shrink, but cracks here don't matter much.

Tongue-and-groove lumber is ideal, but expensive, and getting hard to find. The insanely-priced 2" thick variety is available most places, and will span up to 8' easily at a 45° pitch. Most people who buy this think it'll be extra insulation, but again it doesn't help enormously.

Trim the ends of the decking with a 1" or 2" thick eave rafter of the same height as the main rafters. A 2"x6" will match 4"x6" rafters nicely, without all that weight. Or use another 4"x6" and brace it with an angle piece at the bottom, which is a good idea, anyway. Of course the eave rafters will support each other at the peak.

Eave trim rafter can be supported by an extended plate log or an angle brace from the wall. At right is the Kruger house being decked.

Sometimes log houses were and are, built with the top log plate extended to support this eave rafter at the bottom, but it means a mighty long log. Muskrat Murphy's cabin had 26' plates for this purpose. Traditionally this bit was avoided because older houses didn't have much eave.

Insulation

After you've decked with whatever, staple down a layer of sheet plastic or tarpaper, completely sealing the roof to keep out drafts. It won't help much in insulating as such, or in keeping things dry, since rain can seep down along the shingle nails themselves if your shingles leak. (That's why you use strips of tarpaper, one under each course. If a shingle leaks, the water runs right out on top again, not along under everything till it finds a hole or rots things.)

Insulation should be of a type that traps lots of tiny air pockets, as in Styrofoam, mineral wool or fiberglass. You can insulate between the rafters and finish inside with some kind of wall, if you don't want to look at exposed rafter beams. Or you can put a nailing strip along each rafter, insulate between with a thin layer of Styrofoam and cover with wall, leaving part of the beam showing.

Or you can nail strips, say 2 x 2's, onto the decking over the plastic or tarpaper outside, 8" or so apart, and insulate between, again with something like Styrofoam, that does an acceptable job in relatively thin layers. Then nail the shingles to the strips. You could even use 2 x 4's on edge, and insulate with 4" of fiberglass or rock wool. I like the styrofoam outside, because it's waterproof. (You know, they make cheap ice chests of it). Fiber insulation that's wet is no insulation. Also the foam insulates better per inch thickness, and you don't get particles of it in your lungs, which stay forever.

Again, the early settlers didn't insulate. If ceiling boards, with maybe handmade rugs or bearskins over them upstairs, held heat down in the main rooms, the kids still slept among the elements. Later everything from old newspapers to burlap sacks and cheap wallpaper was applied to inner walls and roofs, but its purpose was mainly to stop wind, and it did not impede the flow of heat through solids.

You've heard about dead-air space, no doubt, and in theory a layer of inert air insulates nicely. But the problem is that this air can circulate, carrying your heat from one confining wall to the other, and away. The idea is to trap as narrow a layer as possible to avoid circulation, but thick enough to insulate--maximum is about 3/4".

Here the roof insulation is laid on top of the decking, between strips or timbers nailed vertically. Shingles will be laid onto the horizontal slats.

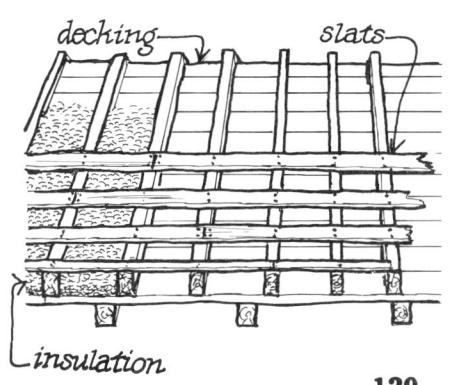

Years ago I used a couple of layers of Celotex, that wood fiber sheeting, as insulation on top of solid decking, and it was fair, but insufficient. Remember, you'll lose most of your heat at the top, so trap it there. An insulated ceiling will keep things warm downstairs if you don't use the loft for anything but storage, but if you live up there, do it to the roof, one way or another.

I like to see exposed beams everywhere. So I prefer a solid deck, with insulation on top, and shingles nailed to strips. Don't nail down through soft insulation. Shingles move around in wind and temperature changes and can work loose.

Shingles

Shingles are sawn or cut; shakes are split or riven.[33] If you split your own, good luck and tell us how it came out when you finally finish. I'm a pretty fast hand at riving shakes, but I cannot compete with the price of lumber yard shakes or shingles. With practice, a wiry individual can split a thousand shakes a day from prime timber, but **that** is precisely the biggest hurdle.

The settlers used cedar, red oak, or cypress if they were far enough south. That virgin growth was fine, but today you're hard-pressed for good, sizeable, clear wood. No knots. Straight. Two feet or more in diameter. Close-grained.

Say you do have a load of red oak blocks, two feet long. Red oak is the easiest of the oaks to split, but not the most durable. You quarter the blocks, using a sledge hammer and wedges. Then split these in two and you have eight very tall pie slices. Split off the point at the heart, and the sapwood and bark, leaving maybe 8" or, if the block is big enough, maybe two or more widths of 8" or 6" or whatever. Now use a froe, an L-shaped tool, to split the shakes along the radial split lines from the heart. That means each shake is a little thicker on the outside, but it's also the only way to do it.

Drive the froe with a hardwood mallet, 3/8" or 1/2" from the edge of the pie slice. Or split the block in the middle, over and over till you have all shakes. Wedge the block into something like the forks of a splitting or riving horse, and pry the shake off with the froe handle.

Riving Shakes

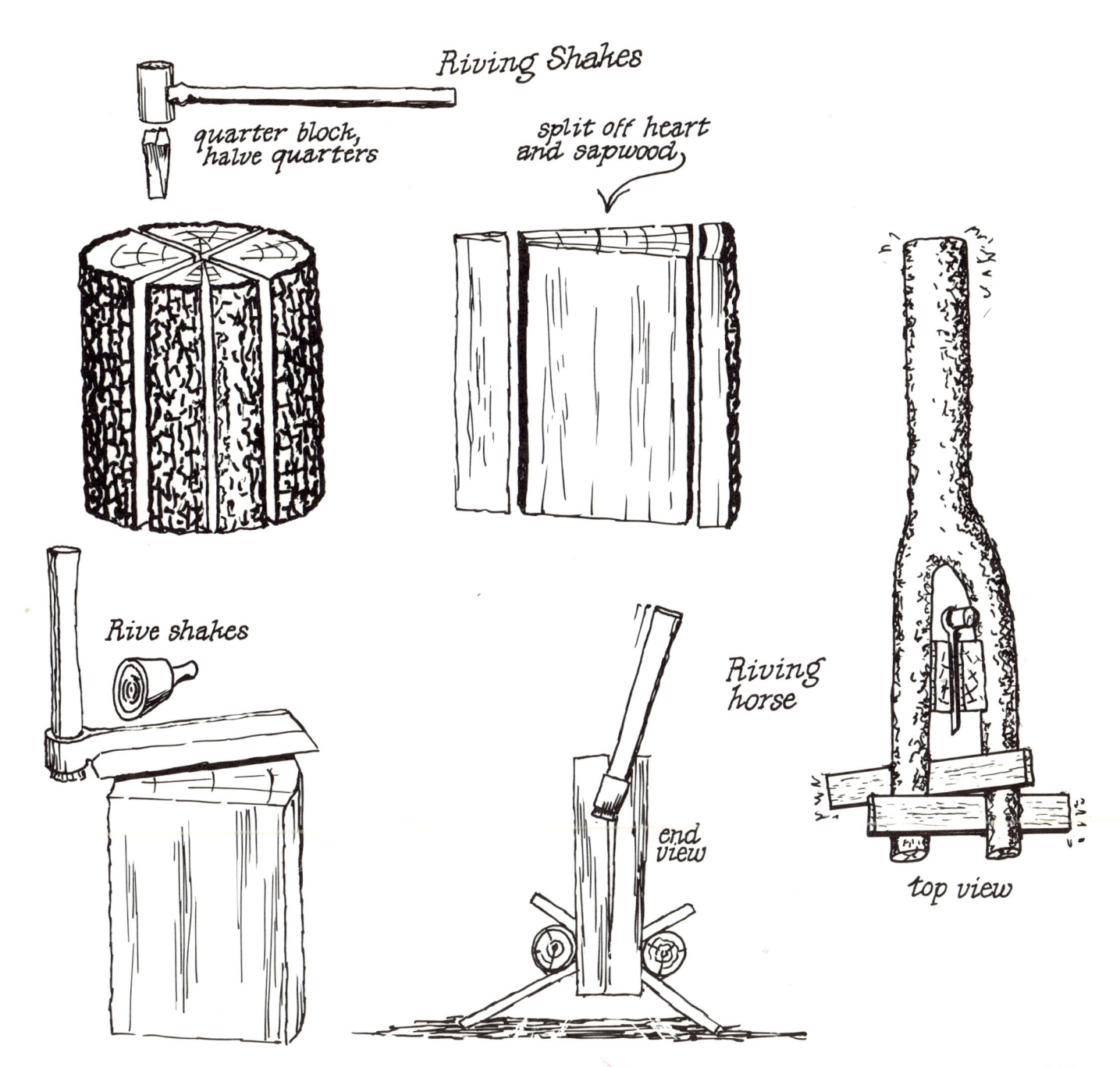

quarter block, halve quarters

split off heart and sapwood

Rive shakes

Riving horse

end view

top view

With practice you'll learn that prying one way runs the split in, and the other runs it out. At first you'll be lucky if the split gets all the way to the bottom without running out. If this keeps happening and you're getting a narrow top and wide bottom to your block, turn the bottom up and work on that end for awhile.

You can split shakes green or seasoned; there are craftsmen who insist that only one or the other will work. Just be sure they season before you nail them up. Shrinking will split them right where the nails go in. There are astrological signs best for this activity, as there seem to be for just about everything, so if you're into this sort of thing, lay them up at the increase of the moon, by all means.[34]

Cedar, cypress and pine are worked differently. Square the block first, then go right across the middle with the froe, a shake at a a time. If the block is large, halve it first. Oak, with its strong radial split lines, will crack down the middle of the shake if split across them.

A word about these woods: Pine will rot quickly unless treated well with preservative, which won't last long itself, in the rain and sun. Cedar, of the native Ozark red variety, is fine if you trim the white sapwood off. The western red brand sold in lumber yards is not as durable as the Ozark cedar. Cypress is fine, where available. Black walnut would do nicely, but let's not kid ourselves.

Cedar that can be riven is almost nonexistent today, except in protected groves, whose owners frown upon its removal. Even red oak is hard to find, so I've switched largely to sawn shingles. Even knotty cedar can be sawn nicely, and oak, if carefully done, can be sawn. I prefer the cedar, partly for the smell, which I never tire of. Cut shingles, sliced with a large mechanical knife, can be bought also, but are quite thin.

In estimating the number of shingles you'll need, figure the square footage of the roof, including eaves. Shingles and shakes are sold by the square or bundle, with a square being 100 square feet, four bundles to a square. If you split your own, figure a mountain of blocks, then multiply that by ten. You still won't have enough.

Lay a double thickness of shingles for the first course at the

The finer craftsmen often shaved the split shakes with a drawknife. This smoothed the wood, allowing for a flatter fit, and also allowed the shakes to be tapered, making it easier to lay them.

bottom, to cover all the cracks. You can saw the first layer in half, use both halves, and save, which is what I do. Lay a strip of tarpaper half the width of your shingle length, under the upper half of each course.

You can, of course, lay a dry roof with no tarpaper or flashing, but one of the truly fine crafts, this takes practice and skill, so I don't advise it. If you're determined to be totally authentic here, remember also that leaky roofs were an accepted fact of frontier life.

You should, ideally, leave exposed only a third of each shingle, but on a 45° roof you can cheat a little. Not as much as half, though. With tarpaper under, using 18" shingles, you can leave 8" exposed, which still gives a 2" overlap on every other course. That's important, because each shingle must cover the crack of ½" or so left between the shingles of the course below it. This means that, with random width shingles, you'll use about the same width up any given section of roof.

Clear? Well, you can't cover a layer of 8" wide shingles, ½" spaced, with 4" shingles, unless you leave huge spaces between. You may use the narrow shingles you'll inevitably find in your bundles, to double up in covering extra wide ones. And, of course, these narrow ones are necessary at the ends, to come out even. Leave ½" or more overhang at the eaves to keep the decking dry.

Nail with two #4 nails per shingle. Cover the nails with the next course and they won't rust away. At the top you may use galvanized nails, since there's no way to cover them.

At the top, too, you'll find it necessary to cut at least one course of shingles, probably two, then finish with a layer on each side laid horizontally over roof flashing. Or go traditional, and leave the last

This is the pattern for laying shingles or shakes. A third of the shingle length or slightly more can be left exposed. Below, wide shingles may be used to cover more than one crack, and narrow ones doubled or tripled over wide ones.

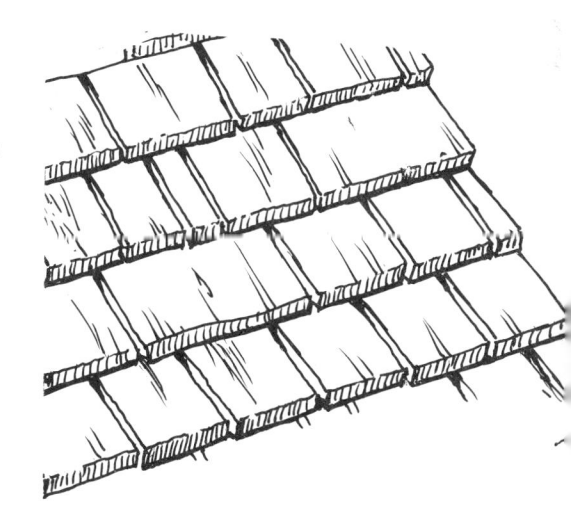

133

Shingle Cap

Turkey Feather

flashing

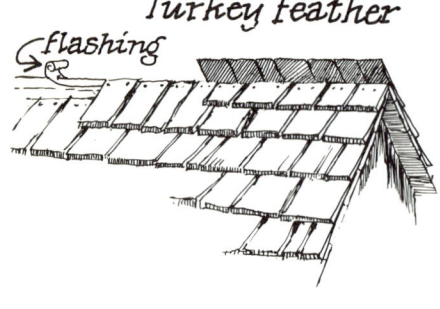

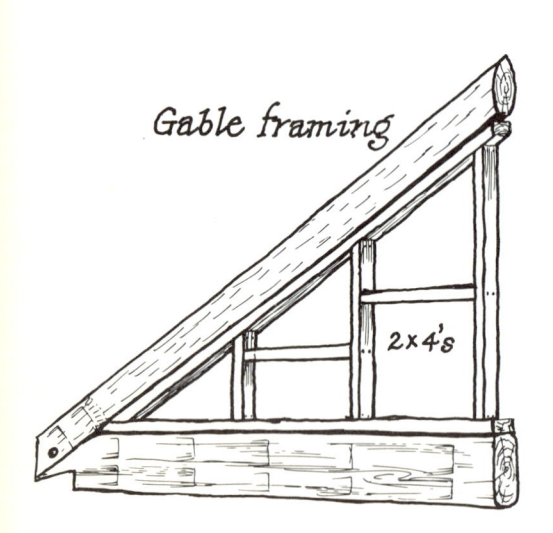

Gable framing

2 x 4's

layer of one side jutting up, away from the prevailing winds. That was called a turkey feather roof, I'm told, and the worn shingles standing skyward on old cabins do look like bedraggled feathers. I've never had the nerve to do this kind of roof on a commercial job, but I will some day. With flashing under, there would be no problem with leaks.

Use flashing in valleys around dormers and wings, and on all ridges. The aluminum kind is cheap and pliable, and less trouble than old offset printing plates or flattened cans. None of it shows.

As a final word on roofs (because it doesn't fit in anywhere else) I'll mention sealing above the top log plate between the rafters. A fitted board known by the delightful name of bird-stop board is used here, nailed flush with the log, extending to the slope of the roof. I use one inside and out, with insulation packed between. By nailing these boards against the sides of the plate, any unevenness on top, compensated for in the rafter mortises, is covered. If you've terminated the rafters at the plate, this isn't necessary.

As another finishing item concerning roofing, you may have thought to leave a section of decking out for the chimney to come up through (I never do, but saw it out later). Anyway, don't shingle this space, usually a 3' wide cut in the 2' eave dimension.

Close the gable ends in conventional studwall fashion, laying a 2 x 4 sill on the top log. With round or unevenly-hewn rafters, spike another 2 x 4 to the undersides of these, to nail the gable wall to. Frame windows conventionally, remembering to leave space between at the fireplace end for the chimney.

Clapboard, board-and-batten, and shakes were commonly used to close the gables. The walls should be insulated, and you will want to finish with interior wall covering. Here I favor a good grade of 1 x 12 lumber, used vertically. It's a simple operation to run this wall material through a spindle shaper or dado blade to shiplap it. This will keep cracks from opening up if there's shrinkage.

With your roof complete, you're just about halfway through with the house. At this point, the pioneers lacked only a fireplace, door, and maybe a floor, but things are more complicated today. You still have windows to do, and stairs, and wiring and plumbing (if any) and cabinets, and boxing in the lean-to, and just lots more.

But the roof is on, so you can get to the flooring, then start moving things in out of the weather. And, of course, you can relax your frenzied pace a bit now that the lid is on, and work along so as to be ready for chinking about the time the logs season and settle.

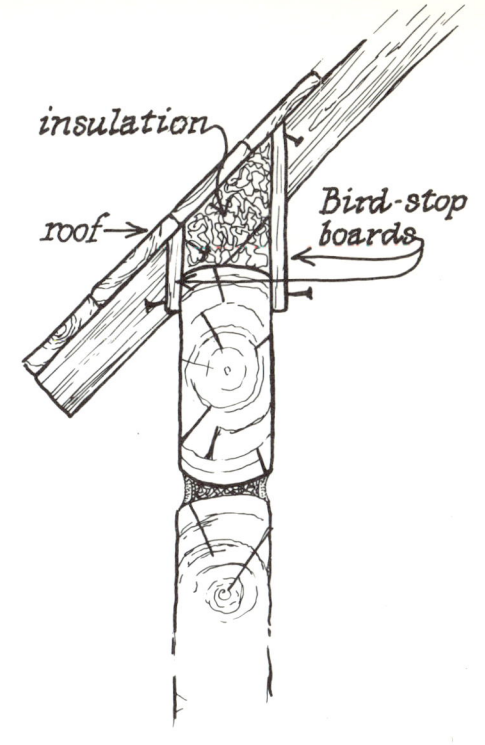

136

CHAPTER TEN

Stone Fireplace

I refuse to build a log house without a stone fireplace.

At best they are the poorest of heat sources, but that's hardly the point. A log house looks somehow naked without a chimney, whether of mud-and-sticks or stone, and the room inside the basic cabin just sort of radiates from the hearth.

Early on, of course, the women cooked at the fireplace, and a crane or iron bar across to hang pots from was standard. As the wood cookstove appeared in the hills and was installed usually in the lean-to, the fireplace didn't have to go all year long. And when the cast-iron heater came, there were log houses built with no fireplaces, heaven forbid.

Muskrat Murphy's cabin is of this type, probably built in the Depression, judging from the materials and style. In restoring it, he plans to add a fireplace, which he knows is nowhere near as efficient as the woodstove was.

I suppose the mystique goes back to our very early use of fire as protection at the cave mouth. Certainly the open fire has historically been a source of cheer as well as warmth. And, of course, the flames were often the principal light source for the settlers, along with their bear fat and bayberry candles.

top view

outside air duct

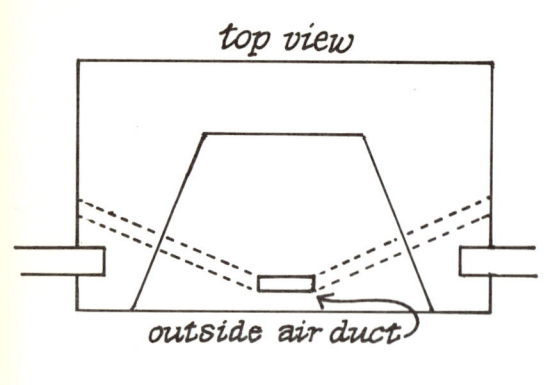

A fresh air inlet does a lot to keep the fireplace from drawing heated air out of the room. Below, ducts from distant corners of the room or house to the heat box intakes, help circulate warm air from the outlet.

warm air outlet

cold air intake *ducts*

joist sleeper

Until recently not much had been done to make a fireplace heat well, and little is done even now. Basically you have a fire in an opening in the wall with a sloped back to reflect some heat, and a narrow chimney throat opening to a wider bell over a smoke shelf to foil downdrafts. Maybe some firebrick as lining, or even a metal box inside, and a damper.

The dual-walled heat box in wide use now simply draws cold air from below, heats it and allows the smokeless air to circulate behind the firebox and either convect naturally or be blown out into the room. That helps a lot.

But still, in order for the fire to burn, large quantities of air must come from somewhere to feed the flames, and go on up the chimney, wasted. This air has always come through cracks around windows, doors, chinking, between shingles and up through open places in the floor. Eliminating these air sources would make it just about impossible to get a fire going.

One of the brightest ideas extant is a duct for outside air to feed the flames, to be closed when there's no fire. The heat still goes up the chimney, but warm air isn't drawn out of the room, and drafts are eliminated. I have a 'Y' passage in concrete beneath the firebrick in our fireplace, with screening over the outside openings to discourage varmints. The air comes in right in front of the fire and does its thing nicely. A device to keep ashes out of it is a simple necessity.

Another improvement using the dual-walled box, puts the cold air inlets ducted under the floor to far corners of the house. This draws cold in, leaving low pressure areas which in turn are filled with the warm air flow from the heat box outlets. If no blowers are used, these ducts should be large, the full size of the inlets themselves. With blowers, you can use smaller ducts, as we did, since the air travels faster. Without these ducts, the circulating heat box pulls air from the room very near the fireplace, and doesn't do much for the distant parts of the house.

A fireplace may be flush with the inside wall, with the structure completely outside. Or it may break into the room and be almost flush against the outside wall. Traditionally, it was largely outside, taking less room space and being simpler to construct. I have built raised-hearth, stone-to-ceiling, floor-level hearth, heat box and just plain fireplaces. I make some compromise with history here, since the old fireplaces did such a wretched job of heating. If you plan to construct a plain fireplace, get exact specifications, since it is so easy to foul the job up.

Catted Chimneys

I have seen, in my youth, mud-and-stick chimneys, but haven't built one. Nancy McDonough, in her delightful book **Garden Sass**, notes the use of mud chimneys largely in the Ouachita Mountains of South Arkansas, while stone was almost exclusive in the Ozarks. Henry Glassie also notes the heavy concentration of "catted" chimneys in the Ouachitas.

Obviously, whatever was the building custom among a group of settlers of similar backgrounds, became the custom of their children, and of later settlers.

Any chimney, even a straight vertical tube, will "draw". The folklore about good chimney construction really applies to a fireplace that will both heat well and not smoke much. The trick is to extract some heat from the fire before it roars up the chimney, and to keep down drafts out.

This dry-stone chimney on the Mulberry River in Arkansas shows excellent craftsmanship. The wider base stones distribute the weight over more area to resist settling.

The catted chimneys are works of art, admittedly, with their mud "cats" and neat mini-log pens, but I will stay with stone. Let their be no talk of brick or concrete blocks.

Traditionally, a fireplace opening was sawed in the end of the log house. The opening began with auger holes to get the saw through, as did openings for windows and doors.

Then large slabs of stone were laid on or in the ground, larger than the hearth/chimney size. These spread the tons of weight over a wider area and minimized settling. It always happened anyway. The chimney settled at a different rate from the house, so chimneys weren't attached to walls. Over the years a crack opened between the lintel stone inside and the first spanner log above it, and this was stuffed with chinking of some sort from time to time.

The ground being wetter and softer away from the shelter of the house, the chimney often tilted away at the top, too. Most unrestored older houses show this, no matter how good the stonework. Although not a log house, the beautiful old Turnback Mill house near Halltown, Missouri, has cut sandstone chimneys of as fine workmanship as I've seen, but they tilt, after 120 years.

Today we dig below frost to firm subsoil, then lay a reinforced concrete slab at least a foot thick and at the very least, twice the area of the chimney base, to start things on. For a 3 x 5 foot chimney base I dig a hole about 5' x 7' at least a foot deep, preferably 18". Then I pour 4"

12"–18" below frostline

chimney slab

of concrete: cement, sand and gravel, mixed 1:2:3. Over this goes a grid of reinforcing rod, ½" or thicker, about every six inches each way, almost to the edges. Then another 4" of concrete, another grid of rod, and a final 4" of concrete.

That's 35 cubic feet of mix, well over a cubic yard, and it means about a pickup truckful of sand and gravel and seven sacks of cement. Plus well over 200 feet of rod (the ends don't reach all the way to the edges).

That's a minimum pad. You see, you'll have tons, truckloads of stone, weighing on a C-shaped area about 9 square feet total. The idea of the reinforced slab is to spread the weight, and also to keep that C-shape from breaking its way down through the slab. Concrete without reinforcing isn't very strong. Not even as strong as dense stone. With steel inside it, it will do amazing thing, like span a ceiling as beams, or become the hull of a boat.

Lay stone in mortar on the slab, just as you did on your foundation footings. Build up solidly to floor height, or leave ducts for fresh air or an ash dump.

You may have built a pier to support the floor joist sleeper end already, or you may want to build the whole fireplace first to floor level. I lay the slab, then go up almost to floor level first, incorporating the sleeper pier. Then I finish the fireplace after the house is up and pretty well settled.

Extend the slab well into the room for hearth footing. It can be less massive here, since it doesn't support the chimney. I bring up stone around the sleeper, through a hole left in the floor to hearth level, then lay flagstones here and into the fireplace, where I switch to firebrick.

If you just want a fireplace to look at, and burn lots of wood in, save the cost of the heat box. Bring the back of the fireplace cavity up and forward, preferably in a curve, to reflect heat outward. This curve should stop only about five inches from the front stone wall, which is the lintel stone, and several inches above its lower edge. Here is where a damper, if any, will go. Dampers are useful mostly to shut out the cold when there's no fire.

Chimney and fireplace profile. Ideally, the narrow throat at the damper should be 1/10 the area of the entire fireplace front. The fireplace cavity is lined with firebrick unless a metal box is used.

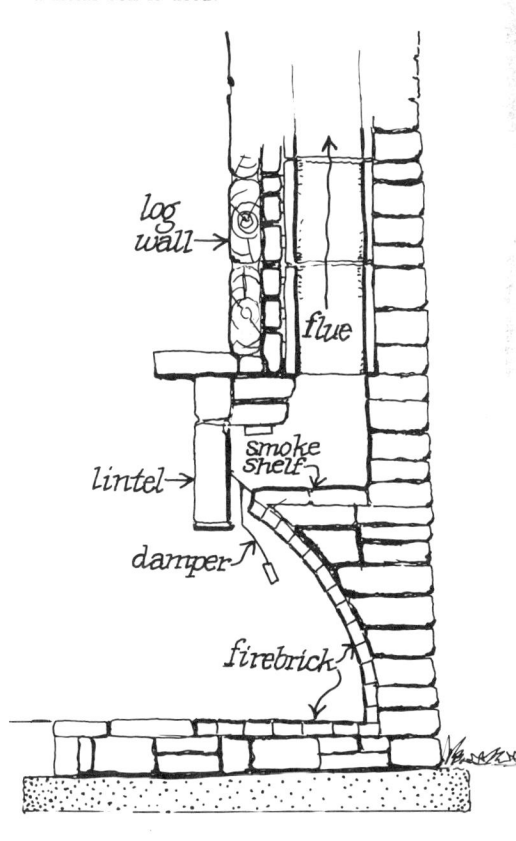

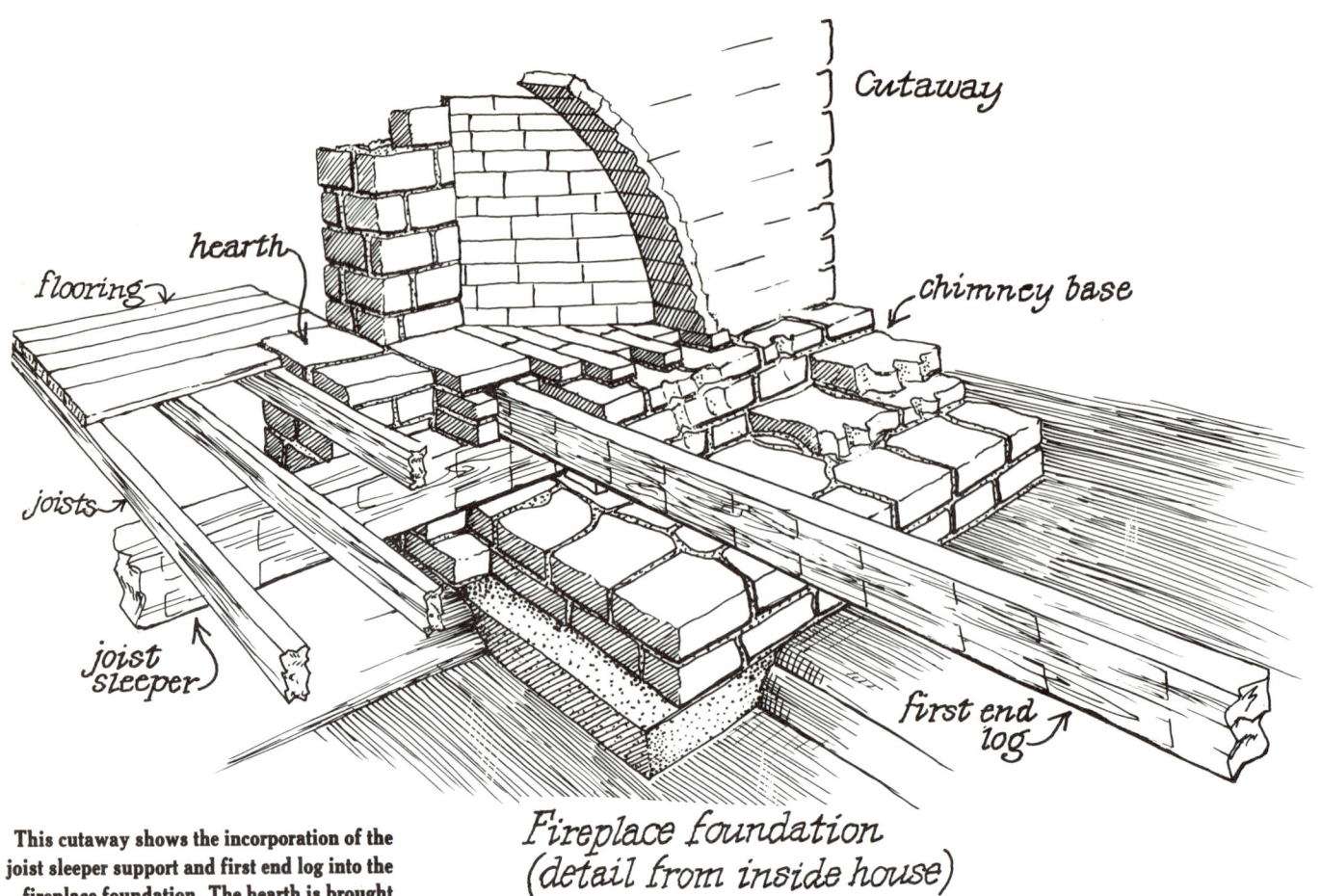

Fireplace foundation
(detail from inside house)

This cutaway shows the incorporation of the joist sleeper support and first end log into the fireplace foundation. The hearth is brought up through the floor.

    Then you drop back clear to the back, leaving a smoke shelf to prevent downward gusts. Above this, narrow the chimney front-to-back to about 8" and go for the sky. The smokeless room theory works a lot like the venturi in a carburetor, constricting the smoke flow at the tight, front passage, then opening out. Downdrafts reach the belled-out space above the smoke shelf and lose their sense of direction.
    The lintel stone should, of course, come down below the top of the curved back so smoke will be more inclined to lift off. This stone should be set on piers built up even with, or inside the walls. I break the inside stonework out from 6" to a foot, enclosing the log ends.

Lintel Stone

Look long and critically for the right lintel stone. A single, massive rock spanning the fireplace opening is a thing of joy and awe. It may be arched or flat, and supported with steel or not. I use a truck spring leaf for an arch, or a heavy piece of angle iron, straight. Neither is really necessary to support a dense stone with some height to it. The settlers often used old iron wagon tires for support, since the big fires needed to heat their drafty cabins sometimes cracked the lintel stone. Settling, too, took its toll of the lintel.

Remembering that this stone may be 4' or so long and weigh 400 pounds easily, get some friends to help lay it. John and I slide the really big ones up a heavy plank that is supported at the fireplace by blocks and a hydraulic jack. When it's in place, we let the jack down slowly, bedding the stone in its mortar.

If your front stonework is, say a foot deep and you can locate only a thin, 4" stone, lay it as a facing, with other stone and concrete behind, supported by the steel. Try to use a stone at least a foot high if you can find it. Height means strength in a span, much more than thickness.

The lintel stone and other indoor stone work can be done last, and are not necessarily joined to the chimney proper. The lintel can be braced or not with steel.

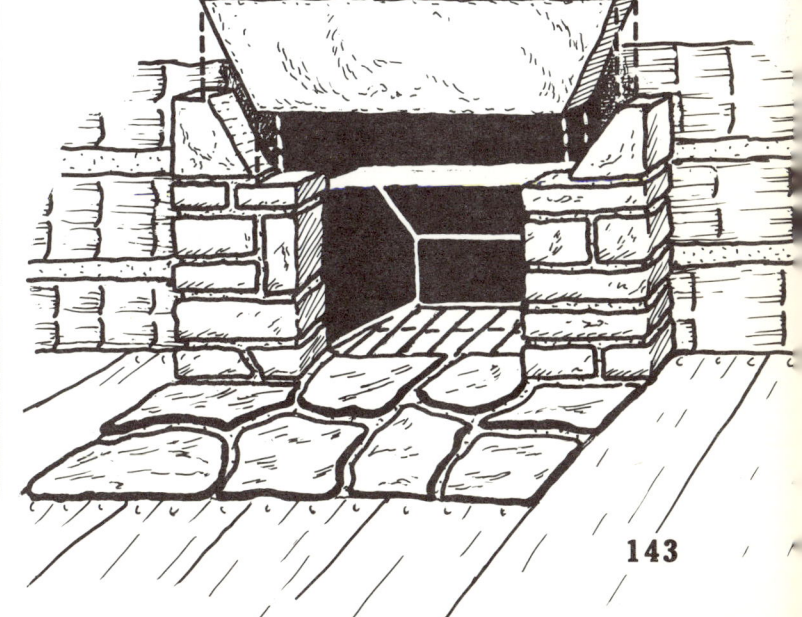

keystone arch

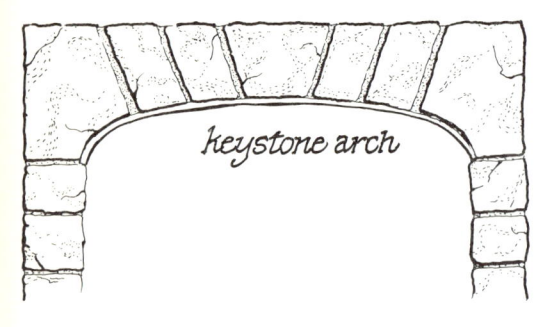

Lacking a single, Cyclopean stone, you may elect to keystone the span, either flat or arched. All this requires is that you build out from each side, on either a temporary or permanent support, slanting each stone back. Fit the keystone in the middle. It will have to compress for the span to fall. Stone doesn't compress easily, and that's what keeps the span up.

Line the inside of your fireplace cavity with firebrick, an expensive but durable substance that keeps annoying bits of hot stone from popping off and ricocheting around the room. Bare stone will also crack completely apart in a raging fire, so don't take the chance. There's a special cement for bonding this brick.

Now, if you really want to get warm at your fireplace, put in a heat box and kiss authenticity goodbye. Set it on a layer of firebrick, and build stone up around it. Don't let the stonework touch the metal anywhere; the expansion will shatter it. Stuff spaces with the asbestos fiber insulation that comes with the heat box.

A word of caution: If you plan to use the metal box, get it before you start up with the stonework. Some have the smoke openings at the back, some in the center, some in front. Obviously you won't want the hot metal right against your logs, so the box design will make a difference in how deep your chimney will be.

Above the heat box, the C-shaped chimney acquires a fourth side against the log wall. This side across the front of the heat box must be supported in mid-air with heavy steel angles, pipe, or grader blade before you lay stone across. Lacking heavy steel, you can cast a concrete beam with reinforcing rod in it, and span the front that way.

Once above the heat box, you may still have to shape a smoke chamber. Check the instructions with your model.

Above the belled-out chamber, if any, you may want to use flue tile. Makes the chimney easier to keep clean and supposedly lets the smoke rise faster. It should not rest on the metal box, but can be set on jutting edges of stones or on angle iron mortared into the chimney. Some masons leave space between the tile and the stone, filling it with dry gravel to absorb expansion. Others leave air between. Still others lay the

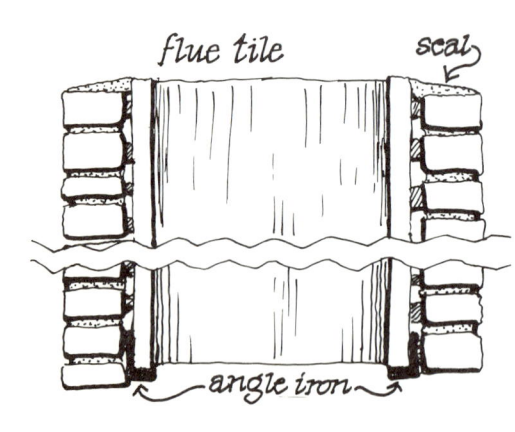

flue tile — seal — angle iron

I cap a chimney that has a metal firebox so rain won't rust it. I usually extend stones upward at least at the four corners, then lay a flagstone over them. It seems to make no difference in the fireplace's tending to smoke. Galvanized sheet iron caps are inexpensive and efficient, too.

This is one way to get heavy stones up onto the chimney. Another way is to use the bigger ones down low and carry smaller ones up a scaffold. Below are two ways to step in a chimney above the fireplace. Each is best supported on steel bars or pipe set into the front and back walls.

stone right against it, ignoring expansion. I rarely use tile, but when I do, I bring the stone close, packing the space here and there tightly with the fiber insulation. Fiberglass batts with paper removed will work. Seal around the top with masonry mortar, so rain won't sog everything.

Step the chimney in a foot so on each side above the large chamber. I usually do it in two or three steps, each reinforced with a steel rod front-to-back. Stonecutters often shaped a 45° shoulder here; evidence of really fine craftsmanship.

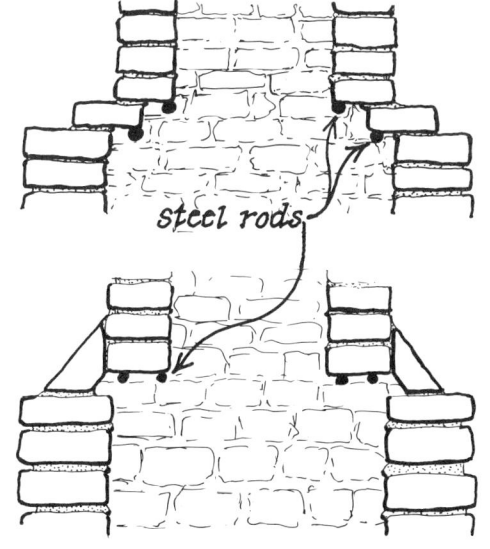

Near the top, too, a bead was stepped out. Sometimes only a thin stone shelf, it was occasionally several graduated steps out, then back in. Earlier, it was believed that this helped deflect wind upward, but it was mostly for decoration. A bead is an indication of the age of a chimney, as is the mortar used. Wide, heavy beads were common in the 1600's.

Of course mud or clay, or even dry stone was traditional in the back country, but lime mortar was general by the 1870's. Modern cement mortar wasn't very evident till around 1900 in the hills, about when the square nails disappeared.

I usually finish the outside work on a fireplace, then work the inside stone, mantel, heat box ducts if any, and hearth. Again, I like for the logs to be pretty well settled before I lay stone against them, inside or out.

Fireplaces take lots of time. You may contract yours out, or even build without one and add it later. Allow most of a summer if you do the job yourself, unless you know your masonry. I know numbers of masons who regularly build a fireplace in a week. I don't. I like for each day's stonework to be thoroughly set up and cured before I pile the next

The Beaver Jim Villines cabin chimney on the Buffalo River in Arkansas. At right, Bill Cameron helps unload sandstone from the nearby woods for the current McRaven log house.

Roughing a chimney with blocks first, to be covered with stone is double work. Any mason worth his salt can do a tight, stronger job with stone alone. Concrete blocks are a building crutch of dubious value and strength.

thousand pounds or so of stone on. I aim for two or three vertical feet a day, with several days between, but you'll have lots of other things to do while this job is going on.

You'll need scaffolding when you get about to eye level. It can be rented or borrowed, but I usually build it of 2 x 4's as I go up. Anything X-braced and strong will do, with planks laid across. A delight to work with is a front loader; into its bucket you can stack stone, mortar, tools and your feet, as you work. They don't reach really high, though, so you'll eventually need something solid up in the sky.

You may, as I've said earlier, build the chimney and fireplace first. Makes it easy to get at, I'm sure, but I've never done it this way, and don't know of any of the early builders' having done it. Again, I'd be concerned with logs settling as they shrank.

Woodstoves

Wood heating stoves are a great deal easier to install. Even the modern Franklin variety requires only a hole in the roof, a thimble to insulate the pipe where it goes through, a damper in the pipe, and some flashing on top. Put a cap on to keep rain out, and you're set. It is a good idea to get one of those asbestos/metal sheets to put under, to catch coals and sparks. Heating stoves are nice to cook stew on too and to heat water.

You can even heat a small cabin with a wood cookstove, which is quite versatile, but its firebox won't hold much, and your indoor plants will freeze before dawn.

One of the neatest ways to heat a house is with a circulating wood stove with thermostat. A load of green wood lasts all night, and the thermostat keeps the heat constant, so you don't have to finger the damper all the time.

We have a 1900 cast-iron heater which goes up in a rear room in winter, where our floors are not heated. This stove puts our fireplace, with all its improvements, to shame as a heat source. But somehow I never put it up till after the first time water freezes back there. You just can't see the embers and feel the cheer as well as you can at the open fire.

I guess it's the cave man in me.

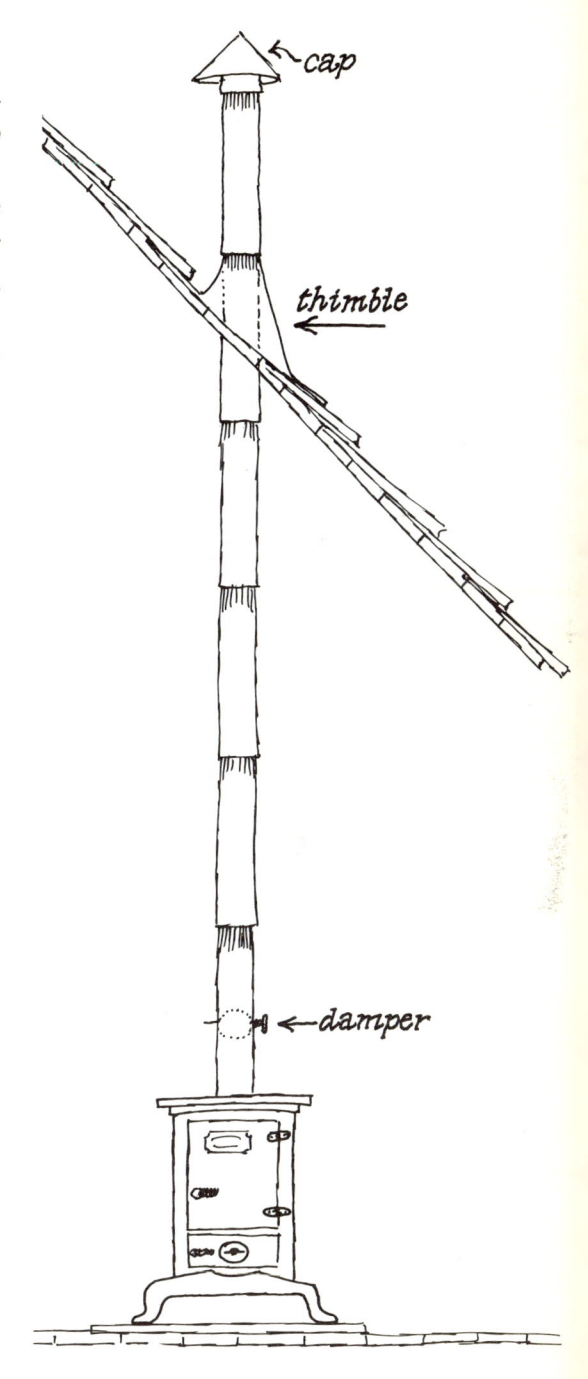

CHAPTER ELEVEN

Floors

Poor folks lived on dirt. And so did lots of other pioneers temporarily, no matter what their solvency, during those first hurried seasons of clearing, getting seed into the earth, and moving out of the wagons that had been home for months.

A dirt floor meant the sill logs were also usually on the ground, so these cabins didn't last long. I have not seen a hewn log house with a dirt floor, and only a few round-log huts, in the wearing-out days of the Depression, laid on dirt.

Publicity in recent years depicting indigent Ozarks children raised in dirt-floored cabins was largely misinformation. I know of temporary camps and communes in which the buildings were set on dirt for awhile, but "back-to-the-earth" movements in the 1970's are hardly authentically pioneer.

Watered and tamped periodically, dirt served well enough, apparently, since many of our ancestors seem to have survived living on it. As soon as possible, however, something more permanent and satisfactory was added.

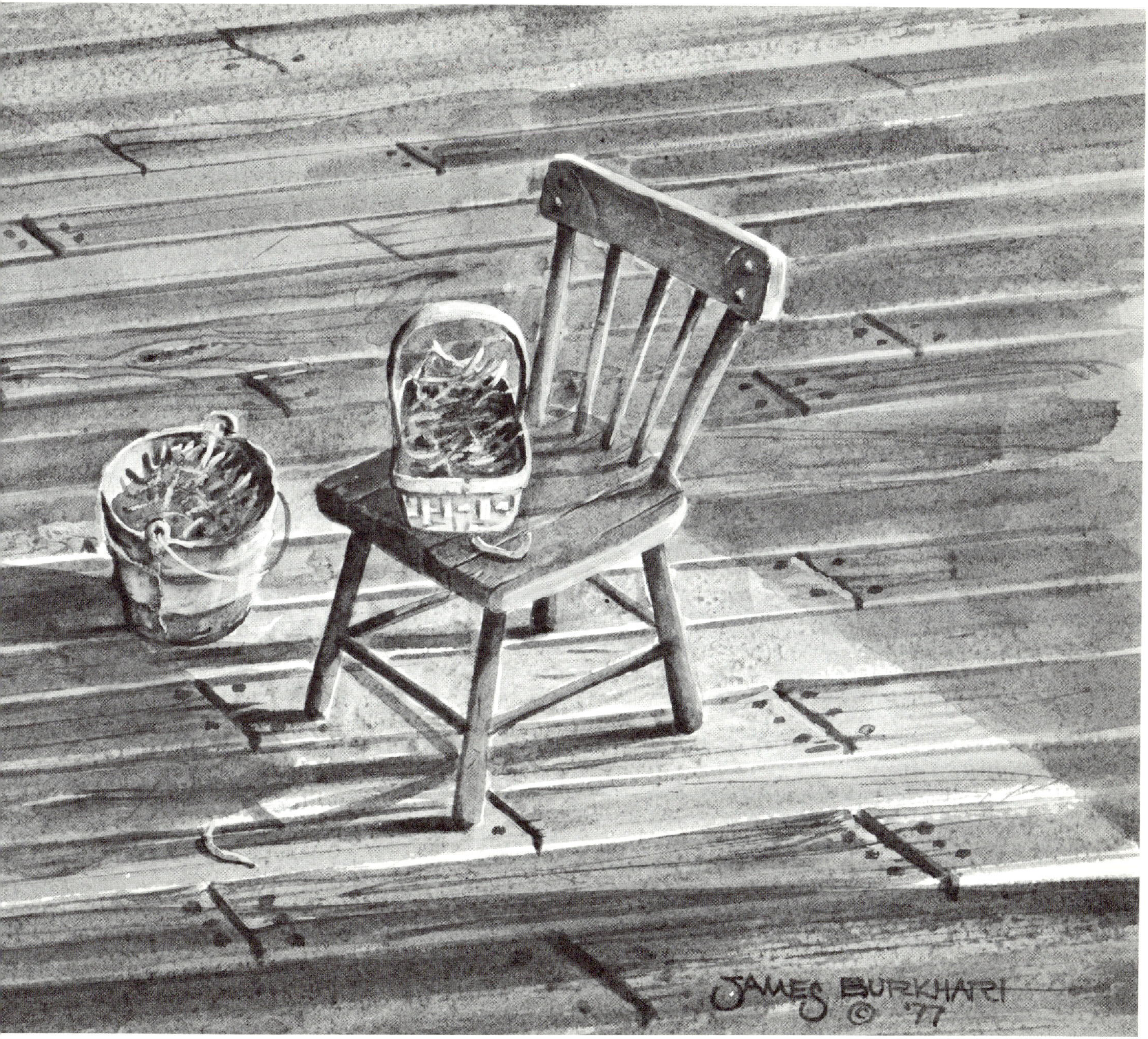
JAMES BURKHART © '77

The puncheon floor in its pure form was round logs split down the centers, with each half laid in the ground, flat side up. The splintery surfaces were worked with an adze to give a rough, but very solid, floor. Sometimes this was rubbed with stones and sand to smooth it further.

Puncheon floor

split logs →
earth →

Again the earth did its work on these timbers, and they did not last. So often the puncheons were raised, becoming a sort of continuous expanse of floor joists, with ends wedged between the sills and next logs up. These raised puncheons were fitted more carefully at their edges, since now drafts and small creatures could enter.

Pine became the favorite flooring among the settlers, as it often was for the logs, where available. A wide pine floor is traditional in older houses, sometimes (again, where available) shiplap or tongue-and-groove, to insure a tight joint even with shrinkage. Oak was more durable, but tended to warp, and was difficult to lay.

Given many decades of scrubbing and the wear of countless feet, pine takes on a rounded mellowness all its own. Wide pine flooring is highly prized by restorers of old houses. I use pine tongue-and-groove in just about every house I build.

The flooring was traditionally laid directly onto the joists, with no subfloor. Here was an intriguing phenomenon that I encountered often in old houses, and could only conjecture on. A series of holes was

When buying tongue-and-groove lumber, be sure to allow for the final width. One-by-six lumber is actually about 5" wide when laid.

150

often bored at random into the top surfaces of the joists, usually about ¾" in diameter. I'd found these both downstairs and up, and puzzled over them for years. When dismantling the Howard pine log house near Kirbyville, Missouri, two years ago, we found them in the sawn ceiling joists under wide pine shiplap.

They are also in the hewn floor joists of the Grigsby house at Arkansas College, and it was here I heard the most plausible explanation. Dr. Dan Fagg, history professor in charge of restoring that house, wasn't sure, but guessed that the holes were for a pry bar, to tighten cracks as the floor was laid. Certainly I have labored long to this same purpose on every floor I've installed, and holes would have made it easier. Since, I've learned that this was indeed standard practice.

I space joists 2' apart, with often an extra one centered with the front and back doors, to take the heavier traffic. Then I lay a subfloor of full one-inch rough-sawn oak or pine, usually insulating under it. Then a layer of tarpaper goes on, and the floor is laid on that. Wide boards

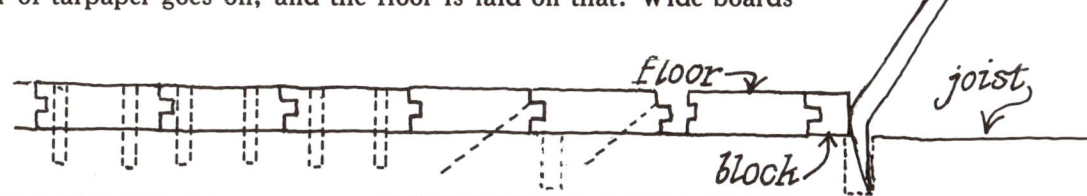

Laying 2" center-match flooring, which doubles as the downstairs ceiling. Boards warp sideways and need a lot of prying into place, where they can be either pegged or nailed.

fastened with pegs are the most attractive, although square nails look good, too. Tongue-and-groove should be nailed through the tongue with finishing nails and a nail set. A nailing tool can be rented from the lumber company to speed this operation.

We've discussed 2" center-matched lumber for the ceiling/upstairs floor. If you use a subfloor instead, and nail to it, use nails short enough not to come through on the underside.

It's a bit difficult to finish flooring off at the log walls with moulding, but if you smooth the worst humps out at floor level you can get a strip of quarter-round to fit tightly, with perhaps some caulking behind it.

In recent years, concrete slab floors have been used in log houses, and have been added to restored older cabins. Sometimes this is painted with masonry paint; sometimes it is left bare, to be covered here and there with rugs. Sometimes floor tile is used over it.

Flagstones

Our house has a flagstone floor, gathered from the nearby creek bed, with some of the limestone as long as five feet and maybe 2" thick. It's a very natural and durable material, though it was not widely used by the early builders. A durable mortar is necessary between the stones; its not being available a hundred years ago may have been why few pioneers used stone.

I lay a vapor barrier of heavy plastic sheeting over the raked and tamped earth, then cover this with sand. Each stone is then bedded flat into the sand, and mortar worked between the edges. As in all stonework, it's a jigsaw puzzle game. There's really no point to a concrete slab beneath a flagstone floor, since each stone must be bedded firmly, and certainly the cement would solidify before an entire floor of stones could be worked into it.

Linda and I had ordered heating cable to lay under our floor, and had put off laying it as the cable apparently languished in some distant warehouse week after week. Finally we could wait no longer, so laid the floor, with Linda perched on a ceiling joist directing my efforts from a perspective.

Sawn joists mortised into wide sill logs are rigid and nearly as strong as hewn joists of greater thickness. Sawn stock produces a more even floor with less work, too.

I cannot overemphasize the importance of this vapor barrier. Without it, stone or concrete act as sponges to draw moisture directly from the earth into your house. Makes a cold floor miserable, and covers everything with a green mold in time. And of course damp masonry has zero insulation value.

Flagstone

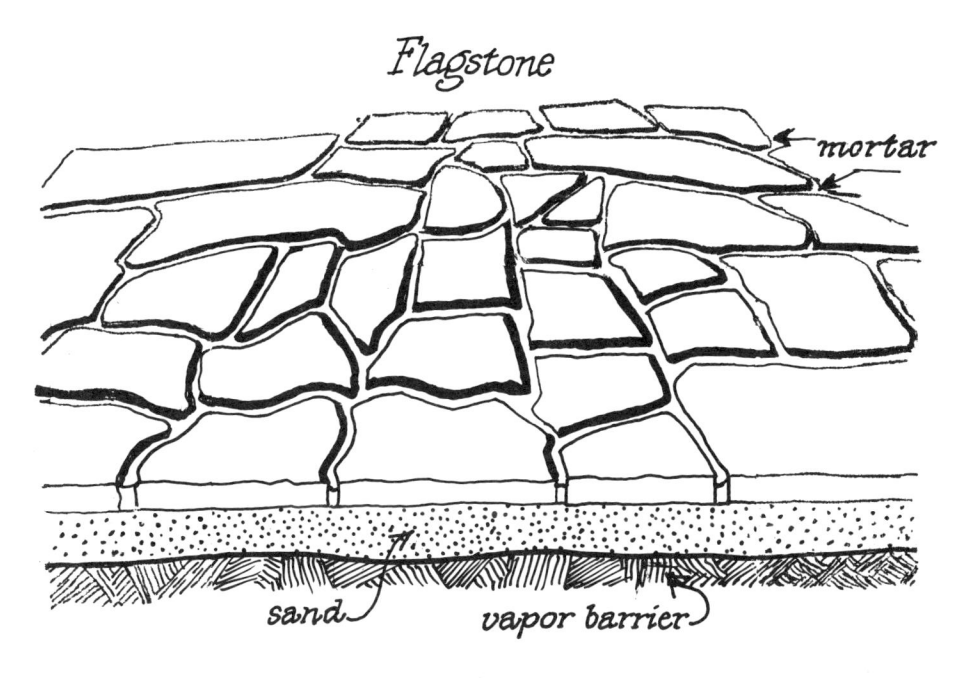

mortar

sand — *vapor barrier*

Flagstones are bedded firmly in sand with a vapor barrier under it. Then mortar without lime is worked around each stone.

Of course the cable arrived as we finished bedding the stones, and we considered leaving it out. But my wife likes to do housework barefoot, so we opted for a warm floor, and for redoing all that work. The cable was some 800 feet of resistance wire, to be laid in rows 2½" apart, crisscrossing the floor. We began stringing it carefully, lifting and replacing stones as we went.

I was not in the best of humor. The temperature was in the 20's that February day, but we persevered. Then, less than a third of the way across, a red tab appeared on the wire, announcing that we'd used up half the cable.

I have been remiss in measuring things, over the years, and had underestimated the 2½". Well, ⅔ of a heated floor wouldn't do, and you can't splice more of this resistance wire, so up came the stones again.

Only this time I couldn't seem to get them back into their places. It grew unaccountably warm in the windowless house as we labored. The hours went by. Wire coiled playfully about our legs and pulled from under the stones.

There is a point beyond which no sane man's patience can extend, especially when his wife is serene and unruffled in the face of exactly the same maddening obstacles. At precisely that point, a group of friends appeared, eager to help. I elected to apply pick and shovel savagely to the lean-to foundation, and those absolute novices had the cable laid and all the stones back in place in half an hour.

Somehow we didn't break the wire anywhere, and, controlled by a thermostat, it serves faithfully like a subterranean electric blanket, winter after winter. It's off when the fireplace heats, then clicks on in the small hours to take away the general chill by morning. Daughter Amanda crawls happily over the heated stones, warmer than vertical folks.

Flagstone can be sealed with masonry sealer, then scrubbed and waxed as often as desired. I will warn you that those beautifully flat stones you selected never seem as smooth when laid, but you get used to it.

We do find that rigid furniture with more than three legs, must be relegated to other non-flagstone floors in the house, or wedged level in a permanent place. We use those flexible wood-and-canvas directors' chairs, from necessity.

The manufacturers of heating cable recommend a concrete slab floor, with vapor barrier and insulation under the cable, and another inch of concrete above. Some of the heat in our floor does go down through the dry sand.

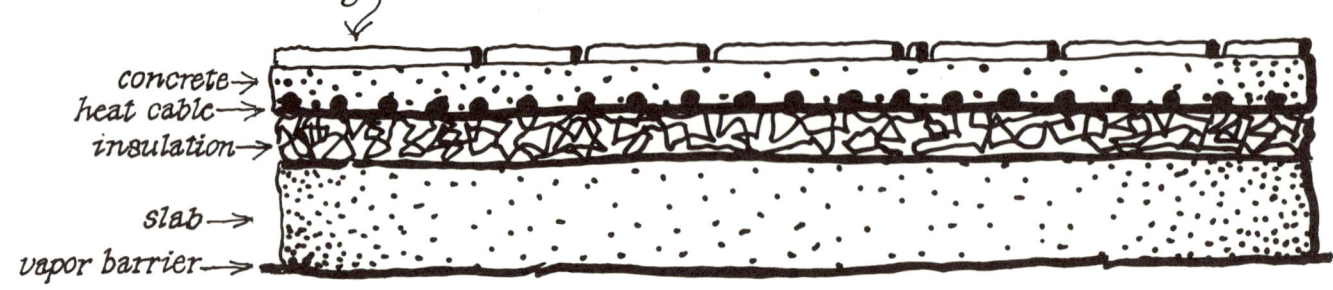

But the 16-foot square living room takes a maximum of 2,000 watts of electricity, and gives good comfort for it. We find general room temperature can be quite low if one's feet are warm.

An addition to our lean-to, containing a small office and the baby's room, is floored with recycled oak flooring, obtained free. It's laid over a subfloor of rough-sawn oak, on oak joists. Recycled flooring requires lots of sanding, since the pieces aren't in their original wear patterns, and you get high and low spots against each other. But it has a glow unlike new wood flooring.

Whatever you do, build your floor strong. Too long a span between joists is no saving. Neither is thin flooring or subflooring. It's embarrassing for your guests to fall through.

The Zent cabin, completed. This is a very nearly authentic single-pen house, used for special gatherings and furnished with Lois Zent's antiques.

CHAPTER TWELVE

Windows and Doors

Along with the treasured pieces of china, wrapped perhaps in a feather bed to withstand the jolting of the wagon, often went a pane or two of glass for the settlers' house. Hand-blown, wavy, thick and so fragile, it traveled west to grace the log house, and was often removed if the family moved on.

Many cabins were built with no glass, the window openings shuttered with split or sawn boards, leather-hinged against the cold. I know of one log house near Gainesville, Missouri, built around 1900 that has only one window throughout, and it has no glass; its shutters hung on forged iron hinges. The Murphys' house, although only some 40 years old, had only one window.

You see, wood was plentiful. Unless it was chopped continually and used, the forest could and did cover a homestead in a few seasons. But iron, and of course glass, were rare and prized. And even where several shuttered windows were cut, they were always sources of drafts and insects, and troublesome to build. So windows were few. But today a log house need not be dark to be draft-free. Use as many windows as you feel belong in your house.

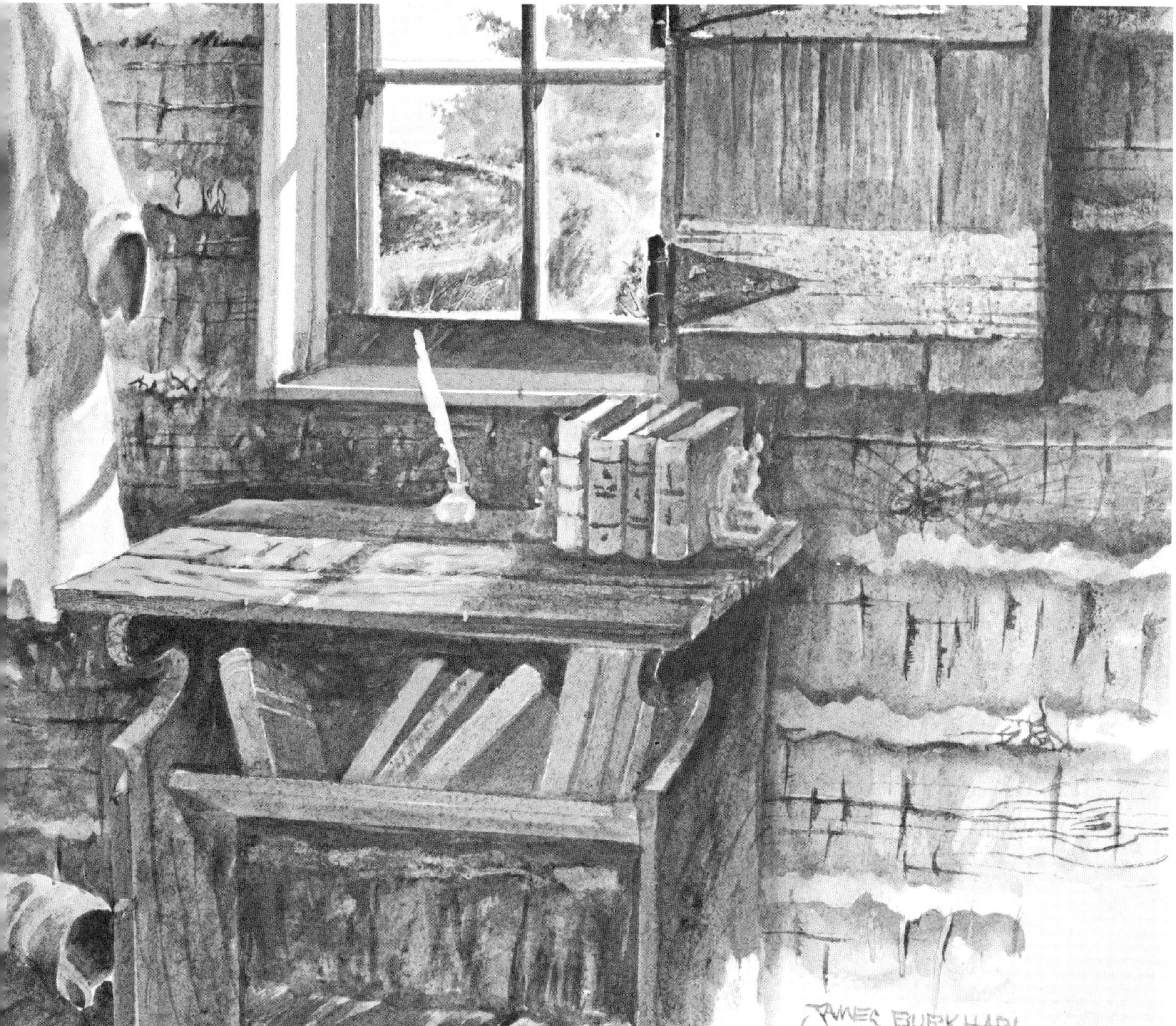
JAMES BURKHART
© '77

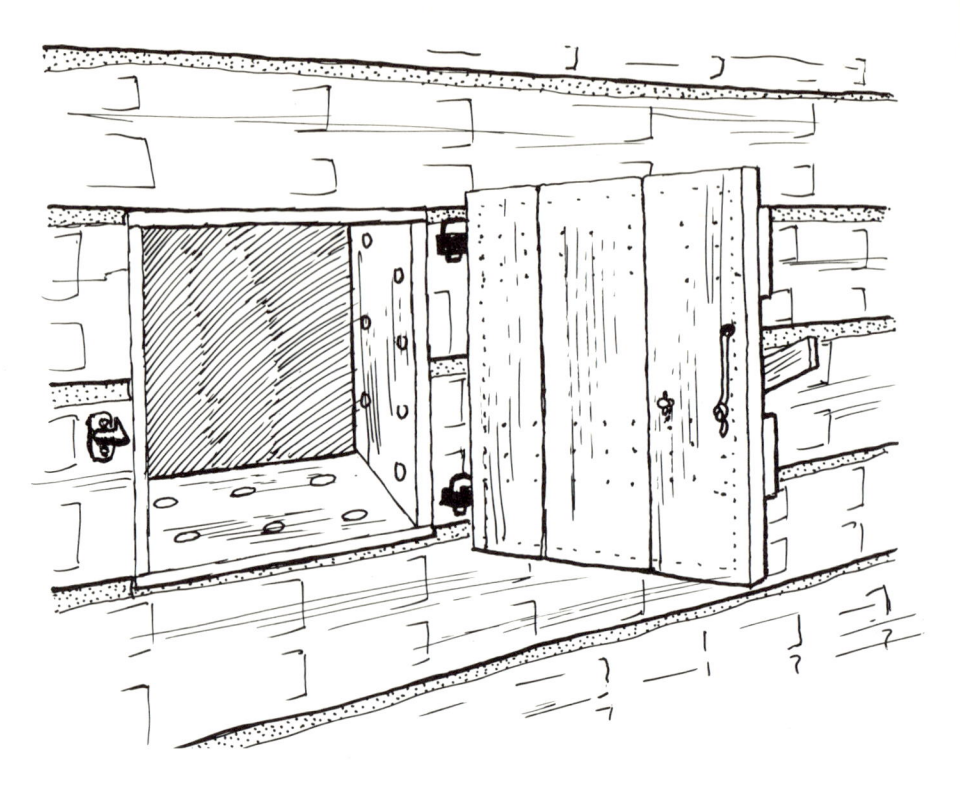

A settler's wooden shutter. Sometimes oiled paper or animal skins were used to let in light. Below is the simple barn sash, hinged for a tight fit against stripping.

Log house builders have always favored small windows, either to save glass, or for the more valid reason that large cuts in a log wall weaken it. So the double-hung sliding sash is not a good idea. Also, if there is enough space for a wood sash to slide, there is enough for drafts.

The cheapest and best-looking window you'll find for your house is called a barn sash. It's just glass and wood, one piece, with as many panes as you like. I prefer small panes, (so did the pioneers) which are easier and cheaper to replace, and because they look better in a log house. I swing them on hinges, against felt-lined weather stripping cut 3/4" square and nailed to the window facing.

It's simpler to hinge windows so they swing inwards, leaving room for screens outside. If you need the space, swing them outwards, but you'll need some device for controlling them through the inside screen. I have yet to fabricate a satisfactory device.

Everyone I know who has a log house with hinged windows, wants hand-forged hinges. I usually install small barn strap or T-strap hinges temporarily, and sometimes I find time to replace them, one by one, as I can get to my forge. At this writing I still have not completed this job in our own house.

Latches, too, can be simple and inexpensive. I use cupboard latches on windows, of the type that lift and drop into a notch. Even simpler is the screen door type hook-and-eye.

You can, of course, avoid just about all the details of window and screen installation by buying the completely assembled units. They come with screens, hinges, latches, and devices for cranking the glass open, all boxed into framing that is simply inserted into a hole in the log wall and nailed in place. Recently, suppliers have limited their design offerings in these units, so make sure you can get the windows you want. For instance, you will certainly want wood, not anachronistic metal. I will warn you that these windows are quite expensive, but by this time, you may be at a stage where your time is worth more than the extra expense.

Window size is a matter for your own taste, within certain bounds. A huge picture window is out of place in a log cabin. We have a double window in ours opposite the fireplace, simply because some of the decayed log notches in that wall had to be re-cut, which meant shortening the logs and enlarging the window space.

Ironically, about the time milled windows became common in the remote areas, the style had changed from the earlier classic small-paned ones to the large, single-paned sashes of the late Victorian period. So, many cabins were given these windows later, and many built in the later 1800's and early 1900's had single-pane windows.

I was surprised to see single glass in the Grisgby House; in the 1870's small-paned windows were still the rule. Dr. Fagg and I examined the workmanship carefully to see if these were replacements, which they evidently were not.

You should keep the same style, if not size, windows in the main house and lean-to. If your house is large enough for dormers, use the

Except in extremely cold climates or where lots of windows are used, double-paned glass is not that much of a saving. Most of your heat loss is upward, through the roof. With a few small windows tightly fitted and adequate heat, you'll be comfortable.

same style sashes there, too.

The Kruger house has its dormers built between 4' centered rafters, with 24" x 37" sashes. Anything larger would be disproportionate in the 28' roof length. Here dormers were almost essential, with the upstairs divided into two bedrooms, walled off from an open area at the head of the stairs. Without the dormers, only one gable window in each room would have been possible.

Dormers allow you to walk up to the outside wall in spite of a low roof slope, and give at least the feeling of more space. They are lots of work to build, however, and you should be a pretty advanced carpenter to attempt them.

Doors

I always build the doors myself, usually with glass in the front and back doors for more light. I build them because I want them more authentic, and because milled doors seldom look right, or can be cut into, to be fitted. Very old cabins had doors that were not angle-braced in the familiar Z-pattern, but had rows of many square nails through the cross boards to keep them from sagging. In time they sagged anyway, as generations of slamming worked the nails loose.

So the Z-pattern became common, as a simple solution, and an attractive one. If you think this has a barn-door look, though, and don't want the nailed version, try your hand at a panelled door. I have built

Three door types

Frontier *Z-Pattern* *Panelled*

several, some of tongue-and-groove lumber, some of plain. I usually brace the corners with right-angle iron straps.

Again, I like wrought-iron strap hinges for house doors, and these can also help brace the wood if long enough. Where a blacksmith was near, the old houses often had iron hinges, from simple loop-and-pin straps to ornate scrollwork, rare unless the local smith specialized in such things.

A wooden hinge is a work of fine craftsmanship. Usually hickory or ash for toughness, it was greased with lard or bear fat, and served long and well. The wooden latch-and-string, too, was almost universal until iron became common. Today I use a metal version of the old wooden latch.

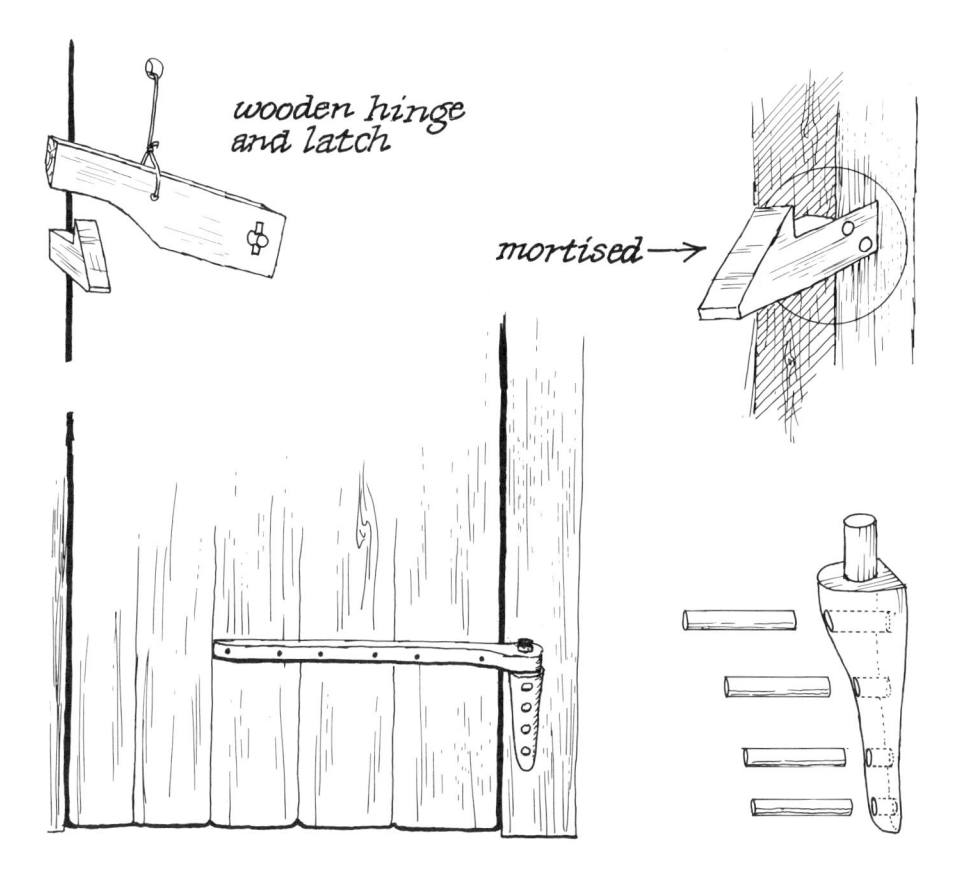

One pit fall in building your own doors is weight. A tight door of more than one layer of wood is heavy, so you may want to concentrate on careful fitting of just one braced thickness.

The wooden hinge and latch were used when hardware was scarce. The latch hook was mortised into the door jamb to allow the door to clear.

You will find many cabins with the patent cast-iron door locks on the outside of the wood, sometimes with white ceramic knobs. (These knobs were sometimes used for nest-eggs in the henhouse). We have these cast-iron locks in our house and they are quite serviceable, except on heavy doors, where they tend to crack when slammed.

I use heavy glass in outside doors, finding plate little more expensive, and much safer than double-strength. If I have access to woodworking machinery, I rabbet the window frame, lay the glass in, then set a thin wood strip against it with small screws. Or use two strips with the glass between. Always angle brace the door in some way to keep stress off the glass.

I close the doors against felt-lined strips as I do the windows. At the sill I use a flexible weatherstripping, which makes a stepped-up threshhold unnecessary.

Interior doors were, of course, unheard of in one-room cabins. When used, I make these, too, often of tongue-and-groove, only one

Door and window facing uprights can be installed after the logs have settled, and then doors and windows themselves put in. This door is a double-thickness tongue-and-groove, nailed with square cut nails.

thickness, where I usually double the outside doors.

The larger and later houses used commercially milled doors, inside and out, available generally for the past hundred years. They were usually pretty thin, and have never seemed to fit the solid look or concept of the overall log house.

Today you can find every kind of milled door, some of which are quite massive and handsome. So, unfortunately, are their prices. If you buy milled doors, do so beforehand. The temptation to save work and time with low ceilings may become strong as you labor, which means shorter doors. Few commercial doors are so constructed that they can be cut down without severe weakening.

A front door can be a really beautiful personal statement. Strong designs in carved wood or wrought-iron as part of your door will set the mood of craftsmanship that is inside.

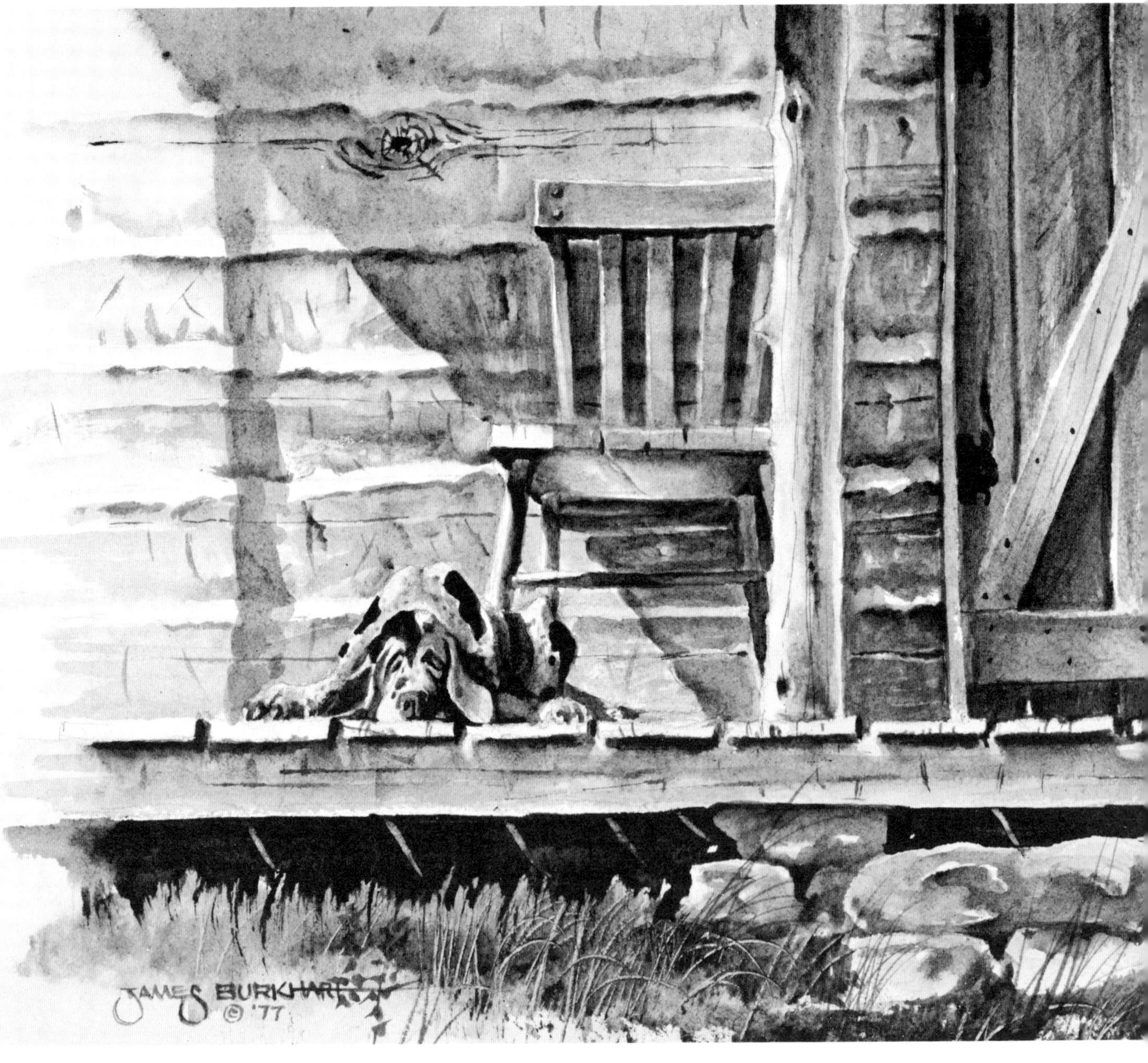
JAMES BURKHART
© '77

CHAPTER THIRTEEN

Porch, Lean-to, Loft

Unless you're a hermit, or more accurately, unless you plan to become or remain a hermit, scrap the plan for just the basic settler's one room cabin. I don't care if you do travel light, or if you want the house only for vacations or for extremely intimate gatherings. One room just isn't enough, given the limits that log length and weight impose. Even a theoretical 40-footer, while possible, would shake every time a door slammed. Too far from bracing corner to corner.

So let's stick to the old basic 16- or 20-foot log pen, whether as a single or half a dogtrot or saddlebag, and do some things to it. First off I won't build a log house without a porch, and have rarely done so without a lean-to. I will admit to a certain laxity in insisting on a loft, always to my regret. Everyone gets cramped for space eventually, and these additions provide the simplest, cheapest expansion, just as they did historically.

Every so often friends will brave our non-road, singly or in groups, for what may become an all-evening impromptu mountain music session. Porch events in warm weather, these move indoors before the fire when it's crisp. The sounds of dulcimer, fiddle, mandolin, mouth harp and guitar lifting out of the hollow remind us again of what this backwoods living is all about.

166

Porches

The settlers used the front porch for everything from drying herbs and produce to talking politics, and courting. Assorted hounds basked here, ready in a flash to scramble full-throated after raccoons, peddlers, or chicken thieves. Harness and saddles always seemed to find their way here, even at well-to-do layouts with spacious barns. And the women **would** hang their shiny washtubs proudly on the porch wall, exactly as they later were to display their new washing machines.

And rocking chairs. Where else, in decent weather, would you have put Granny and her patchwork, maiden Aunt Sarah and her store of gossip, or old Uncle Eli, mumbling over his jug? Of course this furniture moved inside in nippy weather, but in the southern highlands, rocking chairs were out more than they were in.

So you want a porch. Makes the house balance better; keeps the rain from dumping on you while you fumble the door open, arms full of firewood, groceries or somebody else's chickens. And it'll get just as hot inside as it did for the pioneers (every bit as hot if you cook on wood), and you'll need the air.

A porch is simply a heavy floor, usually raised, with a roof extending out from the main house, supported by two or more posts. Visually, the roofline of the porch is the part that's most important, so let's talk about that, first.

There were three basic ways the settlers went about roofing the porch. One was simply extending the main house rafters to six feet or so from the ground, propping them with uprights, and shingling the whole roof together. This "catslide" is neat, with no break in the roof, making it easier to frame up and to shingle. A disadvantage is that, with a steeply pitched roof on the main house, it means a shallow porch.

Another roof design was that of attaching the porch rafters to the house below the main eaves, and extending the porch roof at a flatter slope than that of the house roof. This allowed a deeper porch than the straight-line roof. It also made possible small windows in the upstairs wall, above the porch roof and below the main eaves. Dropping below the main eaves gives less height to work with, however, and a deep

Three Porch Roof Types

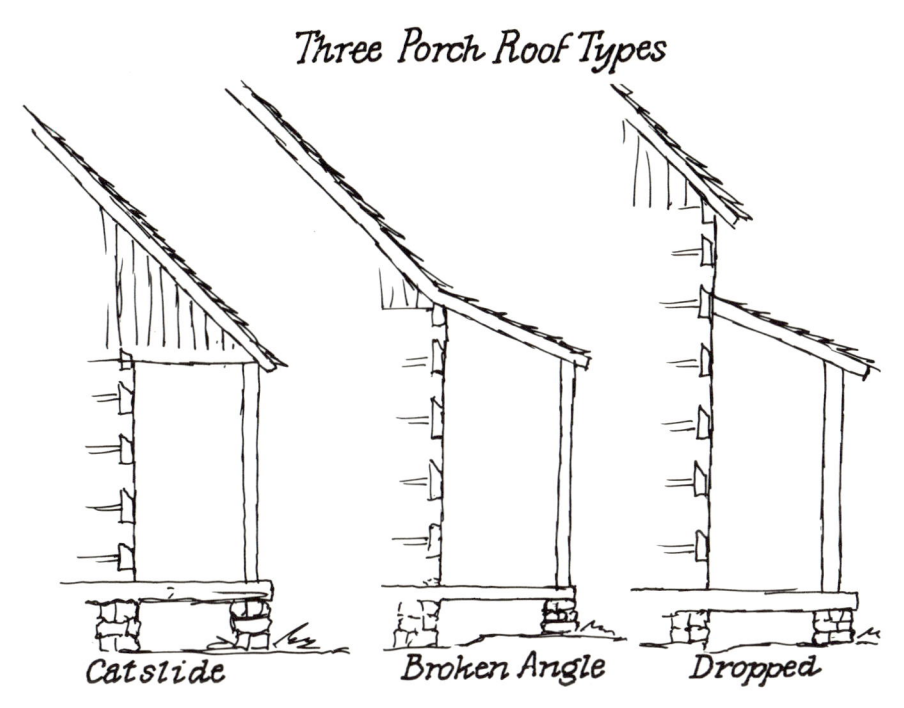

Catslide   *Broken Angle*   *Dropped*

porch still must have a sufficient roof pitch to shed water--say a 1:2½ or 1:3 pitch ratio.

    I prefer still another arrangement, that of the porch roof joined to the main house roof, but at a flatter slope. This gives the maximum height at the house wall, allowing a deeper porch, which I like, still at a sufficient slope. Shingling the joint where the porch roof joins the main roof takes a bit of skill, but I underlay this and the main house roof with strips of tarpaper to be safe.

    The porch roof slope that looks best with your house is a matter for your eye, and as long as the shingles shed water, you have quite a bit of leeway. I spike the house ends of the porch rafters to the ends of the main rafters with one spike each, letting the other ends pivot and hang down. Then I attach the long pole stringer that supports the outer ends of these rafters, to them. Next I get help, if necessary, to raise the stringer, swinging the rafters up until I get the slope I like. Usually I'll use two push poles spiked to the stringer, and I leave these propping up the rafters, until I put in the permanent uprights.

So that I can go ahead with shingling, I usually frame up the porch roof at the same time as the main roof, brace it temporarily, shingle it, but frame and floor the porch later. In pinning the rafter ends to the main house, I use wooden pegs or long spikes, such as gutter spikes. The same fastenings are used in pegging the other ends of the rafters to the long stringer. This stringer itself may be spliced 2 x 4's, since it should be the entire length of the porch, and you may have trouble finding a single timber or pole long enough.

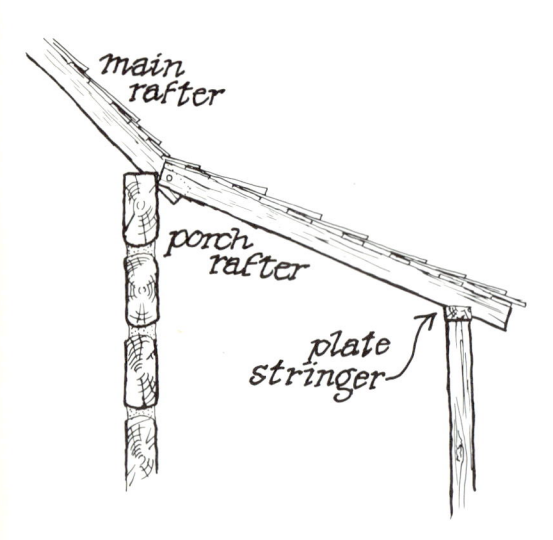

Porch roof rafters can be pinned to the main house rafters and the pitch adjusted by eye. The porch roof at right was braced temporarily until peeled cedar posts were ready.

If you've been efficient and already have the porch floor framed, you can spike or mortise the permanent uprights for the roof in as soon as the rafters are up. Or prop and brace the uprights in place, climb up, nail on the stringer, and lay the rafters that way.

Porches were often afterthoughts, so build yours any way you like. One thing I like to do is slat the roof instead of decking it, and lay the shingles with no tarpaper under them. The undersides of the shingles won't weather much, and if they're heart cedar, you'll smell them for years. From just the right angle, you'll be able to see daylight down through the spaces between shingles, but rain will have to travel uphill to get through.

One thing to remember about porches is that the wind gets under them. All that square footage and toil can easily sail off down the hill in the wind unless you fasten it well. Lag screws help. So do little pieces of angle iron (hand forged look good) to anchor the posts. Since you don't have the tremendous weight to hold the porch down as you do with the logs of the house, consider building a heavy bolt (½" or more) into your stone foundation piers. Bolt the sill down, and fasten the joists and roof uprights to it securely.

You may want to use rough-sawn joists here, or hewn beams. Or just round poles, but flatten the top surfaces if you do. An adze is fine for this, after they're in place. Watch your feet, or they may not stay in place.

If you use sawn stock, a couple of 30-penny spikes through the sill (2"x6" or 2"x8") into the ends of the joists will hold. A nailer 2"x4" along the house sill log will support that end. Or mortise into the house sill, use a heavy porch sill and mortise into that, too.

If you plan to do a lot of jigging on the porch, you may want it stronger. Use a heavy porch sill, and log or heavy beam joists, and mortise or notch them in. Since porches were often added later, and rebuilt or replaced several times over the years, almost anything can be found on older houses. Properly built and maintained, however, your porch should last as long as the house.

Heavy decking, 1½" or 2" thick, is best on the porch. We

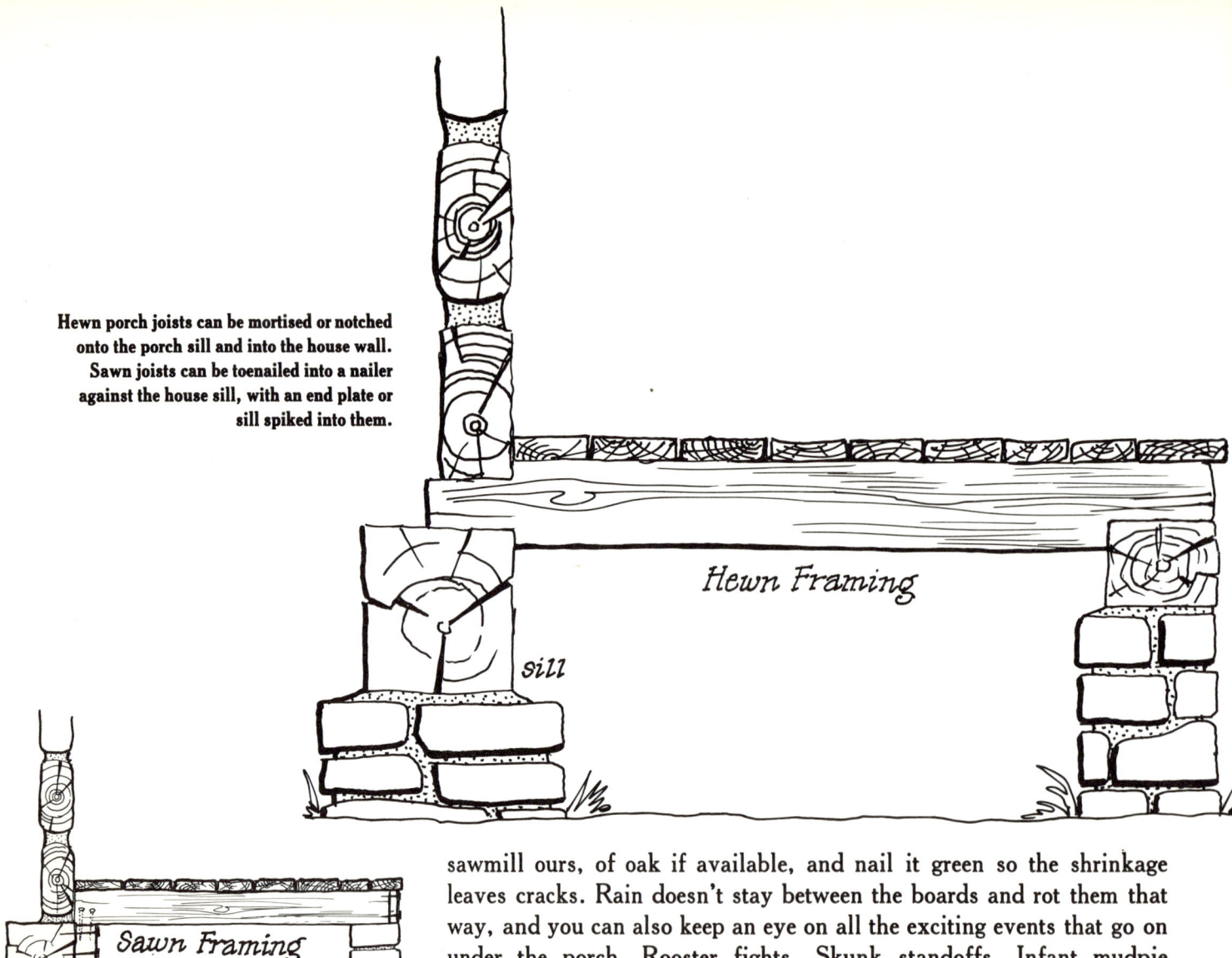

Hewn porch joists can be mortised or notched onto the porch sill and into the house wall. Sawn joists can be toenailed into a nailer against the house sill, with an end plate or sill spiked into them.

Hewn Framing

sill

Sawn Framing

sawmill ours, of oak if available, and nail it green so the shrinkage leaves cracks. Rain doesn't stay between the boards and rot them that way, and you can also keep an eye on all the exciting events that go on under the porch. Rooster fights. Skunk standoffs. Infant mudpie sessions. Snakes, contemplating cabin entry. Also, with cracks, it isn't necessary to slope the porch floor to get the rain water off before you slip on it, liquid or frozen.

Porch steps will probably be out in the weather, even with generous eaves. If it's a high porch, use 2" sawn stock. Oak, cedar, cypress. Walnut or maybe Osage Orange would be perfect, and your grandchildren could grow old on those steps.

High porch and step rails should be strongly braced. They were traditionally mortised into uprights and required no hardware.

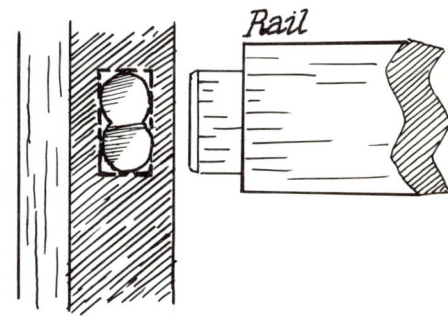

This involves being able to shift the uprights, so you may need to put up a temporary brace or two while you sledgehammer them around.

A low porch needs no more than a couple of nice flat rocks as steps. Don't spoil the whole thing with concrete steps, and don't get too fancy. Marble and wrought iron is a little too much.

Porch rails are a delight. I know of many in the mountains with carved initials and dates in them, and corners worn round from leaning, sitting, and feet propped on them. My favorite rail is a rounded-corner 2 x 4 of cedar heart, usually split out and finished with plane or draw knife. It was usually mortised into the posts at about a 30" height. These mortises were cut with a 2" auger and a chisel. Two holes were bored, one just over the other, and the wood left in the corners of the figure "8" was taken out with the chisel. Do this before you spike down the posts, so you can drive the rails into the mortises at both ends.

If yours is a high porch, bring the rail to the top of the steps, then join it to another for the step rail. The top post of the step rail will probably need no bracing, with rails into it from two sides, but the bottom post, or newel, will. If you don't mind a little shakiness, just spike it to the step framing stringer. I like to extend the bottom tread past the newel post and angle-cut or mortise a brace.

Remember to build your porch for use. If yours has a good view, spend a lot of time here appreciating it. Hold mountain music sessions here. Wear the porch into mellowness; properly used it will have some effect on you, too.

Bill Cameron, right-hand man on our house project, enjoys the front porch and rocking chair.

Lean-tos

These additions were just what their name implies. They leaned against the cabin, and were almost always added later, usually of sawn boards. When that long-suffering pioneer wife finally got her egg money together to buy a cast-iron cookstove, it often went into the lean-to. Kept the heat out of the main house in summer, and was actually a modification of the old kitchen-out-back in a separate building. In a lean-to this didn't do much for fire prevention, but it made more room.

The lean-to is still a good place for the kitchen, and bathroom. It lets you believe that these modernizations **could** have been added later, even if your whole log house is new. There need be nothing very modern looking in the main house if these essential rooms are in the lean-to.

Log cabin kit suppliers have come up with all sorts of ells, wings and spacious goodies for their playhouses, to uncramp the basic cabin, but nothing looks as homey as a board-and-batten lean-to nudging the rear wall. I like them all across the back, inset a foot to avoid covering those dovetail notches.

Spike 2 x 4 studs up the log wall after the logs shrink and settle, set sills on stone foundation corners, mortise or spike in joists, and you're on your way. Better add another stone pier under the back door for extra support at this heavy traffic point. Subfloor the joists as in any construction, insulate under and put your studwall framing up. Tie

The lean-to framing should not be done until the logs have settled and shrunk. Then uprights are spiked to the log wall, and rafters joined to those of the main house.

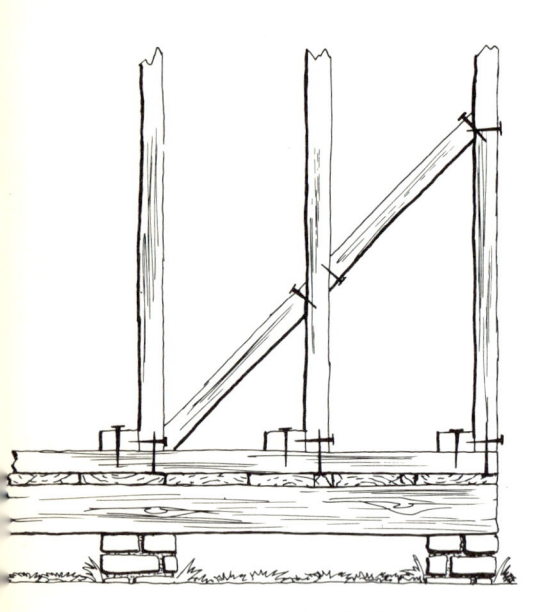

This lean-to is typical studwall construction. The blocks at the feet of the studs are for extra strength, as is the angle bracing.

rafters into house rafter ends as you did with the porch. Deck, insulate, shingle just as with the main house.

Do set in some angle bracing to keep this room from leaning. Modern builders use a sheet of plywood at the corners, covering the rest with fiber board. You'll be happier, and so will I, if you angle-cut 2 x 4's and incorporate them into the studwalls. To insulate, cut the pieces to fit around these angles.

Without this bracing, years of wind and wear will tilt things crazily. I know of lots of old houses with their walls playing dominoes. Of course with angled sheathing under the siding, the bracing wasn't necessary, but with insulation, a double outer wall is really a waste of materials. Another inch of wood won't do nearly as much toward holding heat (in or out) as an inch of foam or fiber.

Procedures in installing windows and doors, inner wall covering, wiring and plumbing, are exactly the same as in conventional modern construction. I suggest board-and-batten outer walls as a visual break from the horizontal lines of the logs, just as for gable end covering. I use random width boards, from 8" to 12", with 3" battens.

Lofts

These delightful spaces exist any time you have a sloped roof above a ceiling, but too often there's only a cramped space under the ridge and lots or wasted cubic footage where the roof slopes to the walls.

In a log house, a usable loft is simply a matter of two or three more logs per wall, and a ceiling strong enough for the upstairs floor. Well, it isn't **that** simple, as we pointed out in the chapter on roofs, but almost.

Of course, the higher the log walls above the ceiling, the more space upstairs, but there's a logical limit. Too many logs gives you a tall, skinny, and funny-looking house. You'll recall that the top course of logs should not be cut into or otherwise weakened for windows. So logs should stop at the upstairs window sills, or go on above the windows at a reasonable level.

Three feet or so of logs, plus a 45° roof, gives you six feet of height three feet out from the wall. Got that? You can shove a bed into that three-foot height, or build closets that bring walls out to head height. If you put in an upstairs bathroom, shift things around so that essential plumbing is located where there's headroom.

Any less than three logs up, cuts your usable space drastically. One log up means you have to stay five feet out from the wall to clear six feet. In a 16-foot house that's only six feet of standing room down the middle, and you may not have that as clear space if you want kingpost support in the middle of the floor.

Lofts are almost necessarily dark, since you have window space only at the ends. No skylights. I have built dormer windows, in those larger houses that can handle them in good proportion. So did the better early builders. But dormers in a small cabin ruin the lines and are pretentious as hell.

In a 50-foot dogtrot, dormers are fine, and give light and a feeling of space, as well as some fine views. They're tricky to build, and mean lots of flashing and lots of weird angles to figure.

Once, faced with the problem of locating an upstairs bathroom (it had to be against a wall so the pipes wouldn't come down into the middle of the living room) I put the shower in a dormer window. The owners loved it, since the house was in the deep woods, with relatively few peeping perverts around.

We've talked about bracing the ceiling joists with king or queen posts from the rafters. If the house is 20 feet or more deep, it's a good idea to use king posts and build a dividing partition around them. That gives you two rooms upstairs, each with its sloping roof. Or, for smaller houses or houses with no upstairs log walls (limiting space), use the queen posts to define a space with headroom down the center.

Since a 45° roof gives you so much height at the peak (13 feet in a 20' deep house with 3' log walls above the ceiling) it's often a good idea to ceil the upstairs, too, and have all that peak for storage. This cuts down on the area you must insulate, too, and allows a flat ceiling here to use conventional insulation above.

Of course you may want to leave out the ceilings altogether. No upstairs. No ceiling joists. Just all that space, soaring off up there.

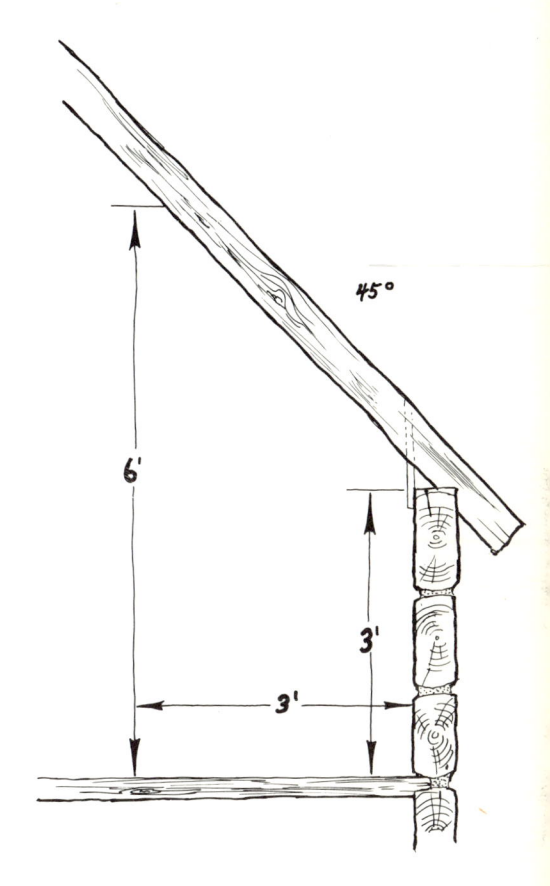

This drawing shows the approximate usable headroom in a loft near the walls. A flatter roof would reduce the headroom proportionately.

Unfortunately, that's what the heat will do, too, in summer and in winter. Aside from that and the 50% reduction in floor space, this is fine. I don't recommend it, and evidently neither did the pioneers, who seemed always to have more warm bodies than space to stow them.

Stairs

To reach the upstairs or loft, you have a variety of choices, all used traditionally. The classic one is a row of stout pegs out from the wall, to a hole in the ceiling. You can nail a ladder to the wall. Or use one of those disappearing ladders. Or build a steep staircase, at the end of the house, always. Front or back, and you'll bump your head before you reach the top.

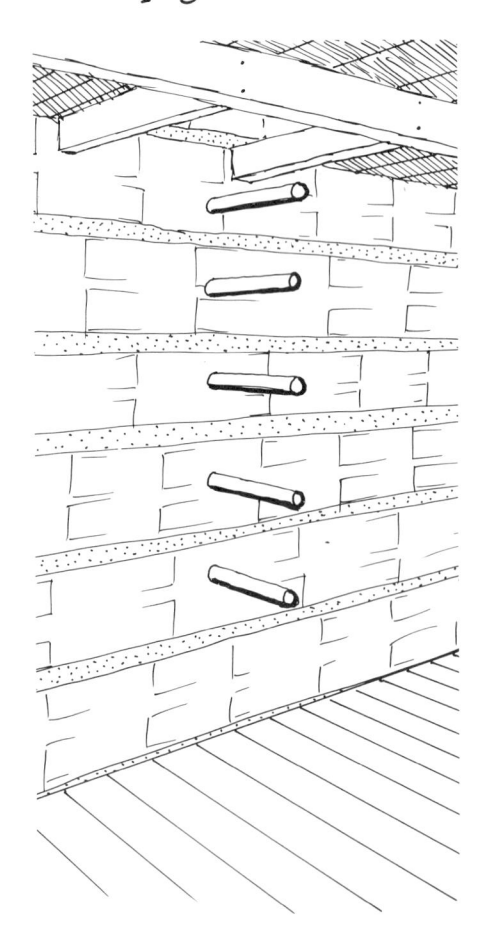

The problem here is the steep angle, since you must have room to get around and onto the steps at the bottom, off at the top, and up seven or eight feet in between. If you plan to move furniture up or down, prepare for a hernia.

I build stairs with a sane pitch, made possible by starting up the front or back wall to a landing well below-head-bumping level, then up the end wall. It uses up a lot of living space, true, but leaves a logical place for a small coat closet downstairs. Upstairs it just takes a lot of space. Try carrying a bathtub, wardrobe, chest of drawers or other bulky mass up or down, and you'll gladly sacrifice the footage. More gladly as the years advance.

Choose your own stair construction. A favorite has always been simply treads nailed into angled cutouts in the side framing stringers. You may prefer treads laid onto nailer strips set inside the framing. Another variation is the treads end-nailed through the framing, with risers for support.

Whenever I attach any horizontal member to a vertical, as with a stair tread, joist end or porch rail, I like to mortise it. This was common before nails were plentiful, and though time-consuming, is stronger.

So consider mortising each stair tread into the framing, with perhaps glue and pegs to help. Stairs should not be fancy and out of place, but are a good place for careful craftsmanship.

Window placement is a mess if you have a languid staircase

peg ladder

Stair types

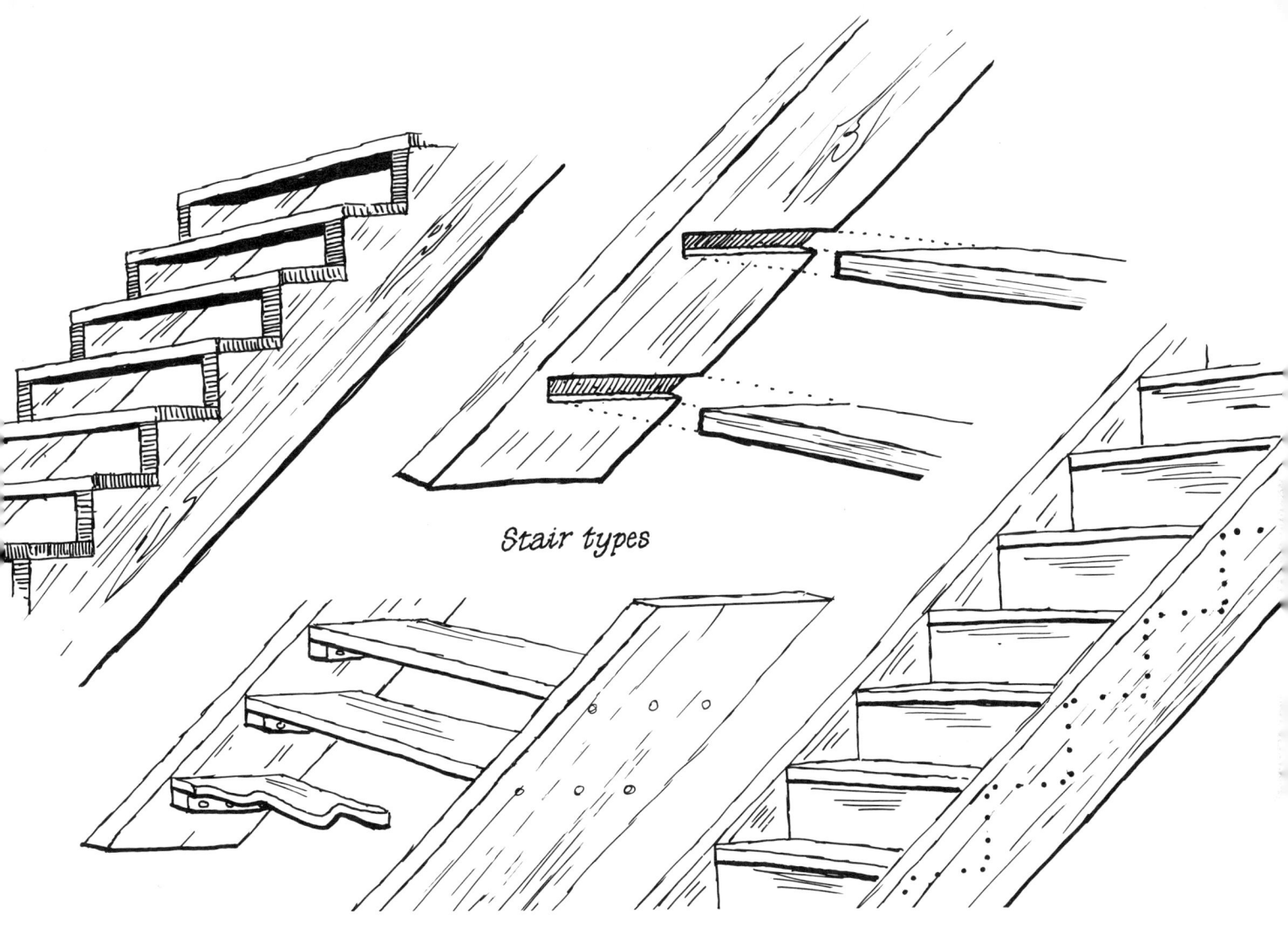

taking up most of two walls. A 9" riser and 12" tread are all right, but anything more gradual, and you have large dark areas where there should be windows, along with more wasted floor space.

A log house we dismantled near Branson, Missouri, for a friend of mine to restore, had the entire staircase wedged between a corner and the fireplace, which was about five feet away.

Of course there was no window in that half wall, and the treads were only 5" deep. You went upstairs on tiptoes, like it or not.

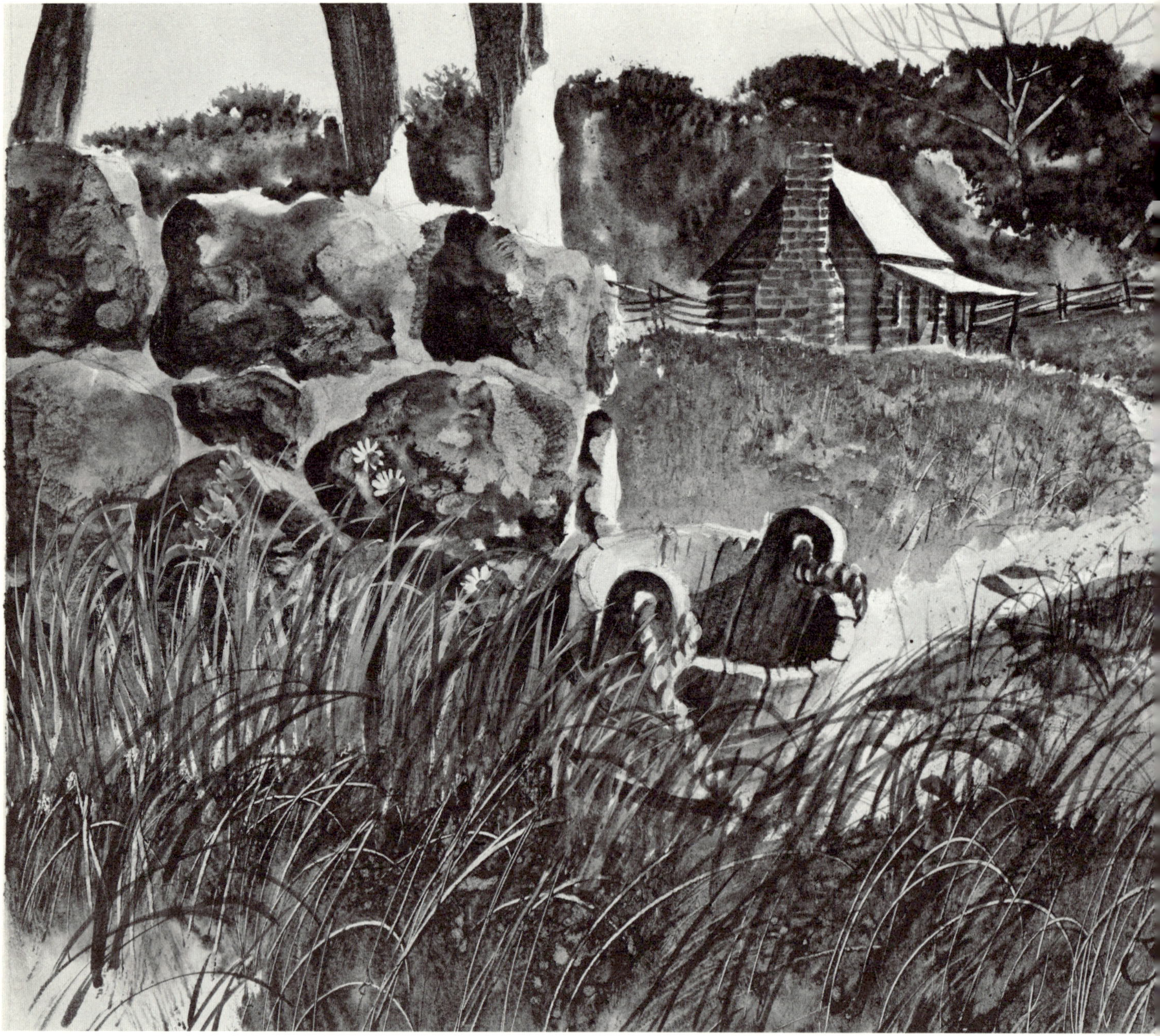

CHAPTER FOURTEEN

Water Supply and Waste Disposal

Water has always been a prime deciding factor in living in the woods. More so, of course, when folks depended upon livestock and crops for their livings, but it's still something major to consider. And now too sewage disposal is perhaps as important. You must have clean water for consumption, and once you do your part to pollute it, everything possible must be done to clean it up for its return to your environment and that of the other creatures.

Let's look at water first. Springs and streams were the prime water sources for the pioneers, but you can scratch both, now. Particularly in the limerock ledge country of the hills. Surface water runs for many miles in crevices and underground channels with almost no filtration. Springs today are a worse risk even than streams, a hydrologist friend tells me, because there's no sunlight to help kill bacteria. A shallow, sunny creek is better, then, but not much, since all the surface runoff gets into it, and there are myriads of water-borne uglies, such as man-made chemicals, that even sunlight won't kill.

Drilled-well bucket

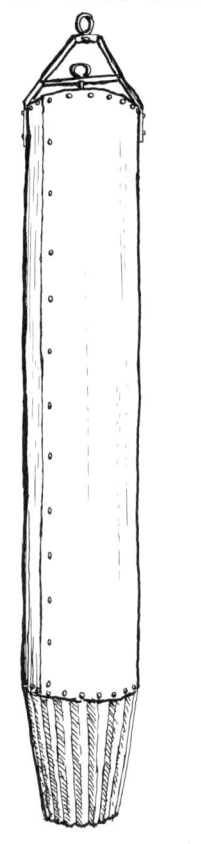

I'm told that there are new laws in some areas requiring casing to safe levels. If so, well prices are apt to go much higher.

You can filter creek or spring water. Commercial filtering systems are available through large hardware stores and plumbing supply houses. You could even build your own sand-and-charcoal filter if you could get the specifications from an engineer or biologist.

Or you can do as several of my friends who live in the wilds do: pump creek or spring water for general use, and haul drinking water. Boiling the drinking water is another solution.

Wells

But all this gets to be a chore. All in all, a well is the best approach to sufficient clean water. A good, deep, drilled well, down to a thick layer of water-bearing sand, nature's best filter. Wells cost money, but a little simple arithmetic will show you how much more you'll spend in a few years on just about any other source.

Well drillers charge, at this writing, around $3 a foot, but that's misleading. Heavy steel casing is necessary to prevent caving in and surface water leakage, and that's often another $3 a foot. Say you drill 200 feet for a sufficient flow of water (12-20 GPM) and you need 40 feet of casing to get past the subsoil and two small cavities in the rock. Seven hundred twenty dollars, so far, and you still need a pump of some sort, piping, and either a gravity or pressure tank. $500 to $750 more isn't too much to estimate, depending on whether you buy a submersible electric pump, a deep well jet pump, a windmill, or a hand pump. Or you may buy a thin, drilled-well water bucket that fills from the bottom, and a lot of rope, depending on how pioneer you want to be.

Alternatives: (1) Dig your own. I have hand-dug a half-dozen wells, in country that had some dirt among the rocks. The water was usually inadequate in volume and quality. And it is a thankless chore to slave away for many days down a dark hole, only to find no water, or to encounter a solid rock layer that steel and/or dynamite won't budge.

(2) Hire a water witcher,[35] to locate underground watercourses that are near the surface. I will say only that I have seen it done successfully, and believe that some of us possess the ability to find water (since probably many of our early ancestors had to find it, or die, and the gift seems to have persisted). But I have also seen dry holes sunk at great

cost of time and labor. Water witchers, or dowsers, seem to have short memories when it comes to their failures.

(3) Low-cost, drill-your-own well drilling rigs, that can pay for themselves on your own well, then make you some money on others. No. Unless you live on sand or river bottom silt, these toys come apart very soon, usually at the first large piece of chert.

(4) Cisterns. Usually leaky, smelly tanks, above or under ground, that invite new and noxious strains of bacteria to multiply. Most are filled from roof gutter runoff, so you can add bird droppings and other wilderness delights to the supply. Ideally, of course, you let it rain the roof clean, then dash out and divert the spout into the cistern. But to be anything like safe, you must dose the tankful with chlorine, which makes it taste like city water, and is probably carcinogenic.

(5) A hydraulic ram from a spring or distant well. This device wastes far more water than it delivers, but requires no power other than that from the water itself as it runs downhill first, in order to be pumped uphill afterwards. That downhill drop is the key, plus enough water so you can waste a lot. Plus keeping the ram from freezing when it's bitter, and keeping sand from jamming it.

Another option is the sand point, which is a screened tube with a sharpened point that is driven down at the end of successive lengths of pipe. They don't go very deep, and stop at the first stone. I used one on the Gulf Coast several years ago, to obtain a scant flow of pretty foul water.

Back to the drilled well and pump. To lessen the cost, two or more of you can go in together on a community well. Sometimes this works nicely, and sometimes, like all forms of communism seem to do in practice, it fails. Just who pays for replacing the lightning-struck pump? And what rights go with the sale of a piece of property dependent on the well? And what happens to your water pressure if I'm downhill, watering my rutabagas?

It can work. My neighbor and I had planned to split the original cost, maintenance and operation of a well for both of us, but we ended by my paying him an arbitrary sum a month until I have my own drilled. It has worked well because we are good friends, with my increasing the amount to cover operation of a washing machine, added when our daughter arrived.

I still recommend that you save your money for a well of your very own. If you have electricity, install a gravity or pressure tank, fed by an automatically controlled pump. No electricity? An overhead gravity tank of say 500 gallons can be fed with a gasoline-driven pump or windmill. That much should last four of you, say a week, depending on how clean you are.

Running water can save you so much time for things you'd really rather be doing, that I don't recommend a hand pump or well bucket. My city-born wife equates civilization with a hot shower and flush toilet, and you need piped water for both. For my part, I was grown before we stopped carrying water from a spring or well, with a respite when my father built a hydraulic ram. I appreciate piped water, too.

One thing to consider in having a well drilled is the machinery involved. An efficient drill rig is huge, and needs a wide road to get to your place and lots of room to set up. I have put off drilling our own well for three years simply because even the smallest, most inefficient rig will require my cutting large trees along my road, then hacking out an open space for the machine to set up in.

And unless you're an expert, don't expect to be able to tell when your driller has reached sufficient flow. You just have to trust him, and since he's paid by the foot, that can be trying. While he's set up, let him go till he's satisfied. Usually he won't sell you more footage than is average for the area. And forget about having the well drilled deeper later if necessary. No driller I know of will do it.

Don't make the mistake a couple I know did. Our mutual hydrologist friend convinced them that sufficient water lay 60 feet down, and they tried to get a driller to go that deep only. Every driller refused to go through the involved business of setting up in their remote location for 60 feet of drilling, and you, too, can count on that. Two years later this couple is still hauling drinking water and pumping creek water with a gasoline pump to an overhead tank for their general plumbing.

Well-drilling can take four hours or three weeks, all for a 200-foot well. Old cable or rotary rigs are slow, loud, usually smaller, and cost just as much. Modern, air driven units work faster, but need more denuded land to maneuver in.

Once finished, most drillers can also put in your pump for a price, before they leave. Don't do this yourself unless you're a plumber, a good plumber.

Before attempting your own plumbing, get yourself some good manuals on the subject. Then investigate the merits of plastic pipe, copper, or galvanized. Explore types of fittings and then cost. Visit other installations. By all means install a master valve and a drain at the low point in your system so you can leave piping dry during extended cold-weather sorties.

Sewage Disposal

Now, what do we do with our newly-polluted waste water?

First and foremost, use as little of it as possible. Diluting eight ounces of human waste with four gallons of water, and then flushing it all into the ecosystem, is dumb. It's led many sensitive souls to the rediscovery of the dry toilet, which may be a privy or a sophisticated compost-producing installation.

And, even though it means extra plumbing, not a few of my woods-dwelling acquaintances have channeled their sinks and shower drains into separate, gravel and sand-filled pits instead of into their septic tanks. This lets the phosphates break down slowly, I'm told, and allows watering of nearby gardens, all without flooding the septic systems.

You may opt for a privy. Yes, you certainly may.

The Swedish dry toilet, or Clivus toilet, is a waterless and (its manufacturers say) odorless indoor affair that reduces all organic waste, including kitchen scraps, to compost, eventually.

Given the world's dedication to conventional indoor plumbing of the flush type, I prefer to work within those principles. I do advocate every means possible to reduce pollution, and here's how:

The septic tank operates on the principle of anaerobic bacteria partially breaking down waste solids. Liquid runoff is channeled through gravel-and-sand filled ditches in perforated pipes, to distribute the effluent as widely as possible. Then it's up to a relatively porous soil to further filter it, and eventually break down the impurities.

Septic system

vent

sludge

gravel-filled ditches

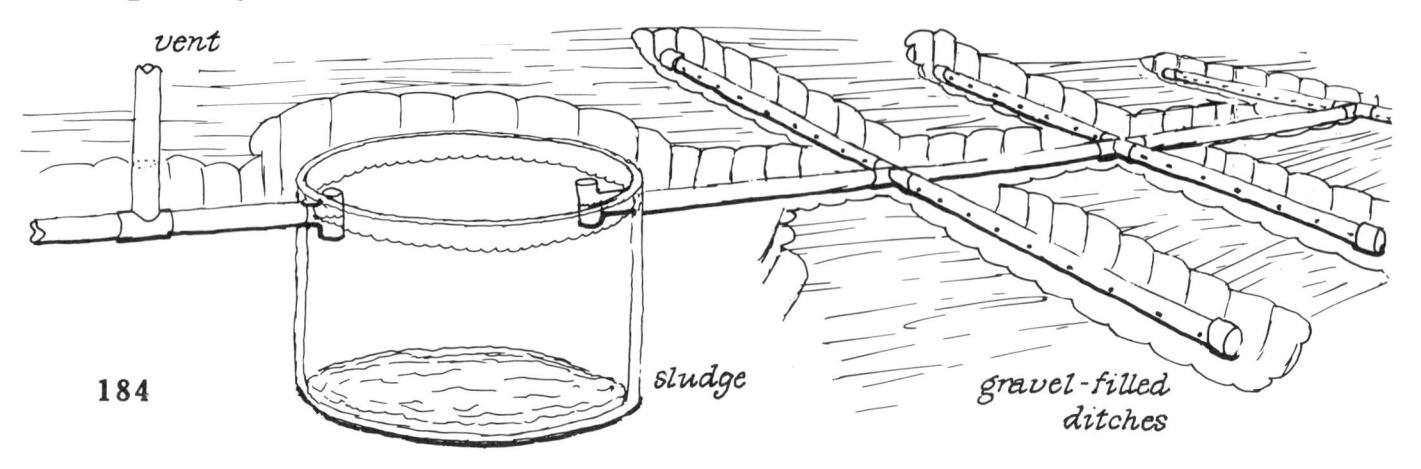

Sludge builds up in the tank, which must be pumped out periodically. How often depends on the volume of solids. A large family, with a garbage disposal, would fill a tank sooner than a hermit with a compost pile for table scraps. In any event, we're talking in terms of years between pumpings.

Anaerobic bacteria are those that can live without a constant infusion of oxygen into the effluent. It is important that both the entry and exit pipes be below the surface of the liquid in a septic tank, and that the entry pipe be on a gradual slope so as not to churn the liquid or break up a noxious but necessary layer of scum on the surface. This below-level porting is done with baffles in the tank itself, or with pipe T's at entry and exit, set vertically.

Good field lines are necessary for any type of liquid waste disposal. If the soil is thin or non-absorbent, you can make it work with several truckloads of sand or sandy soil strategically placed. I have built a series of dry-stone walls down the hill below our house, with tons of sand behind each.

As additional filtration, I pipe the runoff into a chambered filter tank, filled with fine gravel, coarse sand, and then fine sand, before it goes to the distribution area. I also use a system of perforated pipes in the septic tank itself, connected to a small air compressor which is run by an interval timer.

This system is actually an aerobic unit, charging the effluent every few minutes with oxygen to keep the aerobic bacteria alive and working. These bugs break the waste down much more completely, as in a municipal sewage plant, and little sludge builds up in the tank. Field lines are still needed, but not as much, since the oxygen-charged runoff breaks down faster in the soil.

Aeration can be achieved with a compressor, a strong blower, or a deep paddle wheel extending from the surface to well below it, or a combination. With this system, it's important to keep the liquid as near constantly churned as possible, and as charged with oxygen. Inlet and outlet can be at the surface, and it's actually better if a steeply inclined inlet pipe dumps into the tank from above the surface.

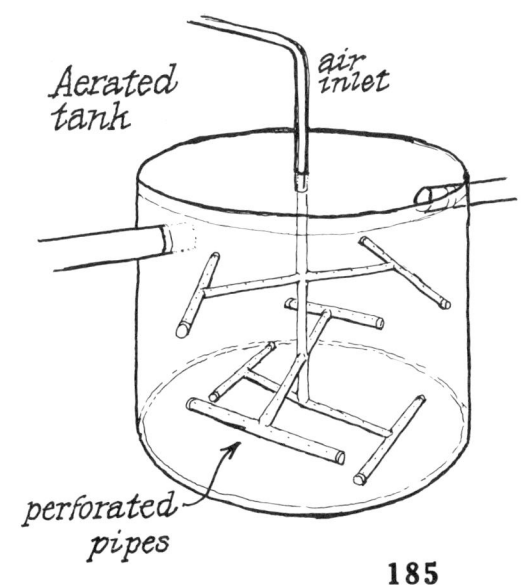

Aerated tank

air inlet

perforated pipes

I've heard of unique aeration devices, among them a paddle operated by a windmill. A compressor could also be powered by wind if you're without electricity.

I experimented with a castoff automobile pollution-control compressor, which gave a low pressure flow of air. In trying to find the best frequency and duration of running it, however, I let sludge build up over the perforated piping in the tank and had to change to a stronger compressor. The diaphragm units used with lightweight paint sprayers work nicely. A variable timer is cheap and easy to install, giving breaks from constant aeration and electrical usage.

If aeration is used, be sure you have adequate ventilation via your vent pipe. Of course that's necessary anyway, to keep from siphoning the water from your drain traps.

On a creek bank or in limerock country where filtering soil is scarce, this is about the only system that will let you use a flush toilet safely. Whether you use a septic tank or aerobic system, there must be no leaks before the runoff stage.

There are a variety of tanks on the market, or you can build your own. The cheapest are the sheet steel tanks treated with tar, which have built-in baffles for anaerobic treatment. These usually are 300 gallons or more, which is about the minimum you should use. Pre-cast concrete tanks are more permanent, but require heavy machinery to install. Some of the more sophisticated aerobic tanks for dwellings may weigh several tons and be 12 feet long.

I usually build my own. Builders conventionally do this with concrete, reinforced with steel wire and poured into forms in place in the ground. This takes a lot of time and cement, but is solid and permanent.

Having read of tanks and even boats built of a thin cement layer with fine wire mesh for reinforcing, I tried it for sewage disposal tanks, and it works nicely. Either dig a hole, preferably round, or set up a cylinder of heavy welded wire mesh on top of the ground, if you're on stone ledges and can't dig. Wrap a layer of fine mesh chicken wire outside and another inside the heavy wire, and use short wires to draw them all together where needed. Lay wire on the bottom too, attached to

This 400-gallon septic tank was built by plastering mortar onto a wire screen set in the ground. The drawings show the procedure for tank and lid.

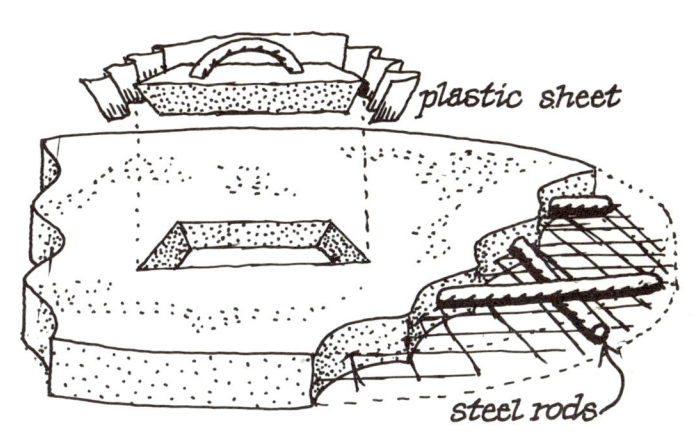

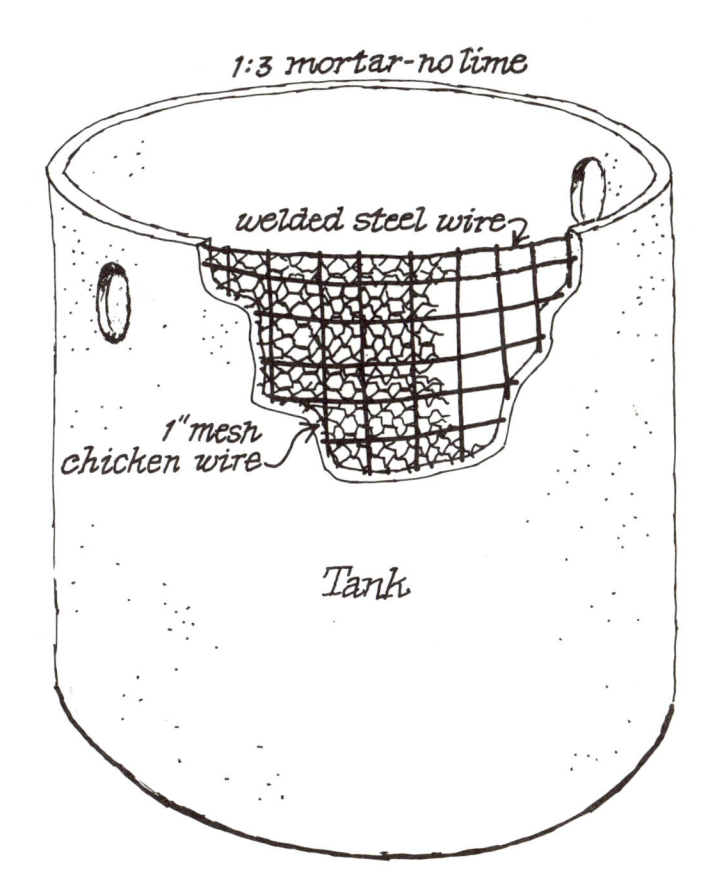

Lid (detail)

plastic sheet

steel rods

1:3 mortar-no lime

welded steel wire

1" mesh chicken wire

Tank

187

the sides.

Use a 1:3 mix of Portland cement and sand (not masonry cement) and trowel it onto the mesh. If in the ground, do it all from inside; if above ground, you'll need a helper with a trowel to push against on the other side.

Do it all at one stint. A cold joint will almost certainly leak, and be weaker. Either spread some mortar on the bottom first, then lay the wire here, or do it with the wire in place, pulling it up and shaking it to get the mortar beneath it and work out air bubbles. Then cover with more mortar.

To play safe, set in an iron bar across the top as you finish the walls, to help support the lid. This lid is cast separately, reinforced with a grid of at least four rods along with the wire mesh. Make it about two inches thick, and leave an opening for cleaning out the tank. I do this by laying an outward-sloping strip of sheet plastic or tin where I want the opening, then reinforcing the space, with a bar for a handle in what will become a sort of hatch. Then I pour the entire lid. When it's cured I can lift the hatch, which fits back exactly. Get help to set the lid in place, then fill in any cracks with mortar.

Be sure to cover both the newly-built tank and lid for six days, wetting at least once a day. If at any time the cement dries out or freezes before curing, the chemical process is halted and it will crumble. Cured properly, ¾" of this type of wall will withstand a medium sledgehammer blow.

If you're near a creek bank or any such ecologically fragile area, coat the inside of your tank with two layers of a special epoxy tar, to prevent leaks, then pipe runoff to an area that has sufficient filtration for distribution lines. Give yourself proper ventilation when you work with this tar; its toxic fumes can send you on an unnecessary trip.

Admittedly, an efficient sewage disposal system is quite involved, requiring either time or money to construct. And you will receive unlimited advice and testimony from the locals, who will tell you of the efficiency of their two oil drums shoved together, or their dry concrete block tanks, or their runoff directly into a gully.

I once laid heavy boards on top of the tank itself to pour the lid on, then cast three iron lifting eyes into it. After it cured, I set up a tripod and block-and-tackle, lifted the lid, removed the boards and lowered it into place with no help.

These are the well-meaning folks who have befouled the once-crystal waterways of our fair country, whose main objective regarding sewage is to get it out of (their) sight. Unless you choose the relatively minimum pollution of a privy, you can easily spoil your own beauty spot, something few of the dumbest of animals do.

John and Sarah Rhiel show off their newly-completed log house at Golden, Missouri, around 1899. With them is granddaughter Jenny Hicks, son Joseph, his wife Suzie, and their son Robert, now 83.

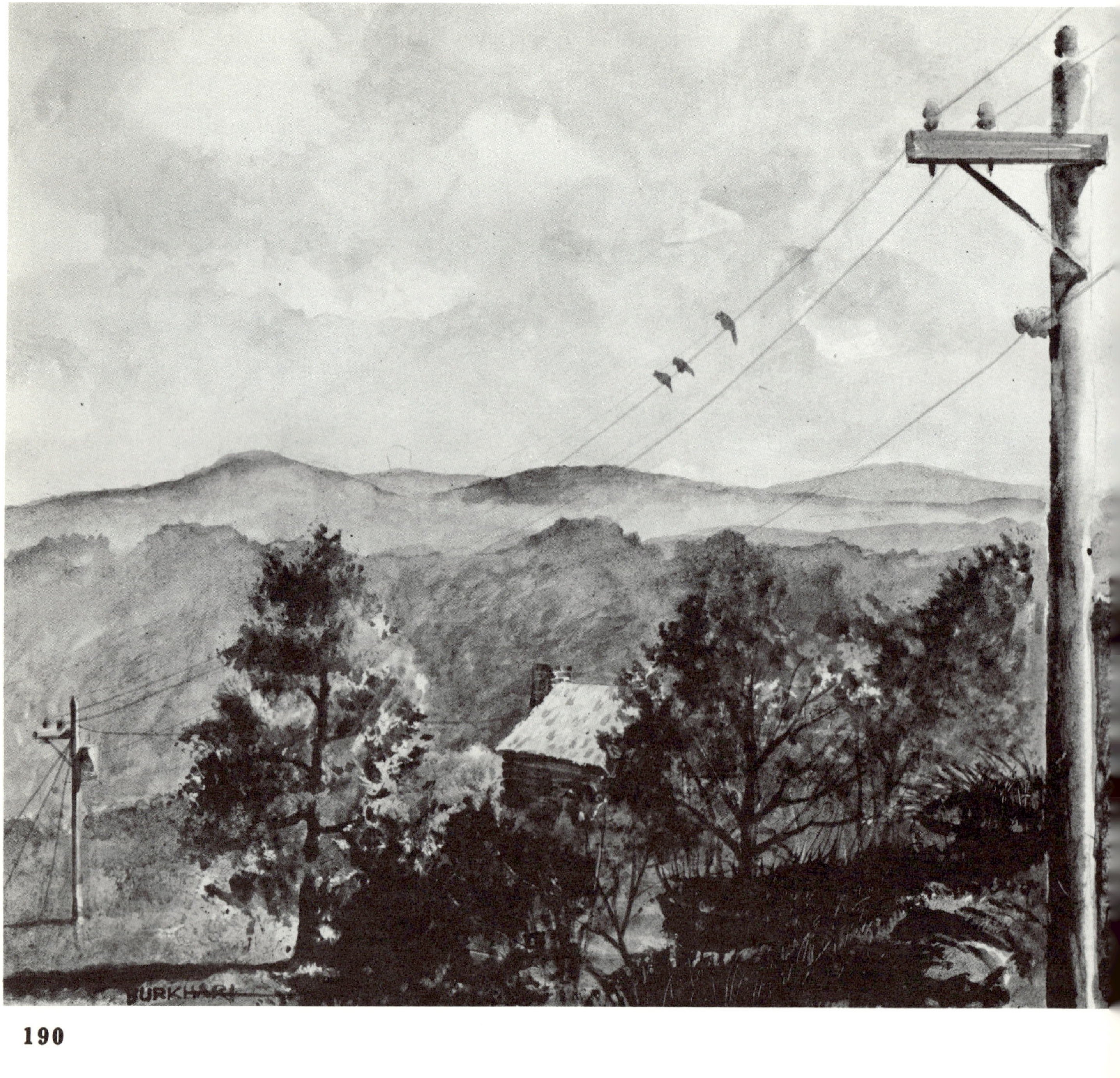
BURKHART

CHAPTER FIFTEEN

Utilities

We've discussed water, and waste disposal, which are often dependent on electricity or some form of power. Now let's talk about what you can do to live with, or without the local utility companies.

Electricity

Electricity is the utility you'll need, or miss, most. I favor cutting our dependency on this form of energy as much as possible, since we have been grossly spoiled in the past two generations by gadgetry that plugs in.

Drawing the line is difficult, however. At our house, we readily do without television, that insidious mindbender, but find a deepfreeze almost necessary. Electric toothbrushes and carving knives and can openers are out, but a water heater, though expensive to operate, is really nice. Air conditioning would be a luxury, but the attic fan in our house works better on sultry days. Then there's cooking and refrigeration, and light, of course, and the stereo . . . Suddenly our electric bill is huge.

Hot water is also available via a coil of pipe in the fireplace chimney leading to a tank. Levels are important here, since the heated water will rise slowly and return to the tank, as cold water enters the coil. It doesn't do any of this very fast.

We have friends who use bottled gas for their refrigerator, water heater and, small cookstove (in summer), use a wood cookstove in winter, and light with kerosene. But they keep a deepfreeze and a washing machine at a friend's house, and have a battery-powered tape player.

I grew up in a log cabin where we had no electricity until I was 15. We carried water, sometimes chilled things in a spring, lighted the house with kerosene lamps, listened to a battery radio and cranked a Victrola. As I remember it, our first purchases for electric usage were lights, refrigerator and water pump.

That's one plateau. You still must cook, but I learned my limited culinary skills at a woodstove, and several of my friends now use wood from October to May. Hot water can be had in reasonable quantities from the reservoir in the cookstove, and you **can** dip in your creek in summer.

Water heater and cookstove require lots of electricity, as does electric heat. You could conceivably generate your own up to this point, but even a small flow is comparatively expensive.

Power companies will usually extend lines only about ¼ mile for one customer. Farther, and they have complicated charges that result in regular, sizeable, minimum bills whether you use the stuff or not. A group of houses in a remote area stands a better chance of receiving the favors of the utility companies than one alone.

Likewise, companies are reluctant to let you bury your power line over a few hundred feet. I always do this for log houses, and 400 feet is the maximum I've been allowed. Seems the voltage drop is on the company after their transformer and before your meter, and they get touchy about such things. Get all specifications from the company if you do it.

I would certainly encourage you to bury your utility lines if at all possible. There is perhaps only one intrusion more obscene in its violation of the serenity of a gently aging log house in its natural surroundings, than electric wires overhead. And that is that embodiment of this age of plastic, the television antenna. Either anachronism will jar

Jane McRaven stokes her wood cookstove from October to May to help cut the cost of utilities. The stove also heats the family's small house.

the sensitivity of all but the most brute-like visitors. You'll want to photograph your house often, too, and there will be no easy way to avoid sight of those bristling umbilical cords to the world.

I might mention that the five families of us who own adjoining land in the National Forest have a mutual agreement not to bring in overhead utility wires (or clearcut, or bulldoze clearings, or build with unnatural materials).

Wiring

If you choose to electrify your new or restored log house, there are a few things to know. Even if you're outside the cities that have strict codes, your local power company will discourage the kind of offhand wiring that could burn your house down. They pay specialists to provide information and suggestions, so go see them.

Find out if the company will even extend their line to your site. Then, if you want to bury the wire, get their specifications. Depending on the usage you and the company man anticipate, you'll need perhaps a 100-amp or even 200-amp entry panel, which connects to the meter base. Different size conduit is required for different amperage.

Do buy a panel with a main disconnect switch, which lets you shut everything off and avoid getting burned. Every electrician I know has at least once turned off the wrong breaker switch and discovered it by burning off the end of his screwdriver on a "dead" circuit.

Three-wire or two-wire-with-ground, 12 gauge plastic-covered cable is standard for house wiring. Staple it with the wide, padded staples for that purpose. Run circuits wherever possible between logs. My brother John usually does the wiring on houses we build and has developed sophisticated methods of concealing circuits. Outlets and switches go right in the spaces to be chinked, and these can be installed horizontally to fit better.

Vertical wiring goes up nicely in a space left by beveling the log ends, to be covered by facings at doors. Sometimes John bores a vertical hole through a log to escape a cul-de-sac at a corner. And with a raised wood floor, lots of the wire can be strung underneath to come up through maybe one log to the outlets.

Wiring for overhead lights is hard to hide unless you've floored the upstairs, with a ceiling downstairs. With open beamwork, I usually try to wedge the wire into the crevice left by the top of a rounded-corner beam. You can get brown or ivory wire that blends reasonably well for places like this.

Power companies frown on the practice of imbedding wiring in concrete, on the theory that acids will eat it or the insulation off it. Maybe they're right; I have no idea what chemicals badger each other in those combinations. Metal conduit can be used here, however.

It's obviously easier to wire a log house or any other house properly before it's complete, so I advise you to go ahead with it. Even the hardiest of my forest-dwelling cohorts entertains schemes to produce his own power someday, and even minimal electricity flows better through adequate circuits.

Do get specific instructions before you wire. It's expensive to have to do it over. There are numerous how-to books on the subject available from library or bookstore.

If you're contemplating cutting yourself off from the utilities, here briefly are some schemes for creating your own electricity. If you're an engineer, you may be able to devise something that will work. Cost goes up dramatically if you produce much flow, however.

1) Windmill charger. Widely used in the 20's and 30's on hilltops and in the plains. An automotive generator or alternator is driven by a windmill to produce a small flow of power, which can be stored in batteries and transformed, or used low-voltage. Erratic, expensive (the batteries don't last long). No good down in a hollow.

2) Water wheel charger. A dependable flow of water can be channeled over a wheel to produce the kind of power that has ground grain and sawn lumber since away back. Any large stream you plan to dam will have some government restrictions on it, probably. Having restored water mills and studied their motive power, I warn of complications.

3) Engine generator. Some very dependable units are on the market, some new, some surplus. Be sure you get a usable wattage and

frequency. And count on noise and lots of fuel. A number of dwellings could be supplied by a high-efficiency Diesel, LP or steam engine-driven generator, but there's the initial cost, and the question of who takes care of it, and when.

4) Solar energy. I don't know much about this form, but it has some intriguing possibilities. Most solar collectors now in use don't lend themselves well to log house rooflines, but smaller, more efficient ones are probably being developed. Keep your eye on this progress; more is being done almost daily. I'd say the power companies' lobbies will probably see to it that not much is done nationally by the government to develop small electric generating units.

When I lived on the Buffalo River some years ago with my older brother and his family, we had a 3,000 watt gasoline-driven generator which we ran a few hours at night. Just about everything there was on LP gas, though: lights, refrigerator, water heater and cookstove.

Gas

Gas is handy for remote areas, either in portable bottles of up to 30 gallons, or in those ugly tanks that now must be above ground. You can haul your own bottles, but a large truck must be able to get near the tank to refill it. And, given a probably continuing petroleum shortage (and industry boondoggles) the price will stay up.

Of course natural gas is out of the question in the woods, unless you generate your own from decaying vegetation, sewage breaking down, or something like a charcoal kiln. Some of our forebears did this for lights, and some enterprising contemporaries are now turning barnyard manure into compost, taking off methane gas in the process.

It should be pointed out that most appliances can be had in gas-burning form, excepting washing machines and stereos, for two. As heat, gas still ranks below wood or coal and above electricity in efficiency.

Communication

You may miss the telephone the least, or the most, depending on your hangups and whether you operate a business, as we do. Linda could not run her publications operation without a phone, and wouldn't want to run her life without one.

Very simply, the telephone company has to be able to reach you if you want the joys of conventional long-distance conversation. Forget a mobile unit; the price is too high. The company will just about always come in on electric company poles, and will let you bury their line in the same ditch as the electric cable, at a reasonable 12-inch distance, to avoid static.

The alternatives are citizen's band radio and shortwave, but of course the folks you want to reach must be within range, and have similar equipment. The wattage required for these radios is quite low, but there are other complications. Federal licensing, for instance, and that same (however low) power supply.

The pioneers solved the problem of communication in a most pleasant way: they went visiting often. Country churches, square dances, quilting bees, house-raisings -- these gatherings were the news centers, of course, and so were the individual visits to borrow fire, lard, or perhaps gunpowder.

A relatively recent rural community news bearer was the late Ted Richmond. He carried books in a pack from his Wilderness Library to hill folks in Newton County, Arkansas. Until the early 50's Ted would set out regularly from his round-log cabin on the north slope of Mt. Sherman, bound for other remote holdings with books and magazines.

Ted lived alone, devoting his life and energies to visiting the hill people, some of whom never quite accepted him. We shall probably not see his like again: the visitor on foot, arriving to cut wood for the ill, to visit long hours, to bring news, and the magic of print.

His cabin is falling into ruins today, and rats have shredded the books and magazines that covered the floor and jammed the loft. He was considered something of an oddity, choosing to live as he did when almost everyone who could was leaving the hills around him.

It will not be many years before the mountains swallow up all traces of him and his work, as well as those of so many of the folks he worked with. In the four years since I visited this site I know the decay process has gone a long way.

Ted Richmond's round-log Wilderness Library goes quietly back to the earth near Mt. Sherman, in the Buffalo River country of Arkansas. Ted was a Depression days homesteader whose mission was to provide reading material for the hill people.

Your log house experience will be a delicious and varied affair, no matter how involved you become. You may be fortunate enough to locate and acquire a silvering cabin hidden in some beechwood glade, and touch it into life again.

Or to begin with the raw earth, in the woods, at the edge of an overgrown field, or even just out of town--wherever there is room for you and your house to breathe. You will soon learn that a hewn-log house is more work and/or expense to build than just about any other structure. That it will exact from you blisters for a lifetime, effort and skill you may not have known you possessed. That building it admits you to a rare and privileged brotherhood of craftsmen, steeped in a love of labor and very near to the living earth.

Or, you may simply find that your sensitivities are tuned to the very fact that some pioneer houses still survive, and you may become aware of their existence. You may drive out of your way now to find them, perhaps deserted, falling into decay.

Spend some time there, now. Now that you understand better the wilderness call our fathers heeded, and the singing of pioneer blood in their veins. Listen for the sound of axes ringing in the frost of morning, and the echo of old lullabies, sung before worn hearths of timeless stone.

Notes

1. (p. 16) Eugene M. Wilson, "Some Similarities Between American and European Folk Houses," **Pioneer America**, 3 (1971), p. 10.
2. (p. 16) D. A. Hutslar, "Log Architecture of Ohio," **Ohio History**, 80 (1971), p. 198.
3. (p. 18) C. A. Weslager, **The Log Cabin in America** (New Brunswick, New Jersey, 1969), pp. 148-150.
4. (p. 18) Fred Kniffen, "Folk Housing: Key to Diffusion," **Annals of the Association of American Geographers.** 55 (1965), p. 561.
5. (p. 18) Warren E. Roberts, "Some Comments on Log Construction in Scandinavia and the United States," in Felix J. Oinas, Linda Dégh, and Henry Glassie, eds., **Folklore Today: A Festschrift for Richard M. Dorson** (Bloomington, Indiana, 1976), p. 445.
6. (p. 19) William Lynwood Montell and Michael Lynn Morse, **Kentucky Folk Architecture** (Lexington, Kentucky, 1976), p. 8.
7. (p. 19) Henry Glassie, "The Appalachian Log Cabin," **Mountain Life and Work,** 39 (1963) p. 8.
8. (p. 19) Roberts, "Some Comments on Log Construction," p. 439.
9. (p. 19) Eugene M. Wilson, **Alabama Folk Houses** (Montgomery, Alabama, 1975), p. 25.
10. (p. 21) Montell and Morse, **Kentucky Folk Architecture,** p. 21.
11. (p. 22) Wilson, "Some Similarities", p. 11.
12. (p. 22) J. Frazer Smith, **White Pillars** (New York, 1941), pp. 25-27.
13. (p. 23) Warren E. Roberts, "The Whitaker-Waggoner House from Morgan County, Indiana," in Don Yoder, ed., **American Folklife** (Austin, Texas, 1976), p. 206.
14. (p. 23) **Ibid.,** p. 197.
15. (p. 24) Henry Glassie, **Pattern in the Material Culture of the Eastern United States** (Philadelphia, 1968), pp. 80-81.
16. (p. 24) **Ibid.,** pp. 64-67.
17. (p. 24) Fred Kniffen, "Folk Housing," p. 555.
18. (p. 25) Glassie, **Pattern in the Material Culture,** p. 113.
19. (p. 25) Nancy McDonough, **Garden Sass: A Catalog of Arkansas Folkways** (New York, 1975), p. 50-52.
20. (p. 25) Hutslar, "Log Architecture of Ohio," p. 192.
21. (p. 25) Montell and Morse, **Kentucky Folk Architecture,** p. 12.
22. (p. 25) Roberts, "The Whitaker-Waggoner House," p. 197.
23. (p. 26) Ibid., p. 207.
24. (p. 26) Ibid., p. 206.
25. (p. 28) Hutslar, "Log Architecture of Ohio," p. 174; see also David Stahle and Daniel Wolfman, "The Potential for Tree-Ring Research in Arkansas," **Field Notes: The Monthly Newsletter of the Arkansas Archeological Society** (February, 1977), pp. 5-9.
26. (p. 35) Wilson, **Alabama Folk Houses,** p. 18.
27. (p. 36) Smith, **White Pillars,** p. 25-27.
28. (p. 41) **Ibid.,** p. 25-27.
29. (p. 43) Roberts, "The Whitaker-Waggoner House," p. 197.
30. (p. 71) Smith, **White Pillars,** p. 25-27; see also Ralph Alan McCanse, **Titans and Kewpies: The Life and Art of Rose O'Neill** (New York, 1968), p. 63-64.
31. (p. 103) McDonough, **Garden Sass,** p. 36.
32. (p. 103) Hutslar, "Log Architecture of Ohio," p. 210.

33. (p. 130) Eliot Wigginton, ed., **The Foxfire Book** (Garden City, New York, 1972), p. 69.
34. (p. 132) Montell and Morse, **Kentucky Folk Architecture,** p. 46.
35. (p. 180) See Evon Z. Vogt and Ray Hyman, **Water Witching U.S.A.** (Chicago, 1959).

References

Glassie, Henry. "The Appalachian Log Cabin," **Mountain Life and Work.** 39 (1963), 5-14.

Glassie, Henry, **Pattern in the Material Culture of the Eastern United States.** Philadelphia: University of Pennsylvania Press, 1968.

Hutslar, D. A. "Log Architecture of Ohio," **Ohio History,** 80 (1971), 172-271.

Kniffen, Fred. "Folk Housing: Key to Diffusion," **Annals of the Association of American Geographers.** 55 (1965), 549-577.

Kniffen, Fred. "On Corner Timbering," **Pioneer America,** 1 (1969), 1-8.

McCanse, Ralph Alan. **Titans and Kewpies: The Life and Art of Rose O'Neill.** New York: Vantage Press, 1968.

McDonough, Nancy. **Garden Sass: A Catalog of Arkansas Folkways.** New York: Coward, Geoghegan, 1975.

Montell, William Lynwood, and Michael Lynn Morse. **Kentucky Folk Architecture.** Lexington: University of Kentucky Press, 1976.

Roberts, Warren E. "Some Comments on Log Construction in Scandinavia and the United States," in Felix J. Oinas, Linda Dégh, and Henry Glassie, eds. **Folklore Today: A Festschrift for Richard M. Dorson.** Bloomington: Indiana University Press, 1976.

Roberts, Warren E. "The Whitaker-Waggoner Log House from Morgan County, Indiana," in Don Yoder, ed. **American Folklife.** Austin: University of Texas Press, 1976, 185-207.

Sloane, Eric. **A Museum of Early American Tools.** New York: Random House, 1964.

Smith, J. Frazer. **White Pillars.** New York: Bramhall House, 1941.

Stahle, David, and Daniel Wolfman. "The Potential for Tree-Ring Research in Arkansas," **Field Notes: The Monthly Newsletter of the Arkansas Archeological Society,** No. 146 (February, 1977), 5-9.

Vogt, Evon Z., and Ray Hyman. **Water Witching U.S.A.** Chicago: University of Chicago Press, 1959.

Weslager, C. A. **The Log Cabin in America.** New Brunswick, New Jersey: Rutgers University Press, 1969.

Wigginton, Eliot, ed. **The Foxfire Book.** Garden City, New York: Doubleday, 1972.

Wilson, Eugene M. **Alabama Folk Houses.** Montgomery: Alabama History Commission, 1975.

Wilson, Eugene M. "Some Similarities Between American and European Folk Houses," **Pioneer America,** 3 (1971), 8-14.

Glossary

adze	smoothing tool with the blade perpendicular to the three-foot handle.
angle brace	any timber bracing a corner, across that corner.
auger	hand boring tool.
barn sash	single sash, simply a wooden frame with glass panes.
beaded beam	usually a ceiling joist ornamented with a groove near each rounded corner; beading was done with a shaping plane.
bird-stop board	board fitted between rafters where they pass over the plate, extending the wall to the roof.
block-and-tackle	series of pulleys roped together to give a mechanical advantage for lifting or pulling.
board-and-batten	vertical siding of wide boards, cracks covered by narrow strips.
board foot	a measure 12" x 12" x 1" or 144 cubic inches. Standard for measuring lumber.
bob truck	truck with one frame, not a truck-and-trailer unit.
broadaxe	wide-faced axe beveled on one side, for hewing.
bunching	grouping logs for loading.
butting poles	part of the roof, poles laid into notches in the top end logs to support weight poles and knees, which held the early shakes in place when nails were not available.
cant hook	a pole with a hook near one end for rolling logs.
catted chimney	one built of dried clay rolled into "cats" laid within courses of small pole pens.
chalkline	string loaded with chalk for making lines.
chamfer	beveled end of a timber.
chinking	the filling between logs; mortar, or short split boards and clay.
clapboards	overlapping siding boards laid horizontally.
concrete	aggregate of cement, sand, gravel and water, usually steel-reinforced.
conduit	pipe for electric wire.
corner-notched	log ends fitted at the house corners.

course of logs	four corner-notched logs at one level around the house perimeter.
crosscut saw	usually a coarse-toothed saw for use across the grain.
cross-haul	a system of chains, ropes or cables for rolling or sliding material up skids.
dado blade	circle saw blade set to weave and make a wide cut.
decking	roof covering onto which shingles are laid.
dogtrot house	a style originally two pens separated by a breezeway, with a common roof and usually fireplaces at opposite ends.
double-hung sash	a sliding window, with halves above and below.
dovetail notch	an angled notch at the end of a log beam or timber, cut straight in and widening to the end.
drawknife	a smoothing tool, two-handed shaving knife drawn toward the user.
dry-stone foundation	stones stacked without mortar to form a base on which to build.
eaves	overhang of the roof.
effluent	liquid waste.
ell	an addition usually at right angles to a house.
entry panel	electric switch box with fuses or breaker switches.
facing	finishing boards used around windows and doors.
field lines	septic tank drain lines, buried level to dissipate runoff liquid.
flashing	sheet metal used at the roof peak and in roof angles, under the shingles to prevent leaking.
floor joists	beams mortised or notched into the sills, onto which flooring is laid.
flue tile	clay pipe used to line chimneys for a cleaner, smoother surface.
footing	wide masonry support in the ground on which foundation is laid.
froe	L-shaped tool for splitting or riving shakes or staves from wood blocks.
full 2 x 4	timber of that measure; lumber company offerings usually measure $1\frac{1}{2}" \times 3\frac{1}{2}."$
gable	the triangular wall space enclosed by the roof at the ends of the house.
gin-poles	pivoting boom of two poles braced by a cable or another pole for lifting.
GPM	gallons per minute, the measure for water flow.
half-dovetail	a log notch with only one outward slope to the end.
heat box	dual-walled metal fireplace liner that improves heat circulation.

hewing	flattening or squaring timber, usually with the broadaxe.
hewing dogs	iron stays driven into logs to hold them steady for hewing.
house raising	the neighborhood gathering to build a house cooperatively.
hydraulic ram	pump that operates on the force of water moving down hill, which transports a part of that water up a higher hill.
joist	timber on which flooring or ceiling is laid.
juggles	heavy chips cut by a broadaxe.
keystone	V-shaped stone at the center of an arch.
kiln-dried lumber	that with the moisture baked out of it.
kingpost	vertical support for the joist down from the rigid roof peak to the midpoint of the joist.
knee	a roof element, short timber laid vertically between weight poles.
lag screw	heavy screw for wood with bolt head.
laths	spaced boards or slats, that serve as a base for covering.
lean-to	three-sided addition to a building, with shed roof, usually in the rear.
lintel stone	stone spanning an opening such as a fireplace.
loft	space upstairs under the roof, attic.
log-sitter	cooperative assistant to keep log steady.
masonry cement	mixture of lime and cement that is mixed with sand and water for mortar.
metal lath	screening used for reinforcing plaster.
mortising	joining two timbers by stepping down the end of one (the tenon) to fit into a hole cut into the other.
nail set	punch for sinking finishing nails below the surface of the wood.
nailer-strips	light timbers fastened to walls to give support for joists ends, flooring ends.
newel	the bottom post to which the stair railing is attached.
notching	cutting away pieces of wood to enable a beam or log to fit to another.
pegging	pinning, as with trunnels.
pens	squares or rectangles built of full-length, corner-notched logs.
pinned	attached with wooden pins or trunnels.
pit-saw	vertical sawmill, powered by steam, water or muscle.

plate	the top timber or log of a wall to which the rafters attach.
plumb bob	pointed weight on a string for locating exact horizontal points.
post-and-beam	type of construction involving widely-spaced, heavy uprights set on heavy sills with heavy plates above.
pry bar	metal leverage tool, crowbar, pinch bar.
puncheons	heavy flooring timbers, originally halved logs with the flat sides up.
purlins	lengthwise roof timbers to which shakes are nailed.
push pole	temporary extension for raising timbers, trusses, rafters.
queenposts	pair of vertical supports down from each end of a horizontal beam near the roof peak.
rabbet	inset groove, as for setting glass in windows.
rafters	beams set at an angle from the plates at the tops of the walls to the ridge, to which the roofing is attached.
rafter truss	triangular structure of two rafters and a horizontal brace or chord; several make up the roof structure.
ridgepole	lengthwise timber supporting the upper ends of rafters, rarely used in early houses.
risers	the vertical surfaces of steps.
riving	splitting, as in shakes.
riving horse	two-branched support for riving or splitting shakes, staves.
saddlebag house	a style originally two pens together at the gable, with a fireplace between.
score-hack	the cuts along a log to the depth it is to be hewn.
septic tank	container in which sewage solids are broken down by bacteria.
shake	a thin split board used as a shingle.
shaping plane	smoothing tool with a shape or design in the cutting blade.
sheave	enclosed pulley for rope or cable.
shingle	thin roof-covering board.
shiplap	shaped-edge boards that fit overlapped, also called half-lap.
shutters	wooden or iron window covers.
sills	heavy base logs onto which the floor joists and walls are set.
skidded	towed along the ground, as in logging.

skids	inclined poles or timbers for loading or raising heavy material.
slats	staves, often described as the widely spaced boards that shingles are nailed to.
sleeper	heavy beam bracing joists, called summer beam when the beam supports the ceiling joists.
smithy	blacksmith shop, often confused with the smith, who works there.
spanner	stringer, any timber reaching from one support to another, spanning an opening.
spindle shaper	mechanized, circular shaping plane.
square	carpenter's tool for determining 90° angles.
staves	split boards longer than shakes.
stone hammer	tool for shaping stone.
stringer	any timber used to span a long distance, usually the side timbers in stairs.
studwall	wall framing of light vertical timbers or studs, attached to a sill, capped by a plate.
summer beam	sleeper, joist support for a ceiling.
tenon	the stepped-down end of a timber that fits into a mortise.
30-penny spike	heavy nail, a size designation, originally 100 could be bought for 30 pennies.
tongue-and-groove lumber	also called center match, t.i.g. lumber, shaped at two edges to interlock.
tread	the horizontal surface of a step.
trunnels	wooden pegs, or tree-nails, used to fasten beams together.
turkey-feather roof	shingle or shake roof with the top row extended above the ridge.
two-foot centers	distance from the center of one joist, stud, or rafter to another.
water witcher	person skilled in finding water beneath the ground.
weight poles	poles holding down shakes before nails were available.
whipsaw	a man-powered vertical sawmill.
wings	additions to the sides of the house.

Index

Illustrations noted **bold**.

A

adze 32, **33**, 37
air ducts 138, **138**
angle bracing
    roof **124**, 125, **125**
    studwall 174, **174**

B

bird-stop board 134, **135**
blacksmithing 40, **40**
broadaxe 32, **33**, 34, 100-102, **101**, **102**
butting poles 32, 36, **36**

C

ceiling joists 35, **35**, 109-115, **113**, **117**, 126, **126**, 150, **151**, 175
chamfer 117, **117**, 118
chimneys
    catted 25, 28, **42**, 139-140
    stone 136-147, **139**, **141**, **142**, **145**, **146**
chinking 27, 42, **42**, 51, 109, 115-117, **116**, **194**, 195
communications 196-197
concrete **90**, 93, **93**, 94, 140-142, **140**, **142**
crosscut saw **32**, **106**, 107, 110, **110**
crosshaul 81, **81**

crutch roof 36, **36**

D

Dawt Mill House (Ozark County, Missouri) 47
doors 41, 156-163, **160**, **161**
dormers **128**, 159, 160, 175
dry stonework 95, **95**, **97**, **139**, 146

E

eaves 27, 28, 107, 120, **120**, 128, **128**, 129
electricity 191-196, **194**
European influence in early houses 16, 17, 18, 19, 22

F

facings 110, **110**, 162
Fagg, Dan (Arkansas College) 151, 159
felling a tree 78, **78**
fireplace 18, 136-147, **138**, **141**, **142**, **143**, 144
flagstone floor 152, 153, **153**, 154, **154**
floor joists 37, 91, **91**, 109-115, **109**, **114**, **138**, **142**, 152
flooring 37, **37**, 38, 41, 114, **142**, 148-155, **150**, **151**
flue tile 144, **144**

Ft. Christina (Wilmington, Delaware) (New Sweden) 18, 35
footings, **90**, 92, **92**, 93, **93**
foundations
    chimney 140, **140**, **142**
    continuous vs. piers 90, 91, **91**, 93
    wall 37, **37**, 65, 88-97, **90**, **91**, **92**, **93**, **95**, **96**, **97**
froe 32, **33**, 40, 130, **131**

G

gables 25, 27, **27**, 36, 38, 41, **41**, 119, 134, **134**
gas 196
Glassie, Henry 19, 24, 25, 139
Grigsby House (Arkansas College, Batesville) 51, 71, 100, 151, 159

H

Harris, Thaddeus 16
heat box 138, **138**, 141, 144
Henderson Cabin (near Ponca, Arkansas) 119
hewing dogs 102, **102**
hewing logs 100-105, **101**, **102**
hinges 159, **161**
history 15-29, 30-43
house vs. cabin definition 8, 15, 16, 17
house additions 20-24, 164-177
house age 26-29

206

house design 66-75
house size 16, 69, 75
house style 20-24, **20, 21, 23, 24, 28,** 69, 70, 71
   central hall 22, 23, **23**
   dogtrot 19-22, **20, 22, 24,** 43, 51, 69, 70, **70,** 71, **72**
   double-pen **20,** 21, **21,** 22, **22,** 43, 51, 69, 70, **70,** 71
   hall-and-parlor 24
   "I" 24, **29**
   saddlebag 21, **21,** 43, 71, **75**
   single-pen (basic cabin) 20, **21, 28,** 69
house raisings **30-31,** 34-37, **53-55**
Howard House (Kirbyville, Missouri) **42, 47,** 48, 151
Hutslar, D.A. 16, 25, 28, 36, 103

I

Ingenthron House (Forsyth, Missouri) **22**
insulation 115, 116, **116,** 129-130, **129, 135,** 145, **154,** 174
interior walls **22,** 23, 24, **39**

J

joists (see ceiling; floor)

K

king post 125, 126, **126,** 175
knees 32, 36, **36**
Kniffen, Fred 18, 24
Kruger House (Viola, Missouri) 91, **91,** **105, 106, 107, 127, 128,** 160

L

lean-to 24, 173-174, **173**
lintel **141,** 142, **143,** 144, **144**
loft 20, 74, **74,** 174-176, **175**
log raising 38, 108, **108,** 110, **111,** 112
log location coding 51, 53
log wall openings 36, 41, 110
logging 76-87
lumber 85, 127, 128

M

McDonough, Nancy 25, 103, 139
McRaven House (Branson, Missouri) **2, 13,** 68, **96, 146,** 172
Montell and Morse 18, 21, 25
mortar 27, 93, 94, 95, 115, 116, **116,** 146
Muskrat Murphy Cabin (Hilda, Missouri) 50, 52-55, **53-55,** 90, 129, 137

N

nails 26, **26,** 110
notches 38, **38,** 39, **39,** 105-109, 113
   compound-angle dovetail 38, **39,** 107
   diamond 38, **39**
   full dovetail 38, **39**
   half-dovetail 25, **35,** 38, **38, 105, 106,** 107, **107,** 113
   half notch 23, 38, **39**
   partition, 38, **39**
   square 25, 38, **39**
   V-notch 23, 25, 38, **38,** 107

notching 105-109, 121, **121,** 122, **122**

P

pegging 26, 27, 35, 38, 41, **41,** 110, 120, 121, **121,** 122, **123, 124**
plumb bob 92, **92**
porch 166-172, **167, 168, 170, 171**
puncheon floor 37, **37,** 38, 150, **150**
purlins 27, **27,** 36

Q

queen post 126, **126,** 175

R

rafters 38, 40, **40,** 120-126, **120-125,** 166-168, **167**
restoration 44-55
Rhiel House (Golden, Missouri) 189
Richmond, Ted 197, **198**
Roberts, Warren 18, 19, 23, 25, 43
roof 26, 27, 36, **36,** 118-135
roof cap 134, **134**
roof decking 126, 127, **127,** 128 **128, 133**
roof pitch 25, 40, 119, **175**
roof style 36, **36,** 134, **134** (see also shake; shingles)
round logs 8, 15, 43, 98, 197, **198**

S

sand point well 181
scaffolding **145, 146,** 147

207

score-hacking logs 102, **102**
seasoning of logs 10, 115, 135, **162, 173**
septic system 184-189, **184, 185, 187**
settling, foundations and chimney 89, 92, 95, 96, 140, 141
sewage disposal 184-189
shake roof 27, **27**, 32, 36, 40, 130-134, **131, 133, 134, 135**
shingles 130-134, **131, 133, 167, 168, 168**
shutters 41, **41, 158**
siding 23, 25, 43, **47**, 116
sills 36, **36**, 109, **109**, 152
site 32, 56-65
sleeper 91, **91, 142**
Sloane, Eric 34
Smith, J. Frazer 22, 36, 71
smoke shelf 141, **141**, 142
social significance of hewn logs 17, 43, 98
stairs 115, 176, **176**, 177, **177**
stone acquisition 85, 86, 94
stone chimneys 136-147
stone foundations 90, **90, 91**
stonework 94, **94**
summer beam 126, **126**

T

tarpaper on roof 133, **133**
tools 32, **32, 33**, 87
tongue-and-groove 113, 114, 128, 151, 152
top plate 38, 121, **121**, 122, 129
trunnels 35
turkey feather roof 134, **134**

V

Villines, Beaver Jim 21, **146**

W

water witching 180, 181
weight poles 32, 36, **36**
wells 178-183
Weslager, C.A. 18, 28, 35, 36
windows 36, 41, 156-163, **158**
Whitaker-Waggoner House (Indiana University) 23, **23**, 24, 71
Wilson, Eugene 16, 19, 21, 35
Wolf House (Norfolk, Arkansas) **20**, 22, 70, **70**

woods, choice of
    flooring 150, 151, 155
    logs 89, 100
    pegs 35, 120
    shakes 130, 131, 132
woodstoves 147, **147, 193**

Z

Zent Cabin (Ash Grove, Missouri) 90, **91, 103, 113, 123, 124, 145, 155, 168**

Acknowledgements

Special thanks to the following people who helped create this book:

Linda Moore McRaven, wife and publisher, for all that implies.
Dick and Laurna Tallman, indefatigable editors, for all their painstaking work.
Pat McRaven, for reading and rereading the initial ms.
George Lankford, for valuable reference material.
James Burkhart, for his paintings and design expertise.
Chandis Ingenthron, for creating drawings from my rough sketches.
Ronnie, Bennie and Oral Owens, of Western Printing, three of the best men I know.
Beth Cadwell, for production work and for the photograph of her great-great grandparents' house on p. 189.
And to my father, John McRaven, from whom I learned to build.

The photographs on pp. 63, 172 and 183, by Charles and Linda Moore McRaven, appeared previously in publications of **The Ozarks Mountaineer**. Used by permission.